AF255644

Astrology, Relationships, and Tarot Spreads

The Ultimate Guide to Zodiac Signs Compatibility, the Celtic Cross, Symbolism, and More for Beginners

Your Free Gift
(only available for a limited time)

Thanks for getting this book! If you want to learn more about various spirituality topics, then join Mari Silva's community and get a free guided meditation MP3 for awakening your third eye. This guided meditation mp3 is designed to open and strengthen ones third eye so you can experience a higher state of consciousness. Simply visit the link below the image to get started.

https://spiritualityspot.com/meditation

Or, Scan the QR code!

Table of Contents

Part 1: Astrology and Relationships

The Ultimate Guide to Zodiac Signs Compatibility

Introduction

Are you looking for a comprehensive guide to understanding astrology in relationships? Do you want to understand how to use zodiac signs and compatibility in your life? Look no further than Astrology and Relationships - The Ultimate Guide to Zodiac Signs Compatibility.

This book combines the latest discoveries about astrological compatibilities and time-tested concepts related to sun signs, planets, and houses. It also provides easy-to-follow instructions on creating synastry charts. With this book, readers can better understand zodiac signs in relationships and apply that knowledge in their lives.

Its comprehensive topic coverage makes Astrology and Relationships - The Ultimate Guide to Zodiac Signs Compatibility stand out. It provides detailed information on all aspects of astrology and compatibility so readers can understand what zodiac signs offer. The book's clear and concise writing style is easy for beginners to grasp the content without getting overwhelmed or confused.

This book provides readers with a comprehensive guide to understanding astrological compatibility. It explains how different aspects of our birth charts – from planets to sun signs, houses, and synastry – affect our romantic relationships. It uses easy-to-understand language combined with clear instructions so even beginners can easily grasp the concepts. Unlike many other books on the market that merely present theoretical information without tangible solutions, this book goes beyond the basics. It provides hands-on methods to help you understand relationships from an astrological perspective.

This book will teach you the fundamentals of astrology and zodiac signs compatibility and help you apply that knowledge practically. You'll learn to read your birth chart and those of your friends or partners to gain insight into yourself and your relationships. We'll explore the various components of astrology, such as planets, houses, and synastry, and how they interact to form powerful connections between two people. Additionally, we discuss tips on strengthening relationships through understanding astrological influences.

The book provides hands-on advice and techniques for readers wanting to delve deeper into the subject. It includes how to interpret synastry charts, how planets influence one another in relationships, and more. This guide gives readers an insider's look at astrology and its implications for their relationships.

Astrology and Relationships - The Ultimate Guide to Zodiac Signs Compatibility is a must-have for anyone wanting greater insight into astrology in relationships. With its comprehensive coverage, clear writing style, and hands-on advice, readers learn everything about zodiac signs and compatibility. So, don't wait any longer. Buy this book today, and get started on your journey to understanding the mysteries of astrology.

Chapter 1: What Is Astrological Compatibility?

There is often much confusion about what it means: astrological compatibility and synastry. But the good news is that this chapter clarifies how astrology, compatibility, and synastry can help us in life. Drawing from the collective wisdom in astrology, this chapter digs deep into the concept of cosmic relationships and harmony. It explores the many benefits of looking at your relationship through an astrological lens. With this knowledge, you can gain insight into yourself and understand your partners better with a deeper understanding.

It's important to learn about compatibility to understand more about your relationships. [1]

What Is Astrology?

Astrology is an ancient form of divination that uses the alignment of stars, planets, and other celestial bodies to interpret their influence on humans. It has been used for thousands of years in many cultures worldwide to predict the future and gain insight into people's personalities and destinies. Astrology uses the movement of celestial bodies to gain insight into human life. Astrologers believe these movements can predict future events and personality traits based on a person's birth chart. They believe the position of planets at the moment of birth directly affects a person's destiny.

Astrology's history dates back as far as 6000 BC when it was practiced by early civilizations such as Babylonians, Chinese, Greeks, and Egyptians. These early cultures believed that celestial events had direct correlations with human affairs on earth, enabling them to predict and interpret the influence of stars and planets on human events.

The methods in astrology vary from culture to culture, but they all study the position of celestial bodies at a specific moment in time. Astrologers use various tools, such as star maps, astrolabes, almanacs, and ephemerides, for calculations. They also use a branch of astronomy known as horoscopic astrology, which focuses on predicting the future based on an individual's birth chart or natal chart.

Astrology is primarily divided into three branches - natal astrology, mundane astrology, and electional astrology. Natal astrology focuses on analyzing the date of birth or nativity. Mundane astrology looks at planetary positions in relation to large-scale phenomena, such as natural disasters or changes in the economy, and how they affect people's lives. Electional astrology (also known as *event astrology*) deals with making predictions by analyzing the potential outcomes of certain activities relating to particular planetary placements and alignments.

Astrologers analyze the planet's positions using a circle divided into 12 houses. Each house is associated with a particular area or aspect in a person's life, like love, career, family, wealth, etc. From this analysis, astrologers can predict an individual's future based on their birth chart. These predictions often take various forms, from major events to more mundane, and are used as guidance for those looking to decide about their life path.

Through its centuries-old practice, astrology has become a powerful tool for understanding the complexities of human experience. Some believe it offers insight into our and others' lives and guides us in decision-making and achieving success. Astrology is an important part of many cultures and helps unite people from all walks of life. Here is some prominent astrology around the world:

Vedic Astrology

Compatibility readings in Vedic astrology determine the karmic compatibility between two people. This examination looks at the natal charts of both individuals and identifies areas of harmony and where they might clash or navigate through challenges together. A compatibility reading aims to provide insight into how these two people can come together as partners and build a strong, lasting relationship.

The most important factor to consider during a compatibility reading is the planets' placement in each individual's birth chart. In Vedic astrology, certain planetary combinations can bring positive or negative outcomes in karmic relationships. Planets like Mars, Venus, Jupiter, and the Moon are important in compatibility readings as their placement influences whether two people have a harmonious or tumultuous relationship.

In addition to examining planetary placements, Vedic astrology looks at the overall birth chart of each person and assesses their energies. Ashtakoota is a system to determine the overall compatibility between two people based on eight different criteria: Varna (social status), Vashya (dominance), Tara (longevity of marriage), Yoni (sexual chemistry), Graha Maitri (mental connection), Gana (personality type), Bhakoota (emotional bond), and Nadi (spiritual connection). A score is assigned to each criterion; based on this score, a compatibility reading is given.

Finally, Vedic astrology also looks at the specific karmic ties between two individuals, which provides insight into their relationship. This analysis can reveal how both people have interacted in past lives and what energies they might bring to their current relationship. It can also identify areas where one person might need to work hard to overcome obstacles or challenges for the relationship to succeed.

Chinese Astrology

Compatibility readings in Chinese astrology determine the best potential for a relationship. By comparing the birth charts of two individuals, insight is gained into their compatibility. A compatibility reading will consider factors like the elements each person is composed of, the Five Elements Theory, and Yin and Yang. These astrology aspects are significant in determining whether two people will be compatible.

The Chinese zodiac signs. [2]

The elements used to define a person's character in Chinese astrology are Fire, Earth, Metal, Water, and Wood, each with its own qualities that influence how someone behaves and interacts with others. Using this information, an astrologer can predict how a person will relate to their partner.

The Five Elements Theory is also used in compatibility readings and focuses on the relationship between the five elements. This theory states that all elements are connected and affect each other, ultimately influencing the success or failure of relationships. If two people possess similar elements, they will be more compatible than those with different elements.

Yin and Yang represent opposing forces in Chinese astrology. Yin represents femininity, passivity, and receptiveness, while Yang characterizes masculinity, activity, and assertiveness. For two people to be compatible, they must balance their Yin and Yang energies. If one partner has too much of either energy, it can lead to disharmony in the relationship.

Compatibility readings are an important part of Chinese astrology and can help those looking for love to understand their potential compatibility with another person. By considering the elements, the Five Elements Theory, and the Yin and Yang energies of two people, you can gain insight into whether they are compatible in a relationship. Therefore, considering these factors when deciding to enter a relationship is crucial.

Western Astrology

Compatibility readings in western astrology provide insight into how two individuals relate to one another. This reading examines the planets' positions in both people's natal charts and compares them to determine compatibility. Compatibility readings are based on numerous factors, including aspects, house placement, sign position, and ruler-ship. Other areas, such as timing, age, and life events influencing each individual's chart, are also considered.

A compatibility reading aims to discover how two people will interact with one another based on their birth charts. It provides insight into what areas they must work on together or separately to maintain a successful relationship. Comparing birth charts assesses the potential for a successful relationship or business partnership.

The most important aspect of compatibility readings is looking at how the planets in each person's birth chart affect their relationship dynamics. This includes looking at which signs and elements are compatible and aspects between the planets, such as conjunctions, squares, trines, and oppositions. Considering how the planets interact with one another when in close proximity is also important when looking at birth charts.

Another factor that must be considered during compatibility readings is timing. If two people's charts show similar planetary placements – but with different time stamps – it could affect the overall outcome of the compatibility reading. For example, if one person has a natal chart with a prominent Mars position and the other's natal chart doesn't have as strong a position, it could mean their relationship is not as stable due to the difference in timing.

What Is Compatibility?

Compatibility describes the ability of two or more items, people, ideas, or situations to work well together. It usually means they can successfully interact and complement each other. For example, compatibility between computer hardware and software components allows them to function together properly. Compatibility in relationships refers to the ability of two people to work together harmoniously and get along despite their differences. It involves having similar values, beliefs, attitudes, goals, and a mutual understanding and appreciation for each other. Compatibility is essential for successful long-term relationships and strong connections between two individuals.

Astrological compatibility describes the relationship between two people based on their Sun signs in astrology. The compatibility between two individuals' natal charts can be evaluated by examining aspects between planets from one chart to another and an overall harmony of energies in both charts. An individual's birth chart is designed to reveal their personality traits, and each sign has a different energy that could be compatible with other signs. Astrological compatibility allows two people to better understand each other's needs and differences and creates a harmonious relationship. It does not guarantee a perfect relationship, but it gives couples a chance to work together constructively on issues that arise.

Carl Jung's Theory of Astrological Compatibility

Carl Jung's study on astrological compatibility began when he noticed a high frequency of relationships between people born under similar zodiac signs. He collected data from approximately two hundred couples, comparing their birth charts' psychological makeup and correspondences.

He found that couples born under compatible signs had more harmonious relationships than those with incompatible signs. He concluded that astrology could be used to help understand the dynamics of interpersonal relationships.

Jung developed his theory of Synchronicity, which states that certain events can be related by meaning or circumstance rather than cause and effect. He theorized that meaningful coincidences might be evidence for an underlying order connecting all aspects of life, including astrology. It means the patterns of astrological compatibility can reflect a deeper, spiritual connection between two people.

Jung's work has since been studied by many researchers and is still an important part of modern astrology. His theory of Synchronicity continues to inspire individuals seeking to better understand the relationship between themselves and their partners. By studying Jung's research on astrological compatibility, we have insight into how Universal forces affect our lives and relationships.

Jung's study of astrological compatibility has proven a valuable tool for understanding our relationships with those around us and connecting with a deeper meaning in life. By exploring his findings, we discover how our birth charts reflect the energies that weave through all aspects of existence.

This research is one example of how Carl Jung's work has contributed to modern psychological understanding. It continues to provide an essential foundation for further study of the relationship between humans and the Universe. His theory of Synchronicity is an important reminder that there are patterns significant in our lives and relationships that connect us more deeply than we previously thought possible.

Concept of Synastry

Synastry compares two natal charts, or horoscopes, to determine the degree of compatibility between two people. It involves looking at aspects between one chart and another to see how they interact and how they might influence the relationship. Synastry is a powerful tool to help you understand why someone behaves in certain ways and indicates areas where you will be most compatible with each other.

The main goal of synastry is to identify and highlight areas of compatibility and potential for growth for each individual in a relationship. Different aspects have different meanings in synastry. Some indicate strong feelings of love, while others point to more challenging times ahead.

Looking closely at the interaction between the two charts explains how two people will get along in their relationship and what they need to do to make it successful.

Synastry focuses on comparing planets and their relative positions and understanding how these combinations affect relationships. Planets represent different energies, and when placed in harmonious or dissonant aspects with each other, they create positive or negative influences in the relationship. Synastry looks at the differences between charts to see what each person can offer the other. For example, suppose one person has a strong Mars-Jupiter aspect in their chart, and another has a weak Venus-Neptune aspect. In that case, this could indicate a power dynamic where one is stronger than the other. Similarly, suppose two people have similar Venus signs. In that case, they might be more likely to share love and affection for one another.

When interpreting synastry, considering all aspects and energies in both charts and how they interact with each other is imperative. It helps you learn why certain aspects of your relationship work and others do not. It provides valuable insight into nurturing a relationship and ensuring its longevity. However, synastry is not an exact science and should not be used as the sole basis for important decisions. Instead, it should be used as one of several tools when considering relationships.

Overall, synastry can offer useful insights into why things happen the way they do in your relationship. It can help identify potential issues and recommend ways to work through them together. Synastry can help you understand each other's needs and desires so you can create a more harmonious connection between you. With this knowledge, you can ensure your relationship continues to thrive on mutual respect and understanding for years.

Benefits of Using Astrology

1. **Exercise Empathy:** Astrology is an excellent tool for empathizing with people. It allows you to understand their inner needs and perspectives on life, which are often difficult to grasp without a deeper understanding of astrological principles. It helps guide conversations toward more positive outcomes and creates better relationships, platonically and romantically.

2. **Strengthen Relationships:** By learning about someone's astrological chart, you discover how they interact with others in different contexts or situations. With this knowledge, you can understand

their motivations better and how best to approach them in conflict resolution or strengthening the bond between two people.

3. **Avoid Strains:** Knowing the tendencies and motivations of the people in your social circle can help you avoid potential strains. For example, someone with a strong Mars influence in their natal chart might act impulsively or be overly assertive; understanding this beforehand helps you manage conversations to prevent misunderstandings or disagreements.

4. **Make Plans for the Future:** Astrology is useful for making future plans. By looking at two people's charts, you gain insight into how compatible they will likely be over the long term. It helps create realistic expectations and understand areas that need extra attention. In addition, astrology provides valuable advice on timing and actions that would be beneficial.

5. **Discover Unseen Paths:** Sometimes, astrology can lead to discovering new paths. By looking at two people's charts and understanding the underlying dynamics of their relationship, uncovering underlying patterns or traits that could be explored further and ultimately lead to a more fulfilling connection between them is possible.

6. **Improve Communication:** Communication is essential for any successful relationship, and astrology helps you pinpoint areas where communication should be improved or strengthened. For example, if someone has a strong Saturn influence in their natal chart, they might stick to rigid rules and be less likely to listen to others' opinions. Understanding this beforehand allows you to adjust your approach and communicate more effectively.

7. **Heal Old Wounds:** Astrology can heal old wounds or resentments, as it provides insight into the dynamics of a particular relationship. With this understanding, individuals can make amends and move forward with greater trust and understanding.

8. **Understand Limitations:** Knowing what areas are difficult for two people to connect on can be useful in understanding each other's limitations and helping them build better relationships. By learning about their astrological compatibility (or lack thereof), they can adjust expectations accordingly, making meeting each other's needs easier without compromising either side's feelings or principles.

9. **Provide Guidance**: Finally, astrology can be useful for guiding others. Identifying potential pitfalls or areas of growth in a relationship provides advice and encouragement to help strengthen the bond between two people, improve communication, and foster mutual understanding. This way, astrology is invaluable for couples looking to build a long-lasting connection.

No matter your beliefs, astrology is an ancient practice that has been a source of guidance throughout history and should be respected and understood rather than dismissed or ridiculed. While it does involve predictions, its main focus lies in providing insight into a person's inner self and potential paths forward, allowing them to move toward their ultimate destiny with greater clarity and confidence. The power of astrology lies in its ability to bring about a sense of understanding and clarity for those who seek it. By looking at the sky and being guided by it, you can gain an insight into your life and the potential paths that could lead toward a greater future. Astrology is ultimately an exploration of our inner selves, which has the potential to reveal more than we ever thought possible.

Chapter 2: You Are More than Your Sun Sign

Navigating our way through the different aspects of astrology can be confusing and intimidating. Fortunately, understanding all the interconnectivity and complexity behind your sun sign, moon sign, rising sign, and descendant is possible with this chapter. Combining insights from these twelve zodiacs helps create an overall picture of ourselves and our unique astrological profile. With this comprehensive analysis of various signs, you gain valuable insight into who we are and what our lives have in store. Through this chapter, we discover how the 12 zodiacs interact with one another to decipher knowledge about ourselves, build relationships and understand situations more clearly.

Your sun signs are also known as your star or zodiac signs. [8]

Sun Sign

A sun sign, also known as a star sign or zodiac sign, is an astrological sign representing the sun's position relative to the stars. It is calculated on the sun's position at birth and determines personality traits and characteristics. Depending on which sign you were born under, your life is influenced by its qualities.

Each sun sign in astrology has certain unique characteristics associated with it. For example, Aries is associated with being bold, courageous, and impulsive. Pisces is associated with being gentle, sympathetic, and intuitive. Each sun sign has different elements attributed to it, such as fire (Aries), earth (Taurus), air (Gemini), or water (Cancer). These elements affect how you view and interact with the world.

To determine your sun sign, check the date range you were born in. Each sign has a different date range that covers approximately one month of the year. For example, if you were born between March 21st and April 19th, your sun sign is Aries. Once you've determined your sun sign, research its associated characteristics to gain insight into who you are and how you might interact with people and situations throughout your life.

Your sun sign is only one part of astrology. Other factors, such as moon signs, rising signs, planets, and houses, further help you understand your personality and life path. Sun signs provide a basic overview of who you are. Still, it's important to remember that astrology is much more complex than just your sun sign.

Knowing and understanding your sun sign can be a powerful tool for helping you make sense of the world around you and gain greater self-knowledge about yourself. It's also interesting to learn more about how others might interact with you based on their zodiac signs. Understanding your sun sign is a great starting point for further exploration into the fascinating world of astrology.

Moon Sign

The moon sign is an astrological concept referring to the zodiac sign the moon was in at your birth. It can be calculated using your date and place of birth and provides insight into your emotional life, mental state, intuition, and spiritual journey.

You need to use an ephemeris to calculate your moon sign. An ephemeris is a reference source of data providing the exact positions of the sun, moon, and planets in relation to Earth. When calculating your moon sign, you must consider the time and place of your birth because each zodiac sign's distance from Earth is different. The moon appears in a slightly different position to our planet, depending on where you were born. Consequently, this impacts which zodiac sign is ascribed to your moon sign. This information makes it possible to look up the moon's position to each zodiac sign on any given day. You can even find easy-to-use online tools that will calculate your moon sign.

Your moon sign can provide insight into how you express yourself, your inner feelings, and your emotional needs. It reveals how you connect with others, your relationship with family, and the comfort of home and close relationships. Your moon sign reflects how you handle change, internally and externally; it shows how attuned you are to your environment and your ability to respond emotionally in different situations. The moon is associated with our innermost emotions, so your moon sign paints a picture of how you approach relationships and the people you are most likely to attract. It also reveals which areas of life need attention, like communication or emotional attachment issues.

Your moon sign can offer insight into how your mind works—what motivates you and how you handle stress. It's also a significant indicator of career potential and the job that might suit you best.

In addition, your moon sign can reveal clues about past life influences and patterns that might still haunt us today. This could include unresolved childhood traumas or relationship issues, which surface later in life.

The moon is often associated with femininity, nurturing, creativity, and intuition – qualities that can be seen through understanding your moon sign. People find they have a deeper connection with their sun sign (the zodiac sign corresponding to the birth date) or identify more strongly with their moon sign instead, particularly if they've experienced significant hardships that have altered who they are.

The moon sign is a powerful tool for understanding ourselves and others and can provide invaluable insight into our emotional makeup. It can help us identify patterns or issues hidden from view otherwise, allowing us to understand who we are and why we do what we do. Understanding your moon sign enables you to connect more deeply with yourself and those around you, unlocking a whole new potential level. With this increased awareness, you will create stronger relationships and success in your chosen path.

Rising Sign

The rising sign, known as the ascendant sign, is one of the most important elements in a person's birth chart. It is a marker of how others perceive an individual and their overall outlook on life. To understand what the rising sign represents and to calculate it correctly, we must first delve into astrology.

Astrology is an ancient practice linking human behavior, events, and natural phenomena to celestial bodies such as planets, stars, and constellations. Astrologers believe our lives are shaped by cosmic energies emanating from these objects in the sky and how they interact with each other. Each object corresponds to – or "rules" over –certain zodiac signs, which, in turn, correspond to parts of our lives like family, career, love life, and more.

The rising sign is the zodiac sign that was rising on the eastern horizon at a person's birth. It sets the tone for how others perceive an individual and their attitude toward life in general. To calculate it correctly, we must first determine when a person was born and then look up which zodiac sign was rising at that time. It can be done with any astronomy programs or websites available online.

Once you have obtained your rising sign, it's important to understand what it represents. Each zodiac sign has certain qualities that can help us understand the personality of the rising sign. For example, Aries is known for its fiery nature and impulsivity, while Cancer is more sensitive and nurturing. Knowing your rising sign's qualities will help you understand how others perceive you and how to respond to maximize positive relationships.

The rising sign is significant in predicting the future. It gives us a glimpse into upcoming opportunities or challenges we might face in our lives. Understanding the energies associated with our ascendant signs allows us to prepare ourselves accordingly and make informed decisions about our futures.

Descendant Sign

The descendant sign, known as the astrological house of the seventh sign, is one of the twelve houses in a birth chart. It is considered an important factor in determining personality and life path. The descendant sign reflects our relationship with others and how we interact with them; it reveals our personal style and approach toward platonic or romantic partnerships.

The descendant sign indicates what partner someone will attract in their life. This can make or break relationships or associations forged between two individuals due to the compatibility, or lack thereof, in each other's traits. Essentially, this part of an individual's natal chart provides information about their relationship needs and how to form a meaningful connection with someone else.

The descendant sign is calculated by taking the sun's degree of the sign at your birth and subtracting it from 180 degrees. The result will be the degree of your descendant. Every zodiac sign has its house or associated area of life. By looking into this particular sector, we gain greater insight into our relationship patterns and tendencies and of potential partners.

Your descendant sign represents the qualities you seek in relationships, platonic or romantic. It indicates the people you're naturally drawn to and what energy you need to feel fulfilled within them. For example, if you have a Scorpio descendant sign, you might be attracted to mysterious and intense people. Conversely, someone with an Aquarius descendant sign might prefer open-minded and independent people.

The descendant sign reveals the energy we bring into our relationships. It represents how we learn to compromise and cooperate with others. Considering that this factor can change over time as we grow and evolve within our current connections is important. Nevertheless, its influence remains strong throughout life.

Zodiac Signs

Fire Signs: Aries, Leo, and Sagittarius

People who belong to Fire signs are passionate, energized, strong-willed, and highly independent. They have an enthusiasm for life that many find exciting and contagious. Generally, fire signs are courageous, confident, self-motivated, and taking the initiative in pursuing their dreams. They require a lot of freedom and are fiercely independent.

Aries (March 21 – April 19): An Aries sun can manifest through ambition, action, and leadership. The moon will help them to feel confident and secure and to express themselves openly and creatively. Meanwhile, their rising sign could bring out their social side and make them more open to new ideas and experiences.

Leo (July 23 – August 22): Leo suns can manifest through confidence, generosity, and loyalty. The moon in Leo helps them stay optimistic about life and encourages them to express their feelings openly and confidently. Through their rising sign, Leos become more adventurous, embracing new challenges enthusiastically.

Sagittarius (November 22 – December 21): Sagittarius suns are independent, adventurous, and open-minded. The moon in Sagittarius helps them stay positive and take risks to achieve their goals. Their rising sign makes them more spiritual and connected to the world around them.

Fire signs, like Aries, Leo, and Sagittarius, typically connect the best with their element; however, each sign has nuances. Fire signs do well with air signs, like Gemini and Aquarius, since they love discussing ideas and debating topics. Air signs' logical nature helps them provide an intellectual balance to the outgoing attitude of a fire sign's personality.

Earth signs like Taurus and Virgo provide a grounding force for fiery personalities and handle tasks in an organized manner providing the structure fire signs need. Fire signs often have many ideas but don't always know where to start or how to make them happen without some help.

On the other hand, water signs like Cancer, Scorpio, and Pisces introduce emotions into relationships a fiery sign might lack. As long as boundaries exist between two parties with different emotions, it can benefit them. In these relationships, both people must understand each other's needs to support one another's goals.

Earth Signs: Taurus, Virgo, and Capricorn

Earth signs are focused on the tangible world rather than ideas or abstract concepts. Their primary qualities are practicality, dependability, stability, and conservative nature. Earth signs focus on building foundations to get things done. They deeply respect tradition and take great pride in their work.

Taurus (April 20 – May 20): Taurus suns are reliable, determined, and resourceful people who love stability in life. The moon in Taurus helps them stay grounded while creating a sense of security within themselves. Their rising sign brings out their softer side; they become more eager to connect with others and try new things.

Virgo (August 23 – September 22): Virgo suns are often recognized as analytical, hardworking, and detail-oriented. The moon in Virgo helps them take a balanced approach to life while remaining organized. Their rising sign could bring out a side of them that loves the outdoors and enjoys connecting with nature.

Capricorn (December 22 – January 19): Capricorn suns manifest through hard work, ambition, and tenacity. The moon in Capricorn helps them create stability while setting boundaries and staying disciplined with their goals. Their rising sign could show they're more outgoing than usual, giving them the confidence to take on new challenges enthusiastically.

Earth signs strive for stability, security, and practicality in their relationships. Earth signs are based on the element of earth, paired with the cardinal quality of being driven and active. Therefore, Earth signs such as Capricorn, Taurus, and Virgo gravitate toward the stability and understanding found in fellow Earth signs. With their shared need for structure and practicality, Earth sign relationships often thrive on mutual understanding and support.

In their relationships with Fire signs, such as Aries, Leo, and Sagittarius, Earth signs provide structure and calmness, which can balance the intensity or recklessness that can be felt within a relationship. When interacting with Air signs like Libra, Aquarius, and Gemini, Earth signs can find a different conversational connection than they are used to due to Air signs' cutting wit. This deepens their relationship and teaches both parties to communicate through emotions rather than strictly logic.

Lastly, Water signs like Scorpio, Cancer, and Pisces would find each other deeply mesmerizing since both are heavily emotional and rely on intuition more than analytical thinking.

Overall, Earth signs can relate to all other elements due to their gentle stability permeating through all the relationships they encounter.

Water Signs: Cancer, Scorpio, and Pisces

People who belong to water signs are known to be emotionally intuitive, deeply sensitive, and highly imaginative. Water signs are often described as dreamers or visionaries since they live in a world of emotions rather than facts. They use their intuition and emotional intelligence to connect with others intimately.

Cancer (June 21 – July 22): Cancer suns are known for being sensitive, intuitive, and nurturing people who care deeply about those around them. The moon in Cancer allows them to comfortably express their emotions openly and honestly. Through their rising sign, Cancers are more outgoing and playful.

Scorpio (October 23 – November 21): Scorpio suns are known for being mysterious, passionate, and intense people who deeply feel emotions. The moon in Scorpio gives them a better understanding of themselves and helps them take risks without fear. Their rising sign could bring out their creative side, encouraging them to express themselves through art or writing.

Pisces (February 19 – March 20): Pisces suns are compassionate, creative, and sensitive people deeply in touch with their emotions. The moon in Pisces helps them feel emotionally secure while also having a strong connection to spirituality. They could be more open to trying new things and exploring the unknown through their rising sign.

Water signs (Cancer, Scorpio, and Pisces) generally have a deep and intuitive connection with one another. Their shared quality of emotionality, empathy, and understanding often creates an attractive dynamic between them.

In contrast, Air signs (Libra, Gemini, and Aquarius) are more likely to bring an intellectual approach to their relationships. This can stimulate water signs as it facilitates new ideas and ways of looking at life that might not have been considered before.

Earth sign relationships (Taurus, Virgo, and Capricorn) benefit from the strong sense of stability from being connected through responsible values and similar goals. The sensuality of water signs meshes perfectly with the grounded roots of Earth signs.

Fire signs (Aries, Leo, and Sagittarius) can represent passion and freedom in Water sign relationships; however, if their differences do not align, they could clash easily.

Overall, each relationship is unique, but when it comes to connecting Water with Earth, Air, and Fire- boundaries need to be respected while adventure ensues on the journey toward growth.

Air Signs: Gemini, Libra, and Aquarius

Air signs are intellectual by nature and strongly need mental stimulation. They love interacting with people, exchanging ideas, and exploring new possibilities. Air signs appreciate aesthetics and beauty; they are gentle and diplomatic in their approach to life. Air signs are generally open-minded and receptive and can easily adapt to different situations.

Gemini (May 21 – June 20): A Gemini sun brings forth a sense of adaptability, intelligence, and the ability to move easily from one thought to another. The moon in Gemini helps them feel emotionally connected with themselves and those around them. Their rising sign could bring out their humorous nature and show that they're open to trying new experiences.

Libra (September 23 – October 22): Libra suns are often diplomatic, fair-minded, and good listeners. The moon in Libra allows them to reflect more on life and their relationships with others. A Libran's rising sign can bring out their sociable side, making them more likely to reach out to new people and try new things.

Aquarius (January 20 – February 18): Aquarius suns are known for being progressive, forward-thinking, and humanitarian people. The moon in Aquarius helps them stay connected with their inner self and think outside the box when tackling problems. Their rising sign could bring out their unique nature; they become more eager to try new experiences and share fresh ideas.

Air signs, like Gemini, Libra, and Aquarius, are among the most sociable astrological signs. They typically enjoy engaging in dialogue and exploring ideas with others, which makes it easy to get along with people with differing worldviews. This can be beneficial when forming relationships with water signs like Cancer, Pisces, and Scorpio.

Water signs rely heavily on feelings rather than logic, which can often be challenging for air signs. However, if they are willing to open their perception a little and temporarily forget their need to make sense of everything, they will find many opportunities to connect with water signs.

Earth signs like Taurus, Virgo, and Capricorn share part of Air signs' desire for structure but also prefer more tangible pursuits. If an Air sign can keep from overly intellectualizing things too much, harmony can ensue between them more easily than expected.

Fire Signs, including Aries, Leo, and Sagittarius, demand excitement in thoughts and actions, which often bodes well with air signs because of their ease at bouncing from theory to theory. As long as the air sign allows enough space for variety, conversations should be lively, likely pleasing everyone involved.

These are only a few ways your Sun, Moon, and Rising signs can influence how you express yourself. Learning more about these aspects of astrology will help you gain a deeper understanding of who you are and how others perceive you. Whether through creative pursuits or reaching out to new people, embracing your unique personality traits allows you to live life with intention and purpose.

Aspects between your natal chart and potential partners' can often yield clues about their compatibility level. If both individuals' descendant signs are in harmony, the attraction and potential for a successful union will be amplified. On the other hand, if they have conflicting signs, it might be more difficult to achieve a balance between them.

Chapter 3: Planets and Houses Matter Too

Confusion can easily arise around the difference between planets and houses in astrology. At first glance, these two concepts appear similar. However, understanding the uniqueness of each is essential in decoding the mysteries of astrology. Planets signify plans for a person's life journey, such as lessons to be learned, obstacles to overcome, and, ultimately, a victory gained. Houses indicate aspects of a person's character and personality determined by their birth, including relationships, career paths, and finances. By interpreting planets and houses together, you gain a holistic insight into an individual's journey on Earth that can provide direction when navigating life's many challenges.

The planets play a pivotal role in astrology.'

Role of Planets in Astrology

Planets play a significant role in astrology and are believed to have the power to influence our lives. Each planet has a set of characteristics, individual energy, and celestial intelligence that shape the character and destiny of those born under its rule. The four main planets in charting astrological data are the Sun, Moon, Mars, and Mercury. Others, like Jupiter and Venus, are also considered important. While many don't think of the sun or moon as planets, they are referred to as planets in astrology because of their immense cosmic power, profoundly affecting our beliefs and values. Since ancient times, humans have looked to the sky for answers to navigate life's complex paths and use the information these planets provide to make educated decisions. Clearly, planets have a strong presence in astrology, providing guidance for those seeking it.

Planets in Astrology

1. The Sun

The Sun is the most important planet in astrology, and its position at a person's birth determines their associated star sign. Often referred to as "the great luminary," the Sun is the central star in our solar system and symbolizes the vital energy we need to live and grow. The Sun is often depicted as a circle with a dot in the center, symbolizing its life-giving energy. It is associated with masculine, active qualities, and its energy imparts a sense of power, confidence, and self-expression.

The Sun is associated with many deities from various cultures. In Greek mythology, Helios was the god of the sun, and Ra was the sun god in Egyptian mythology. In Hinduism, Surya is the deity associated with the Sun.

In astrology, the Sun is associated with certain zodiac signs; its exaltation, fall, or detriment. When a planet is exalted, it is powerful and can use its energy effectively. When a planet is in its fall, the energy can be difficult to control, often resulting in misdirected effort. The energy can become distorted and difficult to use when a planet is to its detriment. The Sun's exaltation sign is Aries - the sign of leadership and courage. Its fall sign is Libra - the sign of balance, fairness, and social justice. The Sun's detriment sign is Cancer - the sign of emotion and nurturing.

The Sun's energy encourages us to be strong, confident leaders and express ourselves authentically. It gives us the inner strength and courage to take charge in whatever situation we are in. The Sun's energy encourages us to be bold and independent but also allows us to find a balance between our needs and those of others. It helps us find harmony and peace in romantic, platonic, or professional relationships. The Sun's energy is vital to our well-being and encourages us to take ownership of our lives, be true to ourselves, and live life purposefully.

2. The Moon

The Moon is a powerful astrology force and the ruler of emotions and feelings. It symbolizes the unconscious, intuition, and the maternal side of life. Its glyph is a crescent shape, reflecting that it is constantly changing, just like our emotions. The Moon is associated with the keywords of security, nurturing, moods, fear, hidden enemies, and personal growth.

The ancient Greeks associated the Moon with several goddesses, such as Artemis, Hecate, and Selene. These deities were linked to intuition, the night, and life's mysteries. This reflects how the Moon encourages us to explore and develop our hidden potential.

The Moon is exalted in Taurus and falls in Scorpio, which reflects how it encourages us to draw out our sense of security and material comfort (Taurus) and to explore our more intense, darker emotions (Scorpio). Its detriment sign is Aquarius, suggesting that the Moon's influence shouldn't be too detached from our feelings.

The Moon is a powerful force in astrology, encouraging us to explore our emotions, nurture our relationships with others, and develop our inner potential. Its energy profoundly impacts our social interactions in love, friendship, or work. Remember to stay open and connected to your feelings while also learning to use them to your advantage.

3. Mercury

Mercury is a planet associated with communication, writing, and intellect. It is represented by the glyph of two crossing circles, symbolic of two minds joining together. This glyph suggests a person's intellectual capacity and ability to communicate and collaborate with others.

The keywords associated with Mercury's energy are communication, ideas, learning, and intelligence. It is often associated with the Greek god Hermes, the messenger of the gods. He symbolized eloquence, wit, and craftiness.

The Mercury is exalted in Virgo and in its fall in Pisces. In Virgo, Mercury's energy is positive, allowing people to think critically and solve problems. In Pisces, the energy is less controlled, suggesting a more creative approach to problem-solving.

Overall, Mercury's energy is communication, intelligence, and collaboration. It encourages people to think critically and develop creative solutions to problems. People with a strong Mercury placement are usually very good at forming and maintaining love-related, friendship-related, or work-related relationships. It influences people to communicate their thoughts and ideas more openly and creatively. When balanced, Mercury's energy brings clarity and understanding to social interactions. Being out of balance can lead to confusion, misunderstandings, and difficulty forming relationships.

4. Venus

Venus is the planet of love, beauty, and harmony. It is represented by the glyph of a circle with a cross on the bottom, symbolizing the female gender. It's connected to divine femininity. In astrology, Venus is important as it speaks of our desires, values, and tastes. Venus is often associated with the many deities of love and beauty, such as Aphrodite, Ishtar, Freya, and Venus, the Roman goddess of love.

The keywords associated with Venus are romance, beauty, grace, charm, socializing, and artistry. It represents our capacity to form relationships and connect with others. It is associated with sensuality, passion, and devotion.

In astrology, Venus is exalted in Pisces, its fall in Virgo, and its detriment in Scorpio. The energy Venus emits is intimacy and connection; it helps us to find beauty in ourselves and others. It facilitates social interactions harmoniously and helps us find balance in our relationships. It encourages us to be open to the beauty around us and the potential for love and relationships. It teaches us to appreciate and cultivate beauty through art, music, or other forms of expression. Venus's energy dedicates us to being more open and loving to ourselves and others.

5. Mars

Mars is an important planet in astrology as it represents our will and ambition. It symbolizes the drive to achieve our goals and the inner strength that pushes us to pursue them. The glyph for Mars is a circle with an arrow pointing upward, indicating the planet's ability to inspire us to take action.

Mars is often associated with the keywords aggression, passion, and assertiveness. These qualities are necessary for us to follow our ambitions and achieve our goals. Additionally, its energy is connected to courage, bravery, physical strength, and leadership.

The deities associated with Mars are Ares in Greek mythology and Mars in Roman mythology. Both were gods of war and violence but also represented courage and strength.

Mars is exalted in Capricorn, indicating that people with this placement are likely highly ambitious and successful in their ventures. It is in its fall in Cancer, suggesting that people with this placement might struggle to stay motivated and find it difficult to pursue their goals. It is a detriment in Libra, indicating that people with this placement struggle to take action and lack the motivation to pursue their ambitions.

Mars is a planet that represents our ambition and drive to pursue our goals. It is associated with aggression, passion, assertiveness, courage, bravery, physical strength, and leadership. Those with strong placements on Mars are highly focused on achieving their ambitions and are usually successful in their endeavors. Those with weaker placements struggle to stay motivated and find it difficult to take action. By understanding Mars's energy, people can use it to their advantage and channel its energy into successful endeavors.

6. Jupiter

Jupiter is the largest planet in our solar system. It holds a special place in astrology due to its strong influence on people's lives. In astrology, Jupiter is associated with growth, abundance, and success. It positively influences humanity's spiritual journey by providing luck, wisdom, and guidance. Jupiter is the "great teacher" because it gives us the power to learn from our experiences and grow.

The astrological glyph of Jupiter is a sign that looks like two curved lines crossed at the base, representing its expansiveness and growth potential. An arc is above the cross, symbolizing enlightenment and luck. This glyph conveys openness to new ideas, seeing beyond limits, and finding joy in learning. Jupiter's expansive energy can push us out of stagnation and unproductivity, encouraging exploration and breadth.

The keywords associated with Jupiter are abundance, expansion, growth, optimism, luck, and joy. These words perfectly encapsulate the energy Jupiter brings to our lives. It encourages us to take risks, explore new possibilities, and trust the universe.

Jupiter is associated with several deities, including Zeus, Thor, and Indra. These gods represent Jupiter's power, strength, and ability to bring us luck and guidance.

Jupiter is exalted in Cancer, demonstrating its ability to nurture and protect those around it. Its fall is in Capricorn, where its influence is weaker. Jupiter's detriment is in Aries, where it can interfere with our ability to take risks and be optimistic.

Jupiter emanates a powerful positive energy encouraging us to take risks and explore new opportunities. This energy benefits social interactions and encourages us to be open-minded and optimistic. Jupiter's influence can bring joy and abundance to our lives, and its energy helps us reach our highest potential.

7. Saturn

Saturn is astrology's planet of discipline, limitation, time, and structure. It is associated with boundaries and rules and is a gateway to the realm of maturity, wisdom, and knowledge.

Its glyph is depicted as a cross above a crescent moon, showing how it brings the physical and spiritual realms together. Its keywords include restriction, discipline, hard work, perseverance, ambition, and responsibility. Some deities associated with Saturn are Chronos, Father Time, and the Grim Reaper.

Saturn is exalted in Libra, giving the planet a sense of balance and harmony. Its fall is in Aries, making it difficult to express individual power without feeling overwhelmed by Saturn's stricter energies. Conversely, its detriment is in Cancer, where its energy can be too overwhelming and restrictive for the gentle sign.

Saturn's energy is associated with focus, structure, and discipline. It helps people stay organized and efficient in their daily activities and more self-disciplined and focused on their goals; however, if overused, Saturn's energy could lead to fear, guilt, and insecurity.

Saturn's energy can affect social interactions with other people. It can lead to isolation and loneliness, and a fear of commitment. In contrast, it helps people build strong relationships and form meaningful connections with others.

8. Uranus

Uranus is a planet of sudden and unexpected changes or upheavals and is associated with revolution and rebellion. It is the planet of unexpected surprises, technological advances, and revolutionary energy.

The astrological glyph of Uranus is an amalgamation of the cross, symbolizing spirit and healing. It is combined with a circle representing eternity. The power of change and uncertainty are associated with this planet and can break down structures and awaken consciousness in those under its influence. Its energy is unpredictable and non-conforming yet charged with creative potential.

Some keywords that describe Uranus's main characteristics in astrology are unconventional, inventive, progressive, rebellious, and unusual.

In mythology, Uranus was the primal god of the sky and the father of Cronus. Other deities associated with Uranus are Hypnos (god of sleep), Thanatos (god of death), and Hekate (goddess of magic).

In astrology, Uranus's exaltation is in Scorpio, and its detriment is in Taurus. Exaltation means a planet or sign displays its highest potential, while detriment indicates the opposite. In this case, Uranus is most powerful in Scorpio, a sign associated with intensity and transformation, so it is ideal energy for inspiring changes or innovations. Uranus's energy is weak and limited in Taurus, a sign associated with predictability and stability.

Uranus brings an energy of unpredictability, sudden shifts, and unexpected surprises. Its influence can bring a sense of liberation as it encourages people to break free from the norms and restrictions of society. Its energy can be disruptive, creating chaos and turmoil in people's lives and interpersonal relationships. It is associated with subtle and powerful changes that can cause major transformations in people's lives.

9. Neptune

Neptune is the planet of dreams, illusions, and delusion. It predicts the state of people's inner spirit, consciousness, imagination, creative potential, and enthusiasm for art and music. As a result, it is often connected to spiritual activities and the exploration of mysteries or secrets.

Neptune's astrological glyph comprises the crescent moon, an infinity sign, and a cross. It symbolizes the planet's deep connection with intuition, faith, and understanding, making it one of the most enigmatic signs in astrology. The trident tied to its symbol speaks of its power as ruler of the sea and master of divine wisdom.

The keywords associated with Neptune include spirituality, creativity, inspiration, transcendence, and imagination. It is closely related to the gods Poseidon and Neptune in Greek and Roman mythology, respectively.

Neptune's exaltation is found in Pisces, and its fall is in Virgo. Its detriment is found in Leo, making it the opposite of our Sun's sign. So, while Neptune's energy can create an environment of spiritual fulfillment, it can also be deceptive and lead to confusion and disorientation.

When Neptune is in its fullest expression, it brings creative energy and a sense of awe and wonder. Therefore, it can be very helpful in social interactions, exposing a sense of harmony and understanding. On the other hand, its dark side can cause confusion or alienation among others. Neptune's main contribution to astrology is its ability to tap into the energies of our inner spirit and creativity. Its expansive nature brings out the best in us and helps us reach our potential.

10. Pluto

Pluto is considered a "transpersonal" or spiritual planet. Pluto's glyph is a circle with a crescent at the top, representing the hidden power of the planet and its influence on life. The crescent also resembles a scythe, symbolizing Pluto's ability to sever what no longer serves us. An orb at the base of the circle rests, representing Pluto's authority over the mysteries of life and death. Together these symbols reflect Pluto's deep-seated role in transformation and regeneration in our lives. It represents transformation, rebirth, power, regeneration, elimination of the old, and creation of the new.

Pluto is associated with the keywords transmutation, regeneration, transformation, power, and death. It is associated with certain deities such as Hades, the Greek god of the underworld, and Orcus, the Roman god of death.

In astrology, Pluto's exaltation is in Scorpio, its fall is in Taurus, and its detriment is in Leo, indicating it is strongest in Scorpio and weakest in Leo. When a planet's energy is exalted, it bestows its fullest potential. In contrast, its energy is blocked or weakened when it is in fall or detriment.

Pluto's energy can positively affect a person's life if used constructively. It can bring about powerful transformation and help gain a deeper understanding of oneself and others. On the other hand, Pluto's energy can lead to control issues and power struggles if used destructively. It can cause manipulation and destruction in relationships.

Pluto is a powerful planet that can bring about sweeping changes in a person's life. It is associated with the power of transformation and can help gain insight into their darkness and the darkness of others. Be mindful of Pluto's energy and use it constructively to create positive change. When used wisely, its power can be harnessed to create something beautiful and meaningful. It symbolizes the hope that something new can be born even in the darkest moments.

Why Are the Moon, Mars, and Venus Considered the Most Revelatory In Synastry?

In synastry - comparing two birth charts to determine compatibility - the Moon, Mars, and Venus are considered the most revelatory planets.

The Moon reflects emotions and feelings, showing how two people interact on a deeper level, how they comfort one another, how they react to each other's needs, and how their day-to-day lives are in sync. Mars is a planet associated with passion and aggression, revealing how two people interact passionately. It reflects sexual chemistry and the intensity level of a relationship. Venus is all about love, affection, and beauty. It represents the harmony between two people, the attraction, and how they express their love. It shows how two people compromise to make the relationship work.

These three planets show the connection between two people and if a relationship is harmonious. They indicate how well two people understand each other, how in sync their emotions are, and why certain dynamics work between them. They reveal what is necessary for a relationship to succeed. Ultimately, looking at these planets in synastry can determine whether two people are truly compatible.

Astrological Houses and Their Relevance

The astrological house system is an ancient practice to interpret a person's character, relationships, and career prospects. It looks at the position of planets in twelve segments of the chart called houses. Each house corresponds to an area of life, so it can give insight into how to approach these specific areas and possible outcomes.

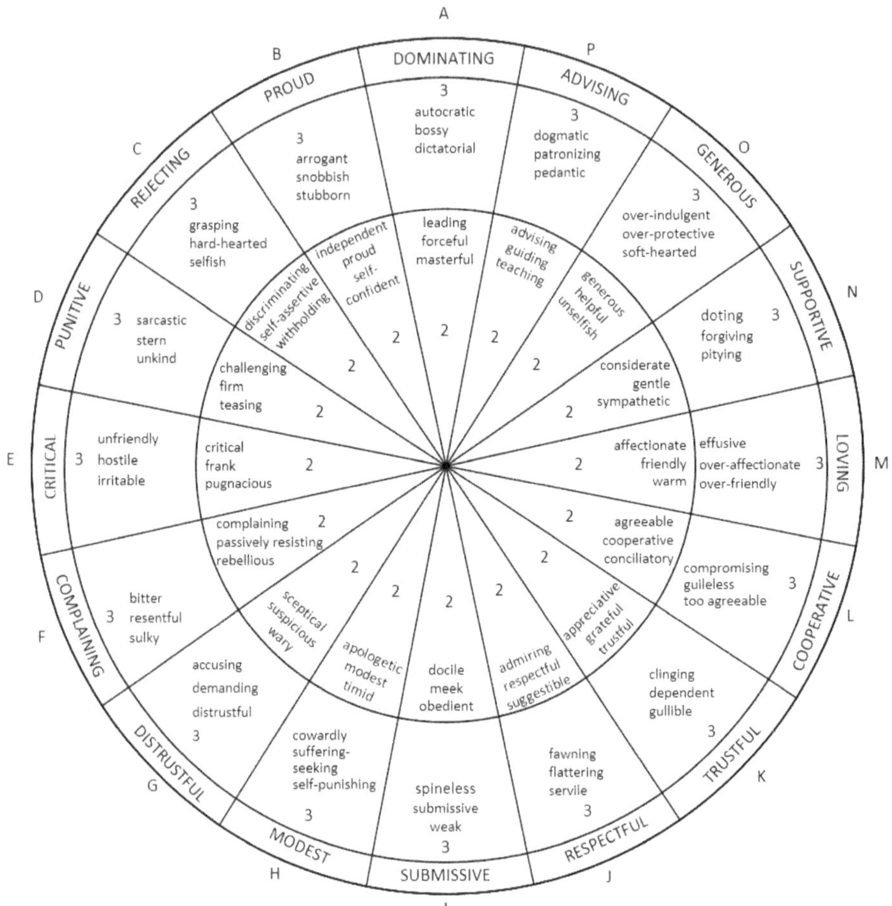

The astrological houses in detail. [5]

The first house is associated with the self and first impressions, indicating a person's appearance and how they appear to others. It gives insight into a person's health and well-being. The second house is associated with material possessions and values, while the third house rules communication and relationships. The fourth house governs the home, parents, and psychological foundations, and the fifth house is associated with pleasure, creativity, and self-expression.

The sixth house rules service to others, work life, and health habits; the seventh deals with partnerships, the eighth looks at a person's finances and legacies, and the ninth is concerned with philosophy and higher learning. The tenth house governs public recognition, social status, and career, the eleventh deals with friendships, hopes, and dreams, and the twelfth house is associated with spirituality.

When predicting compatibility through the astrological house system, pay attention to how planets are distributed throughout each house. Suppose two people have several planets in compatible houses. In that case, this suggests they may have a strong connection and will understand each other deeper. On the contrary, if many of their planets are in incompatible houses, this could suggest some difficulties or misunderstandings between them.

When determining compatibility between two people through the astrological house system, the best indicator for understanding and a successful relationship is a strong match in their respective houses. Houses that should be focused on more include the 7th house (describing partners in relationships) and the 5th house (focused on creativity, children, and romance). Houses like the 4th house focusing on home and family matters can show how well two individuals will get along in a domestic environment. Paying attention to these particular areas gives invaluable insight into a potential coupling and if they are compatible.

The Importance of the Lunar House in Astrological Compatibility

The lunar house in astrological compatibility is vital because it helps people determine their planet's position concerning one another. By exploring the positions of the celestial bodies and their impact on external influences, astrologers gain insight into relationships between two individuals. The lunar house aligns planets by reflecting how they interact with each other and the significant aspects that shape people's lives. Comparing the birth charts of two individuals provides information on their compatibility. This understanding especially benefits potential couples who want to save themselves from a relationship disaster. Further, understanding astrological compatibility allows couples to identify patterns and behavior tendencies that would otherwise go unnoticed in their relationship. Ultimately, gaining knowledge of astrology through the lunar house empowers individuals with extra tools for deciding about their life practices and personal relationships.

Chapter 4: Going Deeper through Synastry Charts

If you have ever been curious about how two people in a relationship can be so compatible or why some relationships don't last, synastry charts can be the answer. A synastry chart provides the analysis necessary to understand why the two individuals can complement each other or why they experience difficulties. Although many people find synastry charts and their analysis confusing, this chapter will guide you through the steps of creating and understanding your own synastry chart. This chapter details how to assess planets, signs, houses, and aspects between two birth data to comprehend their relationship better. There is no one-size-fits-all approach to learning about synastry charts and reading them; however, with knowledge from this chapter, you gain an idea of where to begin to grasp its mysteries.

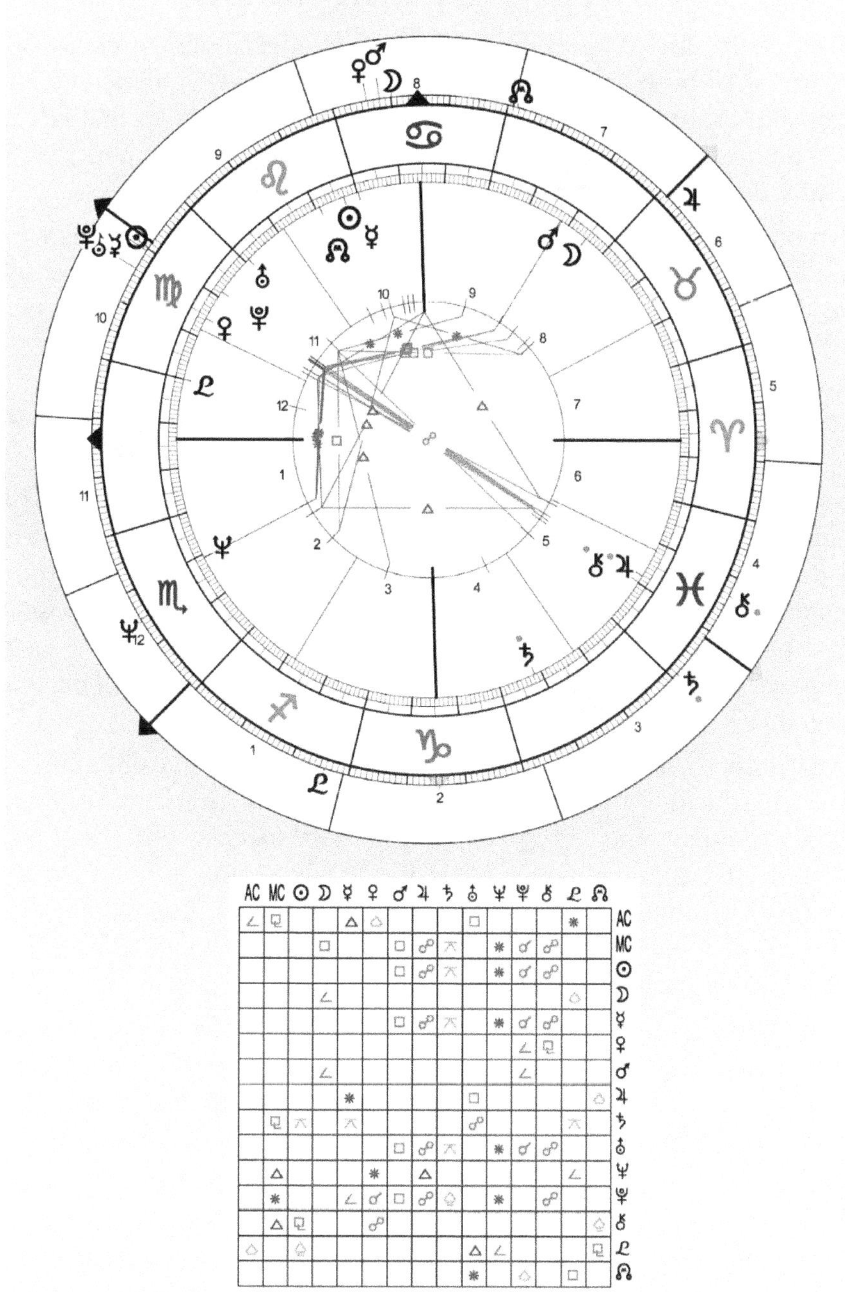

Synastry chart. [6]

Concept of Synastry Charts

Synastry charts, known as compatibility charts or relationship horoscopes, compare the birth charts of two individuals to understand their relationship dynamics better. Synastry is based on the belief that celestial bodies influence and indicate correlations between people's personalities, life paths, and destinies.

Synastry charts are created by overlaying one person's natal chart onto another's and looking for aspects (the angles) between them. Aspects show how planets in one person's chart interact with those in another's chart; they reflect potential areas of harmony and discord between two individuals. Two people's astrological signatures might differ, but if their chart placements form harmonious aspects, their relationship can be more successful.

Generally, conjunctions (0 degrees) and oppositions (180 degrees) are considered the most important aspects in synastry charts. However, trines (120 degrees), sextiles (60 degrees), and squares (90 degrees) are equally important. Conjunctions indicate a merging of energies, while oppositions show a push-and-pull dynamic; trines create an easy energy flow; sextiles encourage growth and exploration; and squares bring challenge and tension that is constructive or destructive.

Synastry is by no means an exact science, and it should never be used to make hard-and-fast decisions about a relationship or its future. Rather, it provides insight into how two people relate to each other and helps them understand their union's dynamics. It offers clues as to which areas of the relationship need extra attention and care. Ultimately, synastry charts give us tools for self-reflection and understanding to help us build healthier, more harmonious relationships.

In addition to providing insight into individual relationships, synastry can compare a group of people to understand their dynamics. It is especially helpful for couples or business partners to better grasp their relationship and how it fits into their greater community's context.

Synastry charts are an invaluable tool for understanding the complex nature of relationships. By studying these aspects, we gain valuable insight into how two people interact with each other and what potential areas of harmony and discord exist between them. With this knowledge, we can cultivate healthier, more successful partnerships with those around us. Although they should never be used to make definitive decisions about a relationship, synastry charts help us comprehend the dynamics in our lives.

Ways to Create Your Synastry Charts

Creating a synastry chart to compare the compatibility between two people can be a complex task. However, many software packages and tools are available to simplify the process. This chapter explores some popular options for calculating and interpreting synastry charts.

One of the most comprehensive software packages for creating and analyzing synastry charts is Astro-Vision Astrology Software. This program includes an extensive database of astrological information with an easy-to-use interface for creating synastry charts. It includes detailed interpretations of individual planets in natal and transit charts and their introspects. Additionally, it features customizable report creation with graphical representations of the chart data and compatibility indicators.

Another popular option for creating synastry charts is Janus Astrology Software. This program offers numerous features designed to make charting easier and more accurate. It includes an extensive database of astrological information, such as natal and transit planets, introspects between them, house placements, midpoints, asteroids, and fixed stars. Additionally, it provides detailed interpretations of individual planets in natal and transit charts with compatibility indicators. It offers customizable report creation with graphical representations of the chart data.

Free online tools are available for those looking for a simpler way to calculate synastry charts without purchasing software or signing up for a subscription service. There are several online chart services; one of the most popular is Astrodienst's Synastry Chart Calculator (https://www.astro.com/horoscope). This tool allows users to enter two birth dates and compare their compatibility with a simple chart. It provides basic interpretations of the planets in each person's natal chart and their introspects.

For those wanting to go beyond a simple chart comparison and dive deeper into the complexities of synastry analysis, AstroMatrix (https://astromatrix.org/)offers a comprehensive suite of software packages and tools specifically designed for this purpose. Their Synastry Matrix program (https://www.positiveastrology.com/synastry-matrices-collisions/) includes astrological data from natal and transit charts and detailed interpretations of individual planets and aspects. Additionally, it provides customizable report creation with graphical representations of the chart data and compatibility indicators.

Finally, for those interested in exploring the ancient art of using astrology to assess the potential success or failure of a relationship, AstroSynthesis (learn more here: https://www.astrosynthesis.com.au/) is another comprehensive software package available. This program includes an extensive database of astrological information with detailed interpretations of individual planets and aspects. It provides customizable report creation with graphical representations of the chart data and compatibility indicators based on traditional synastry methods.

Many options are available for calculating synastry charts and understanding their implications. One can better understand the potential compatibility between two people by taking advantage of these various tools and resources. However, no software or tool can make up for the individual insights and intuition to truly understand a relationship. Ultimately, it is up to you to use these tools to understand a romantic, platonic, or other relationship. With the right approach and resources at your disposal, you can gain valuable insight into how compatible two people truly are.

Calculating Synastry Charts

Synastry charts compare two people's natal charts and provide insight into their relationship. A synastry chart is a powerful tool for understanding the dynamics of a relationship; it reveals how each individual's planets interact with the other person's chart. The combination of these two energies can help understand and improve relationships. Several methods can be used to calculate a synastry chart, but they all involve comparing one person's birth chart with another's.

One way to begin analyzing a potential relationship is by using transits when a planet in one person's chart interacts with the other person's planets or points during the relationship. This method can assess how well two individuals are likely to get along and if any areas of conflict could arise.

Another way to calculate synastry is by looking at aspects. Aspects are when two planets in one person's chart form an angle with each other and interact with a planet or point in another person's chart. Several aspects can be used to calculate synastry, such as conjunction, sextile, trine, square, quincunx, opposition, semi-sextile, and sesquiquadrate. Each aspect's meaning depends on what it connects in both people's charts.

The third way to calculate a synastry chart is to look at midpoints. Midpoints are when two planets in one person's chart interact with the same planet or point in another person's chart. They provide insight into how each individual's energies blend and potential areas of growth or challenge.

Finally, considering the houses and signs when calculating synastry charts is important. Houses represent different areas of life, such as home, relationships, careers, and finances. Looking at which house each person's planets fall into will reveal how they interact with each other in various aspects of life. Signs represent different elements and qualities that influence our personality, behavior, and outlook. Looking at which sign each person's planets fall into provides deeper insight into how they interact with one another.

Calculating synastry charts is a complex process, but once you understand the basics, it can be a great way to understand relationships. By studying transits, aspects, midpoints, houses, and signs, you get an in-depth look into how two people's energies interact and what areas of growth or challenges arise. With this knowledge, you can better understand yourself and your relationships with others.

How to Read Synastry Charts

Before taking a deep dive into a synastry chart, it is important to have some background knowledge of the core elements of the chart. Those include understanding the planets and aspects used. Planets represent different areas of life, while aspects tell how they interact in your relationship. They are the building blocks that make up a synastry chart and provide insight into how two individuals will interact. To get the most out of reading a synastry chart, it is important to have a solid understanding of what planets and aspects mean.

Planets and Luminaries

Synastry's most important planets/luminaries are the Moon, Venus, and Mars. The Moon is one of the most important planets in synastry because it represents our emotions and how we naturally respond to a situation. Placements of the Moon in one's chart will determine what type of relationship they need and seek out and their natural responses to stimuli. The Moon can show us where we find comfort, security, and intimacy. It also reveals our emotional triggers, which can be beneficial in navigating conflicts within a relationship.

Venus is another major planet/luminary in synastry that signifies love, attraction, beauty, and harmony between two people. Its placement in both partners' charts will reveal whether or not they are attracted to each other on an emotional level. It also shows us the type of partnership that would fulfill both individuals. Strong connections between Venus placements in the two charts could indicate their lasting bond.

Mars is the third most important planet/luminary for synastry, representing sexuality, passion, aggression, and drive. Mars placements can be telling when assessing how physically compatible two individuals are with one another. A strong connection between Mars placements could mean that these individuals would have intense physical chemistry with each other. Mars also provides insight into how one person might handle or react during arguments or disagreements with their partner.

Finally, the Sun and Ascendant are key factors when looking at the compatibility between two people's personalities. The Sun sign reflects an individual's core character traits while the Ascendant describes their outer demeanor or appearance; these qualities may attract others or provide an initial spark even before any conversation occurs between them. Comparing these placements in synastry can help uncover complementary qualities that could potentially form the foundation for long-term relationships built on mutual understanding and respect for each other's needs and desires.

Important Aspects in Synastry

Conjunction: The conjunction is formed when two planets are in the same sign, creating a direct connection between them that can be either beneficial or challenging depending on the exact planetary energies involved. This aspect amplifies both planets' expressions, often to an intense and powerful degree. A conjunction can represent an opportunity for growth and transformation, with both planets combining their power to create something entirely new.

Trine: When two planets form a trine aspect, they form an angle of 120° between them – forming a near-perfect connection. This is considered one of the most beneficial aspects, as it allows for harmonious energy exchange between the two planets involved. It also creates a supportive environment where challenges can be overcome easily and effortless growth is possible. Trines usually indicate luck and good fortune, allowing situations to unfold naturally in one's favor without any extra effort.

Sextile: Sextiles are formed when two planets are at an angle of 60° from each other. This aspect is generally considered more helpful than challenging. It usually indicates favorable circumstances in which one can succeed with minimal effort or disruption to their normal routine. People with sextiles in their charts often find themselves blessed with good luck and positive outcomes without exerting too much energy toward achieving them.

Square: Squares occur when two celestial bodies form an angle of 90° from each other, creating tension between them that must be balanced to move forward. Squares typically require active work to resolve issues or progress further; they can signal areas needing attention or signify challenges that must be addressed before true alignment can happen. They also offer the potential for growth by understanding how different forces interact and balancing opposing energies within oneself and others.

Opposition: Oppositions form when two celestial bodies are 180° apart from each other, creating a direct link between them but also strong tension due to their conflicting energies. Oppositions often reveal difficult truths about ourselves or our relationships as we learn how our values clash with those around us. However, when approached properly, they can provide valuable insight into our motivations and help us broaden our perspective on life's nuances by forcing us out of our comfort zone into a place of greater understanding over time.

Quincunx: Quincunxes occur when an orb of 1-2 degrees separates two celestial bodies, forming an incomplete relationship that needs further exploration to reach its full potential. Quincunxes can indicate hidden obstacles or karmic lessons yet unresolved; they challenge us to look beyond the surface level to uncover what lies beneath so we may have a deeper understanding of where we stand energetically with others and ourselves alike.

It is also important to understand the different aspects of synastry and how they might indicate compatibility between two people. Most commonly, the Sun, Moon, Ascendant, Venus, and Mars are considered when analyzing a relationship.

When evaluating the Sun-Moon connection, it is important to consider how both parties' energies interact. The Sun represents our core identity, while the Moon reflects our inner emotions and needs. A harmonious connection between these two planets indicates an understanding of each other's core identity and emotional needs. Similarly, an opposition or square can indicate difficulty understanding or empathizing with each other's feelings and needs.

The Ascendant symbolizes how we outwardly express ourselves to others, so a strong aspect between this planet and the Sun or Moon can help establish an easy flow of communication within the relationship. Trine and sextile aspects tend to create more harmonious energy between partners than their oppositions or squares do.

Venus is known as the planet of love, beauty, pleasure, and companionship. Aspects between Venus and Mars signify sexual attraction, while trine and sextile aspects create a harmonious connection; however, too much comfort within this connection could lead to a lack of excitement in the relationship. Harsh aspects such as squares or oppositions may bring conflicts but greater passion into the relationship as well.

Finally, aspects between the Moon and Venus or Mars show how emotionally in tune with each other two people are. While trines and sextiles represent smooth communication where both parties understand each other's emotions without effort, squares or oppositions can indicate misunderstandings that can strain the relationship if not properly addressed by both partners.

Houses

When comparing birth charts in synastry, the 1st, 5th, 7th, and 8th houses of each person's chart are particularly important. These houses are associated with relationships and intimacy, so if any of a person's planets fall into one of these houses in their partner's chart or vice versa, it can be seen as an indication of a closer and more intimate relationship between them.

The 1st house (ascendant) is the most visible house in a birth chart and is associated with beginnings, identity, and self-expression. This house can represent how two people interact or present themselves to one another in synastry. It shows how each individual interprets the other's behavior and what kind of impression they make on one another when they first meet. This house also looks at how both partners respond to life's challenges together and what values they share.

The 5th house is associated with creativity, passion, pleasure, romance, and children. In synastry, this house looks at the degree of passion between two individuals and their shared interests. It looks at how much fun they have when together and how well their emotions mesh. It also examines whether they express themselves creatively in relation to one another and any potential for having children together.

The 7th house (descendant) is associated with partnership and commitment. In synastry, it looks at whether two individuals can agree on important issues, such as goals, values, or beliefs, which will form a strong bond between them over time. Aspects between planets in this house indicate how willing both people are to compromise for the sake of their union overall. For example, suppose Mars from one person falls into the 7th house of the other. In that case, it could show heated arguments or clashes between them. Still, it could also signify that both people are willing to fight for each other out of love instead of fear or resentment.

Lastly is the 8th house, which looks at two people's ability to trust one another deeply by exploring each other's vulnerabilities behind closed doors. This includes understanding each other's hidden desires and secrets as well as physical intimacy but also extends past these elements, such as opening up about emotions that one has difficulty expressing out loud, like sadness or anxiety. It represents an almost sacred bond between two people where nothing goes unsaid or unrealized, even if it may initially be uncomfortable for either party. The 8th house offers insight into the level of trust within a relationship and whether both parties feel safe enough around each other to open up completely without judgment or fear that something will be taken advantage of or used against them later on down the line.

Step-by-Step Guide on How to Read Synastry Charts

Step 1: Understand the Basics – Before reading a synastry chart, it is important to understand the basics. Synastry charts are astrological diagrams that show how two individuals interact. They look at how the zodiac signs of each individual influence one another and can be used to gain insight into relationships. Additionally, these charts compare aspects such as planets, signs, and houses between two people to identify potential areas of conflict or harmony.

Step 2: Gather Data – To start reading a synastry chart, you will need to gather data from both individuals' birth charts. You need the exact time and location of birth for each person to accurately compare their respective planets, signs, and houses. Once you have this information, you can draw up a synastry chart with both individuals' positions plotted onto one diagram.

Step 3: Analyze Aspects – The comparison of planets, signs, and houses is known as an aspect. Each aspect has its own meaning, which can help shed light on a relationship dynamic between two people. Two people's aspects can be considered harmonious or challenging depending on their interpretation. For example, a trine (120-degree angle) might indicate a strong understanding between two people, whereas an opposition (180-degree angle) could somehow signify tension or conflict.

Step 4: Interpret Houses – Synastry charts also consider the house placements of both individuals within the chart. These houses represent different areas of life, such as career, travel, or love and romance, which can provide further insight into how two people relate to each other in specific regards. By looking at what house placements overlap between the two charts, it is possible to gain insight into how those areas might manifest in the relationship dynamic between them.

Step 5: Look For Patterns – When examining a synastry chart, it is helpful to look for patterns across all aspects being compared between the two persons' charts rather than focusing purely on individual placements alone. This means looking for common threads, such as multiple difficult aspects indicating potential challenges in the relationship or harmonious connections pointing towards understanding and connectedness instead. By looking at patterns across multiple aspects, it is easier to gain an overall sense of how these two individuals may interact with one another rather than just looking at individual elements separately from one another.

Step 6: Draw Conclusions – After considering all these factors, it is possible to start drawing conclusions about how these two personalities might interact with one another based on their respective birth charts when put together in a synastry format. It is important to analyze each aspect being compared and think about why certain connections might exist between these two natal diagrams to draw meaningful interpretations from them. Doing this should give you some idea about the dynamics between these two individuals, allowing for better understanding and communication within their relationship going forward.

Overall, it is essential for individuals involved in any kind of relationship to understand significant aspects found in synastry as these will likely have great influence over their compatibility as a couple moving forward. It is also pertinent for them to pay attention to any possible challenge points posed by harsh planetary connections. That way, they may be aware of what obstacles they may need to overcome should they decide to take their partnership to the next level, whatever that may entail for them individually or collectively as a unit.

The complex dynamics of love and human relationships can be better understood through synastry. Since nothing so profoundly affects our lives as our contact with others, synastry must be approached with thoroughness and an open mind. Consider all synastry aspects to obtain an accurate assessment of a relationship.

Chapter 5: Aries and Taurus

Aries is a fire sign, and Taurus is an Earth sign; both are more different than they are alike. This chapter analyzes the first two zodiac signs, presents their strengths and weaknesses, and how they impact your personality as the sun, moon, rising, and descendants signs. This information is the first step to exploring their compatibility with the rest of the zodiac.

Aries. [7]

Aries

Glyph

An Aries glyph or symbol is a ram's curved horns representing the sign's main characteristics. The horns symbolize Aries's take-charge personality and not letting anything stand in their way. These individuals use their "horns" to push against challenges or obstacles. Like rams, known for their aggressive behavior, Aries people have a bad and explosive temper.

The rams have a sacred history. In ancient Egypt, they lived in temples and were associated with the gods, making Aries worthy of its place as the first of the zodiac signs. Ram is a symbol of power, one of the main characteristics that define Aries. It showcases Aries's fiery, unstoppable, and stubborn personality.

The ram signifies Aries's ability to achieve anything they set their mind to and be go-getters. The horns are associated with "cornucopia" (the horn of plenty in Greek mythology), which connects the sign with fertility and abundance.

Dates

From March 21st to April 19th.

Key Phrase

"I am"

These words are fitting for the first of the zodiac signs. They show Aries's awareness of their individuality, who they truly are, and their strong belief in themselves. Similar to the ram, Aries is a leader who always takes charge. When their competitive side takes over, they can win any competition or challenge they face. This attribute makes them leaders who develop their own definition of success and who they want to be. "I am..." and whatever comes next reflects their unique and true identity.

Strengths

• Headstrong	• Direct
• Brave	• Innocent
• Fearless	• Independent
• Powerful	• Strong sense of justice
• Assertive	• Forgiving

Aries individuals have a competitive side and a desire to win. Hence, they are successful in all their endeavors. They always advance in their careers, and since they don't like taking orders from anyone, Aries work hard until they become bosses or CEOs or start their own businesses. An Aries never shies away from a challenge; they thrive on them. They find challenges exciting and a perfect escape from boredom and routine.

As the first zodiac sign, Aries is born to lead, not follow. They have leadership skills and strengths that inspire people. A confident and brave individual, Aries usually takes the initiative and leads others. Even if they lack experience, people usually trust Aries to handle any situation.

Aries are highly energetic and passionate individuals, and their enthusiasm usually rubs off on the people in their lives. They act as role models to their loved ones and push them to accomplish their goals, overcome challenges, and live the life of their dreams. People usually gravitate toward Aries because of their magnetic, positive, and interesting personality. They bring excitement wherever they go, whether at a boring party or job Aries will make anything fun.

They approach everything with a full heart, either all in or all out. They have a zest for life; you can feel it in their actions. Once they decide to do something, nothing and no one can stop them. They have the passion, courage, and strength to achieve their goals. The word impossible doesn't exist in their dictionary.

Having a strong sense of justice and an argumentative personality, they will stand up for their loved ones against anyone who mistreats them. An Aries will never accept injustice and will do whatever it takes to make things right.

Although they have a bad temper, Aries quickly forgive and don't hold a grudge. If you want an honest opinion, ask Aries. They are direct and say it as it is. Aries doesn't sugarcoat the truth, which is a trait many people appreciate. As a fire sign, they are bold and fearless. They jump into anything without thinking, a trait that some consider a strength, while others find it a weakness.

Weaknesses

- Bad-tempered
- Aggressive
- Controlling
- Self-centered
- Selfish
- Loud
- Blunt
- Impatient
- Pushy
- Impulsive
- Mood swings
- Inconsistent
- Arrogant

Stubborn and aggressive, Aries can be difficult and frustrate those around them. Not everyone is as competitive as they are, which can lead to many arguments and friction in their relationships. Arrogant individuals, Aries want all eyes to be on them as they crave attention. Although some people appreciate Aries's excitement, some can find them overwhelming. Aries hate boredom and enjoy shaking things up in social situations. However, quiet individuals who prefer a stable environment don't always appreciate their constant enthusiasm. As a fire sign, Aries can be hot-headed and prone to losing their temper.

Sometimes, they have a "my way or the highway" attitude, especially at work. Their competitiveness and willingness to do anything to achieve their goals can make them come off as selfish. They also don't have the patience for people who lack motivation or initiative. Although some people appreciate their blunt personality, others wish Aries were more diplomatic.

Aries are impulsive individuals who usually act without thinking and make rushed and bad decisions. They don't consider the consequences of their actions, which can get them in trouble. Aries can be hot and cold and impulsive in their relationships. They can fall in love quickly and fall out of love without warning, confusing their partner.

Pet Peeves

Impatient individuals, Aries's biggest pet peeve is waiting. They hate waiting in line, walking behind a slow person, getting stuck in traffic, waiting for a seat at a restaurant, or anything that tests their patience. They can't stand people who hold them back, prevent them from achieving their goals, or interfere in their spur-of-the-moment decisions.

Blunt individuals, Aries can't stand passive-aggressive behavior as they consider it as lying. They prefer others to air their grievances even if it leads to a big fight. Positive individuals, Aries can't tolerate the negativity of passive aggression.

Ruling Planet

Aries is ruled by Mars. In Roman mythology, Mars was the god of war, perfectly representing Aries' brave and fearless warrior side. Mars is the planet of action, initiative, passion, and energy, all traits that describe an Aries. Aries' confidence in their abilities and believing there is no one better to get the job done results from Mars's impact. The red and hot plant influences Aries's impulsiveness, intensity, passion, hot temper, and take-charge attitude. Mars provides them with the leadership skills and energy that drive them to accomplish their goals and makes them unstoppable in the face of challenges.

Aries as a Sun Sign

As a sun sign, Aries motivates and inspires other zodiac signs to grow. Helpful individuals, they provide guidance and advice to their friends and co-workers. They love to be number one and be showered with compliments and praise. Aries will help you as long as it doesn't interfere with their goals. However, they are prone to jealousy when others advance over them.

They enjoy chasing after the object of their affection. Aries are bold and flirty and don't hesitate to express their feelings. However, they get bored with the routine that often accompanies relationships. They will do anything to recreate the old magic. It can be anything from preparing a nice surprise to creating drama. Aries sun sign is compatible with Leo, Sagittarius, Libra, Pisces, Virgo, and Gemini. It is least compatible with Cancer, Capricorn, Taurus, Aries, Scorpio, and Aquarius.

Aries as a Moon Sign

Moon Aries are creative, optimistic, and intelligent individuals. They have a plan for every aspect of their lives, like advancing in their careers or making their relationships work. They believe they can accomplish anything. However, they can get frustrated if they fail to achieve their goals. When their competitiveness takes over, they can't help feeling jealous and do whatever it takes to win. They crave excitement and novelty and find comfort in new situations, a competitive environment, or anything that gives them an adrenaline rush.

Aries moon brings passion to relationships. Even if you have a quiet or introverted nature or an unadventurous or cool sun sign, you will still be passionate, even if it's on the inside. You will have a hot and explosive temper that results in intense arguments and yelling.

Aries moon is most compatible with the Sagittarius, Leo, Aries, Libra, Aquarius, and Gemini moons. They are least compatible with the Taurus, Cancer, Virgo, Scorpio, Capricorn, and Pisces moons.

Aries as a Rising Sign

If Aries is your rising sign, you are an independent, opinionated, and brave individual. Most people are probably intimidated by you due to your powerful presence that commands a room. You would rather ask for forgiveness than permission, so you act first and apologize later. An Aries rising individual has strong instincts that never fail them.

Aries rising signs are compatible with Sagittarius, Leo, and all fire and air risings. They are least compatible with Virgo, Pisces, and all Earth and water rising signs.

Aries as a Descendant Sign

Aries descendants are the opposite of the Aries zodiac. They aren't as bold and will let others take the first step, especially in romantic relationships. Making a strong first impression is significant for them, so they usually pay attention to their appearance and behavior around others and dress to impress. They are very calm and patient, but they struggle with making decisions.

In relationships, they want someone who can inspire them and bring out the best version of themselves.

Taurus

Taurus.⁸

Glyph

Taurus's glyph is a circle of a bull's head and its curved horns. The bull symbolizes the Taurus's slow and steady nature. Like its symbol, Taurus is intense, passionate, powerful, tenacious, strong, and calm. However, they can have a destructive temper like a raging bull if provoked. As a result, they thrive in calm environments. They have a "bull-head" that pushes them to achieve their goals. Like the slow bull, they are very patient individuals who don't like to be rushed.

Dates

From April 20th to May 20th.

Key Phrase

"I have"

Tauruses are grounded individuals who focus on the real world instead of having their heads in the clouds. They respect everything the physical world has to offer and believe in the power of ownership. Taurus individuals are usually aware of all their possessions. They have a materialistic side and enjoy buying new things and living luxurious lives. A Taurus loves saying, "I have a new car, new phone, new outfit, etc."

Strengths

- Trustworthy
- Level-headed
- Enduring
- Driven
- Persistent
- Determined
- Steady

- Tenacious
- Tasteful
- Solid
- Patient
- Responsible
- Committed
- Generous

Tauruses are reliable and loyal individuals. Calm and patient, they take their time before deciding or taking action. As a result, they usually make the right choice and are regarded as sensible people. They like to do things at their pace and see no point in being in a rush. Tauruses understand that delivering the best results takes time. Whether it is their love life or career, a Taurus doesn't mind waiting. They respect other people's needs and will give them space and time to make their own decisions. Determined individuals, Tauruses get things done, accomplish their goals, and tie loose ends.

They enjoy living a luxurious life, so they work hard to afford the lifestyle they crave. However, they are also smart with money and invest it to secure their future. Tauruses are fun people who enjoy laughing and spending time with their loved ones. Although they love spoiling themselves, Tauruses know when it's time to have fun and when to pull back and focus on work.

Tauruses are stable and always have their feet on the ground, which makes them predictable. However, they aren't boring people, but they will always come through for others and keep their word. People can always depend on a Taurus because they are reliable individuals. They are extremely loyal and will always be there for their loved ones.

They are laid-back individuals who avoid stress and enjoy relaxation. People love spending time with them because they are chilled and savor every moment. Regarding their goals, no one is more focused or determined than a Taurus. They will do whatever it takes to achieve their objectives and are usually very successful. Whether it's people or work, Tauruses are committed and never give up on their hearts' desires.

Weaknesses

- Stubborn
- Possessive
- Narrow-minded
- Selfish
- Indulgent
- Inability to change
- Materialistic
- Gluttonous
- Fanatical

Tauruses, like their animal symbols, are very stubborn. They prefer a stable environment and are very resistant to change. Trying to convince a Taurus to adjust to something is exhausting because they will resist or agree at their own pace, which can frustrate their co-workers and friends. Once they set their mind to something or make a decision, it is impossible to deter them. It can create discord in their professional and personal lives. Their love for stability is a double-edged sword, as it can prevent them from taking risks or trying new things.

They are perfectionists and set themselves high standards. However, if their work isn't good enough, they will beat themselves up about it. Patient and calm, Tauruses don't easily get angry, but it can result in aggressive or destructive behavior when they do. Narrow-minded individuals, Taurus don't accept other people's opinions or points of view. They must always do things their way because any other way is wrong.

Tauruses are overprotective of their relationships and belongings, which can make them possessive. Possessiveness is how they remain in control of situations and prevent change and unwanted surprises. In relationships, they can get too attached and very trusting early, leading them to depend on others.

Their inability to change, love for comfort, and chill attitude can make Tauruses prone to laziness. They get stuck in their comfort zone and resist any chance to grow. Their overprotectiveness, possessiveness, and stubbornness are why they come off as self-centered and selfish.

Pet Peeves

Tauruses don't like to be rushed or given a project with a close deadline. They can become stagnant and shut down when they can't do things at their own pace. Impracticality is another pet peeve that frustrates Tauruses. They like to have a plan, schedule, and the necessary information to get things done. They don't think highly of reckless people who don't plan in advance. For instance, people who always leave the house with uncharged phones annoy Tauruses. They consider it reckless and irresponsible behavior.

Ruling Planet

Venus is the goddess of love and beauty in Roman mythology. Venus, the planet of pleasure and luxury, rules Taurus. The planet reinforces Taurus's sensual nature, materialistic nature, indulgence, and expensive taste. It influences Taurus's generous, harmonious, and affectionate personality. Tauruses gravitate toward fine art, nice perfumes, delicious food, and anything that entices their senses. Venus encourages Tauruses to spoil and treat themselves to the finer things in life. Since Venus is the goddess of love, it drives Tauruses to be committed and loyal in their relationships. Taurus individuals have Venus to thank for their charming, creative, and likable personalities.

Taurus as a Sun Sign

Tauruses are hard workers who only put effort and time into rewarding endeavors. They prefer artistic and creative careers that encourage self-expression and independence. As much as they work hard, Tauruses play hard, too. They take long breaks to focus on their well-being and self-care and relax, and probably how they got a reputation for being lazy.

Taurus thrive when they are in love. They prefer the stability and comfort of a relationship. Thanks to their calm nature, Tauruses prefer a peaceful environment away from conflict and drama.

People with Taurus as their sun sign are most compatible with Capricorn, Virgo, Scorpio, Taurus, Gemini, Cancer, and Pisces. They are least compatible with Aquarius, Leo, Aries, Libra, and Sagittarius.

Taurus as a Moon Sign

Taurus moon people believe they deserve the best of everything. They often reward themselves after finishing a big project or exercising and dieting for a week. Confident individuals, the Taurus moon often trust their inner voice and are led by their instincts. Their biggest fear is uncertainty, especially in relationships. If they have to relocate, break up with their partner, or leave their job, the Taurus moon will struggle and feel lost.

Regarding self-care, Taurus moon people know how to pamper themselves. They will spend the day at the spa, treat themselves to a luxurious meal, or buy fancy scented candles. They will most likely stick with whatever they choose since they don't like trying new things.

Taurus moon is compatible with the Taurus, Cancer, Virgo, Scorpio, Capricorn, and Pisces moons. They are least compatible with the Aries, Gemini, Leo, Libra, Sagittarius, and Aquarius moons.

Taurus as a Rising Sign

These people are strong-willed, dependable, and fierce. They are active individuals who like to stay busy and create new things. They enjoy activities like knitting, cooking, or gardening. Taurus-rising people prefer to be around those who understand their need to take things slow. Once they trust someone, they establish a connection with them. Taurus's rising signs are compatible with Pisces, Virgo, Capricorn, Cancer, Taurus, and Scorpio. They are least compatible with Libra, Aries, and other air and fire signs.

Taurus as a Descendant Sign

Taurus descendant people are mysterious, intense, and passionate. Traditional individuals born under this sign care about special occasions, holidays, and anniversaries. They prefer to be around someone with similar ethics, values, and beliefs. They are prone to jealousy and pride, which can impact their relationships. Taurus descendants are attracted to beautiful partners to show off to others. They want to be with someone they can trust and be their truest self around.

Aries and Tauruses are different in many aspects and can seem opposites. However, these two can still be compatible as opposites attract. However, not all signs are different, like Aries and Taurus; some share many similarities.

Chapter 6: Gemini and Cancer

Gemini is an air sign, and Cancer is a water sign. While Gemini is the life of the party and enjoys socializing on the weekends, Cancer is a homebody who prefers a quiet evening at home.

This chapter will cover the third and fourth zodiac signs so you can decide if you are compatible.

Gemini

Gemini.[9]

Glyph

The Gemini glyph depicts the Roman number II, representing the famous twin stars Castor and Pollux. These stars symbolize Gemini's duality. The Twins represent its creativity, ingenuity, and strong communication skills. They also symbolize Gemini's indecisive personality, as they often change their minds. The twins' duality showcases the exchange of ideas often associated with this sign. Adaptable and flexible, Gemini can sometimes confuse people into thinking they have two different personalities.

The twins also represent the duality of many Gemini women. They can be loving, sweet, and passionate, but suddenly they become cold and distant. It isn't easy to understand a Gemini because of their dual personality; however, this duality is a unique quality no other zodiac sign possesses.

The pillars at the top and bottom of the glyph signify the unity between intuition and intellect. They also point in different directions symbolizing how Gemini's brain works. People born under this sign often bounce from one idea to another and have various desires to fulfill.

Dates

From May 21st to June 20th.

Key Phrase

"I think"

Communication, ideas, and thoughts define this sign. A Gemini's mind never stops thinking. They entertain many thoughts because they believe nothing is more powerful than having a curious mind. Gemini people are known for their intellect, making the words "I think" pretty fitting for them.

Strengths

- Communicative
- Intelligent
- Creative
- Connected
- Adaptable
- Insightful
- Inquisitive
- Flexible
- Versatile
- Knowledgeable
- Agile
- Attentive

Charming and social butterflies, Geminis are great conversationalists attracting people with their wit and charisma. They are fun with magnetic personalities and usually have many friends. Geminis aren't emotional individuals. They are more concerned with thoughts and ideas instead of feelings. Like Aries, Geminis can't tolerate boredom, so they always come up with fun things to do.

Thanks to their curious nature, Geminis are very knowledgeable. They like to learn about various subjects, so they appear smart and interesting. However, their knowledge is usually superficial. They want to learn about many things, so they jump from one topic to the next before fully understanding.

Creative and witty, Geminis can become successful entrepreneurs and journalists. They are risk-takers who never shy away from a challenge. Geminis have a way with words and can easily express their thoughts and avoid any misunderstandings. Due to their duality, they can see both sides of an argument.

Geminis want to live life to the fullest. Easy-going and flexible, they are always up for an adventure. They thrive in new situations because they are fast learners and want to stay busy. However, if the activity isn't stimulating, they will lose interest.

Geminis are the perfect employees. They are multitaskers, clever, and inventive; they can think on their feet and calmly handle tough situations. They are problem-solvers who can look at a situation from different perspectives and develop out-of-the-box solutions.

People born under this sign are known for their sense of humor. Confident, intelligent, and quick-witted, they are always prepared with a funny comeback. People are drawn to Geminis because of their natural charisma and mysterious personality.

Geminis are very energetic, and they don't like to sit still. They have a wanderlust and are eager to explore the world. Their energetic personality rubs off on their friends and family, who are always enthusiastic about accompanying Geminis on their adventures.

Weaknesses

- Superficial
- Talkative
- Inconsistent
- Exaggerating
- Cunning
- Restless
- Deceptive
- Unorganized

Although their duality makes them intriguing, it can frustrate those around them because they can change their personality at any moment. Since Geminis only focus on the rational side of things, they can appear cold and unemotional. They have a short attention span and can juggle many projects simultaneously without finishing any. Geminis get bored easily and lack the discipline to follow through with anything.

Self-worth is significant for Geminis; they want to stand out wherever they go. They use their charm and charisma to make up stories about themselves or exaggerate the truth. If a Gemini isn't in the spotlight, they will leave, making them seem selfish.

It isn't only topics or projects that Geminis find boring; they can also get tired of people. Many of their relationships are superficial because they don't take the time to know someone or have deep conversations with them. Being in a relationship with a Gemini isn't easy. They are indecisive and struggle with commitment. One day, they can be madly in love with someone but will lose interest soon after.

Geminis are very clever individuals, which can spell trouble for others. They can easily understand and read people and use their gifts to manipulate them and get their way. At first, a Gemini can be friendly and sweep you off your feet. However, they have a hidden agenda. For instance, your Gemini coworker brings you a gift or charms you to work an extra shift so they can leave early. A Gemini will also resort to lying if it will benefit them in achieving their goals or getting what they want from others.

People born under this sign can be devious. They use their dual personality and intelligence to play games and tricks on others. Geminis will maintain a mystic persona to keep people guessing about them. However, their behavior doesn't only impact others. It also affects them. Unreliable and impulsive, they can often get in trouble.

Geminis struggle to make decisions because they usually see all sides of a situation and usually take their time to weigh their options before deciding. Although this frustrates others, this process benefits Geminis as they usually make the right decisions. People born under this sign want to experience everything in life, so they rush into things without considering the consequences.

Pet Peeves

Never interrupt a Gemini. These knowledgeable and great conversationalists always have something interesting to say. They can get slightly angry if you interrupt them or interject their opinion. Geminis find interruptions rude and will often forget what they are saying.

Ruling Planet

Gemini is ruled by Mercury, described as the planet of communication, a perfect fit for this sign. In Roman mythology, Mercury was the god of interpreters and the messenger of the gods, hence the planet's association with communication. Mercury influences Gemini to express themselves and share their opinions. It encourages them to learn and expand their knowledge.

Gemini as a Sun Sign

Having Gemini as your sun sign means you possess a diplomatic personality and can act as an excellent intermediary between groups. Geminis are upbeat people who support and inspire others to succeed and be their best selves. Fun individuals; they want everyone to join in and have a good time. If sun Geminis land a career they love, they could be workaholics. They don't mind the extra work as long as they succeed and advance in their careers.

These individuals can be players and jump from one relationship to the next. However, when they meet their match, someone as intelligent and can carry a conversation with them, they are in it for the long run. Gemini is represented as twins, indicating how they value partnerships. Committed Geminis are very loving and loyal.

They are compatible with Libra, Leo, Aquarius, and air and fire signs. They are least compatible with Pisces, Virgo, Sagittarius, and other water and Earth signs.

Gemini as a Moon Sign

Gemini moon people need to express their emotions through talking or writing. They usually struggle with dramatic or challenging situations. Gemini moon people have high self-esteem despite showing off and exaggerating. They can be moody and confused by their own feelings. Gemini moon people are very kind, and others genuinely enjoy their company. However, they struggle with opening up to others and being vulnerable. They want to appear mysterious and fascinating because they fear their true personality will alienate or disappoint their loved ones.

They are compatible with Sagittarius, Leo, Libra, Aquarius, Gemini, and Aries moons. They are the least compatible with Pisces, Cancer, Scorpio, Virgo, Capricorn, and Taurus moons.

Gemini as a Rising Sign

If Gemini is your rising sign, you know what to say in any situation and when to remain silent and let others talk. At work, these people can easily work alone or in a team. However, they might walk away if their teammates don't listen to or respect their opinions. When they fall in love, they never tire of listening to their partners and learning everything about them.

Gemini-rising people are compatible with Libra, Aquarius, Leo, Sagittarius, and Aries ascendants. They are the least compatible with Cancer, Pisces, and Earth signs.

Gemini as a Descendant Sign

Gemini descendant people love their freedom and hate feeling confined or controlled in a relationship or a job. In relationships, they can be possessive and resort to lying. These individuals usually see the big picture but miss the details. An equally intelligent partner will open their eyes to the things they fail to pay attention to and can learn from each other. They look for intellectually stimulating partners with similar communication skills. Gemini descendants want to be around creative people who keep things exciting.

They are most compatible with Air signs.

Cancer

Cancer.[10]

Glyph

Some people think a Cancer glyph is the number 69 or two opposing *sixes*. However, it depicts the crab's claws. The word "Cancer" is Latin for crab, and it perfectly represents people born under this sign. Crabs have a tough exterior but are soft on the inside. Similarly, Cancers are fierce protectors of their loved ones but very kind and compassionate. Crabs use their claws to hold onto things. Likewise, Cancers enjoy remaining in their comfort zone and hate taking a different path.

Dates

From June 21st to July 22nd.

Key Phrase

"I feel"

Cancers feel their emotions deeper than other signs. They are empathetic individuals who can easily feel and relate to others. Cancers usually know their emotions and can easily express them, so "I feel" is perfectly fitting.

Strengths

- Nurturing
- Healing
- Enthusiastic
- Compassionate
- Adjustable
- Supportive
- Sociable
- Loving

Cancers are extremely maternal, loving, and nurturing individuals. They are very loyal to their loved ones and take their relationships and friendships seriously. Compassionate individuals, Cancers love unconditionally and prefer the comfort of relationships and being around people they trust. When in trouble, your cancer friend will rush to your side. Even if they are busy, nothing comes before their loved ones. They are giving individuals who enjoy sharing everything they have with their friends and family. If a friendship or relationship ends, it breaks their heart.

They have a sense of humor that some people don't understand because Cancers can find a fun side in any situation, even when others fail to see it. Cancer knows how to make their friends laugh and lighten the mood during difficult situations. Cancer is the only sign that can relieve people's pain by providing them with comfort and a sympathetic ear. Their empathetic nature makes them attuned to other people's emotions, and they know what others need during moments of grief. Warm and compassionate individuals, Cancers genuinely care about others.

Whether advice or a shoulder to cry on, Cancers will always support their loved ones. They make others feel safe by nurturing and protecting them, especially when struggling. Unlike Geminis, Cancers are committed to relationships. Selfless individuals, they will put your needs above their own.

Cancers are very creative individuals with vivid imaginations. They see the world differently and usually develop unique ideas or solutions. When given a project or a task, Cancers will stay on it until it's finished. Ambitious and determined, they work hard to succeed and advance personally and professionally. Although they don't seem like it, Cancers have strong leadership skills and never shy away from a challenge.

Cancers don't forget; this doesn't mean they hold grudges, but they can remember details about others and often reminisce about their past. They listen to their intuition and don't pay much attention to the rational side of an argument. Some people think Cancers are psychics because of their ability to read others. However, they are merely intuitive with high emotional intelligence. It is hard to deceive a Cancer because they can tell what others are thinking.

Weaknesses

- Emotional
- Dependent
- Irrational
- Moody
- Unorganized

- Indirect
- Lazy
- Passive aggressive
- Conceited
- Can't Let go

In relationships, Cancers can be very needy. They constantly want their partner's attention, making them overbearing and clingy. Cancers are very devoted to their loved ones but fear abandonment. They will do anything to prevent a partner or friend from leaving and sometimes resort to lying.

Although they are forgiving individuals, Cancers never forget and struggle with letting go of the past. They can forgive you for hurting them but will never forget the pain you caused. Cancers will not bring it up during an argument but will relieve the pain and reopen the wound when alone. Like a crab, Cancers retreat into their shells (solitude) whenever someone insults them or hurts their feelings. However, they will never tell you their feelings are hurt. Cancers want to appear tough and hide their sensitive side, but it makes them seem moody. They can suddenly get angry or lash out at others, confusing people. However, this frustration results from their hurt feelings. So, they become private individuals who keep their vulnerable side hidden from the world.

Their empathetic nature also impacts their mood. One minute, they are friendly and chatty, then suddenly, they become quiet and want to be left alone. They are highly sensitive people, always attuned to their environment. They can get overwhelmed by something others don't even notice. Cancers are insecure individuals who obsess over other people's opinions of them. They depend on others and rely on them for decision-making since they usually second-guess themselves.

This kind and sweet sign have a dark side. Cancers can be manipulative, resorting to passive aggression or guilt-tripping to get what they want. If anyone threatens their safety or sense of security, they will use manipulation to gain control of the situation. If you cross a Cancer, they will first understand and see things from your perspective. However, if this doesn't work or you cross them again, they can be very vindictive.

Pet Peeves

Cancers are caring individuals with good memories, so they will never forget anniversaries, birthdays, or any significant dates. However, it irritates them when others forget. It hurts their feelings when a best friend forgets their birthday or a partner forgets an anniversary. They might even stop talking to them. Although they are devoted to their loved ones, winning an angry Cancer back is very hard.

Ruling Planet

The moon rules cancer. Like the moon impacts the tides, it also influences their emotions, so they deeply feel everything. The moon is considered a celestial maternal figure, reinforcing Cancer's caring and nurturing side. People born under this sign value their family and home life and provide their loved ones with comfort and safety.

Cancer as a Sun Sign

Cancers don't merely work to succeed. They want to make enough money to support their family. Although they are hard workers, they will find time to relax and care for themselves. Cancer's moodiness can impact their relationships. They fall in love fast and hard but fall out of love just as easily. When they commit to someone, they open up to them and reveal their vulnerable side. However, it takes them time to trust and feel comfortable around others.

The Cancer sun sign is highly compatible with Taurus, Cancer, Virgo, Scorpio, Capricorn, and Pisces. They are least compatible with Aries, Leo, Libra, Gemini, Sagittarius, and Aquarius.

Cancer as a Moon Sign

Like Cancers care for others and understand their feelings, they secretly want to be treated the same way. Cancer moon people are very loving to their partners; however, they struggle to end a relationship even when it is clear things aren't working out. They are so eager to start a family and build a home that they refuse to see when it's time to walk away.

Cancer moon is compatible with Pisces, Scorpio, Capricorn, Taurus, Cancer, Virgo, and Pisces moons. They are least compatible with Aries, Gemini, Leo, Libra, Sagittarius, and Aquarius moons.

Cancer as a Rising Sign

Cancer risings are approachable individuals. During conversations, they are usually immersed and give their undivided attention to their loved ones. They prefer the comfort of home or sitting at a cozy cafe with a friend rather than going to a loud and crowded club. They have an introverted-like personalities, so they usually like to recharge and spend time with themselves after social interactions. Cancer needs an understanding partner who will support them as they deal with their intense emotions and mood swings. Cancer-rising thrives in creative careers where they can learn and grow.

They are compatible with Pisces, Scorpio, Capricorn, Taurus, Cancer, Virgo, and Pisces ascendants. They are least compatible with Aries, Gemini, Leo, Libra, Sagittarius, and Aquarius ascendants.

Cancer as a Descendant Sign

Cancer descendants want a sensitive partner they can depend on in relationships and who provides security and comfort. They prefer a quiet environment where both partners can focus on each other's needs. They won't tolerate a competitive partner. They crave stability and struggle when their personal or professional life is on shaky ground. Although they usually offer others advice, they are reluctant to accept guidance from their superiors.

Like any zodiac sign, Gemini and Cancers share some differences and similarities. Both share many attractive qualities, making them popular among their peers. They should forgo their manipulative tactics and show others their true nature and vulnerable side.

Chapter 7: Leo and Virgo

If you want to learn more about the world of Zodiacs and what it means to be a Leo or a Virgo, look no further. A true Leo is confident, enthusiastic, and ambitious. A Virgo is often analytical, practical, and reliable. Both signs have unique traits and characteristics that make them stand out among the other horoscope signs. Keep reading further for a deeper understanding of these two fascinating zodiac signs. It could be your key to unlocking the power of your star sign.

Leo

Glyph

The glyph of Leo, the astrological sign associated with summer, consists of a circular loop with a curve crowding its perimeter. This loop symbolizes the eternal cycle of life; no beginning and no end. It symbolizes protection, for encircling and shielding what is inside this eternal circle. The curved lines that crowd under the circumference are quite cunningly thought out. They represent strength, charisma, and pride, fundamental character traits of a

Leo.[11]

Leo, as does the lion's head, which crowns the circle. It is portrayed by an ancient Greek deity, Zephyros, who had aspects associated with divine kingship and great personal power. The glyph sums up Leo's proud – yet fiercely protective – streak.

Dates

July 23 to August 22

Key Phrase

"I will"

The key phrase associated with Leo is "I will." This phrase reflects the intense passion, courage, and desire for success those born under this sign exude. Leos have a strong drive to reach their goals and aren't afraid to take risks. They possess a creative spark and grandiose vision, often leading them to develop innovative strategies in business and other areas of life. Leos are naturally confident, which helps them stay optimistic despite obstacles they encounter toward their objectives. The "I will" phrase captures the spirit of Leos perfectly - confident, determined, creative, and willing to face challenges head-on.

Strengths

- Boundless Confidence
- Hearts of Gold
- Loyal to their Tribe
- Infinite Creativity
- Profoundly Courageous
- Amazing Leaders

Leos have an unrivaled self-confidence, unparalleled to other signs. They are brave and courageous and know they can handle any situation life throws at them. This confidence allows them to take risks when others would not and to be incredibly successful in all aspects of life. Furthermore, Leos often have great strength mentally and emotionally, enabling them to make mistakes and learn from them quickly. They have an unshakeable sense of determination, and their drive never fails, allowing them to achieve the heights they set out. Their natural desire for leadership gives Leos a competitive advantage over others as they think objectively and lead with compassion and consideration. Leo's boundless confidence and strengths make it one of the most remarkable signs of astrology.

Leo is traditionally known as the sign of courage, and these brave people possess a remarkable trait - they have hearts of gold. A generous spirit is their best quality that shines through their actions, thoughtfulness, and kindness. This heartfelt generosity can open doors and create connections among people of all ages, making them popular in any social circle. At its core, Leo's heart of gold is rooted in its established value system. These individuals know what's right and act with conviction to ensure these values are kept alive. A level of self-discipline is connected to their ability to stay true to their moral code, which sets them apart from other signs, showing their strong and trusting characters.

Having strong values and principles, Leos are renowned for their unwavering loyalty. Those born under this sign are highly dependable and trustworthy. People admiring the lion-like personality of Leos are attracted to their confidence and commitment to their convictions. This strong and passionate energy allows Leos to work toward their goals with tremendous success. In personal relationships, Leo's loyalty results in an intense sense of fidelity that strengthens the bond between them and those they love. They take every initiative to ensure their friends, family members, and loved ones feel secure because they feel immense satisfaction. Leos exhibit a specific loyalty that is unbreakable and soulful.

Leo is known for their creative and lively energies, making them prone to channeling these qualities into infinite creativity. For Leos, this means having the power to express themselves through artistic endeavors, problem-solving ability, and an overall bright outlook on life, inspiring others. Leos are fueled by confidence and an enthusiastic spirit that keeps them coming up with innovative solutions to even the most complex problems. These natural-born creators are drawn to social circles and value the connections they have access to. Whether for professional or personal reasons, there's no doubt that Leo's charisma will take them far. Leo's passion, powerful personality, enthusiasm, and original ideas help them thrive while exploring the endless possibilities for being creative in unique and impactful ways.

Leos possess a profound, courageous trait because of how assertive, determined, and confident they can be. Their strong-willed attitude often lends itself to having the determination to achieve success. Leo is a fire sign with abundant energy and a competitive spirit, allowing them to take risks when needed and never back down from a challenge. They adapt very firm views about different issues, so outside influences or opinions rarely change their minds. Most importantly, Leos have a deep understanding of the world around them. They know their strengths and weaknesses, allowing them to find ways to support what they know should be done in any situation. Their ability to stay brave in the face of seemingly impossible odds truly makes Leo profoundly courageous.

No wonder those born under the constellation Leo are seen as strong, confident leaders; it takes immense courage and self-assurance to be a part of history. With their sunny dispositions and irrepressible spirit, those wielding Leo's power have taken the world by storm since ancient times. Representing qualities of strength, courage, and ambition, many leaders throughout the ages have been Leos. From Pharaohs and Ancient Roman Emperors to renowned artists and modern-day billionaires, the boldness of this sign has been a shining beacon in every era. Those who share this lionhearted trait can take comfort in having a shared ancestry with some powerful figures who demanded attention and admiration even amid intense obstacles.

Weaknesses

Leos have some weaknesses affecting their lives, relationships, and experiences. Here are six of the most common weaknesses associated with Leo:

- Pride
- Insecurity
- Impulsivity
- Vanity
- Self-centeredness
- Stubbornness

Pride is one of the biggest weaknesses of the Leo sign. They overestimate their abilities and underestimate others. It leads to arrogance and a lack of humility, which hurts them more than helps.

Despite their prideful exterior, Leos often suffer from deep insecurity and fear of failure or rejection due to their heightened sense of self-worth. It leads to jealousy toward others who seem to be doing better than them, making it difficult to form meaningful connections.

Leos are often impulsive, making decisions without thinking things through and acting on their emotions rather than logic. This impulsivity can lead to bad decisions that could have been avoided had they taken the time to think about the consequences of their actions.

Leos are quite vain, focusing too much on their physical appearance and material possessions to feel important or valued by others. They might appear shallow and narcissistic, which turns people away, even if it isn't intentional.

Leos are selfish and self-absorbed, focused mainly on their needs and desires without considering the feelings or perspectives of others. It is difficult for them to form meaningful relationships with people, as they don't always see things from other people's perspectives.

Leos are incredibly stubborn and set in their ways, so they have difficulty accepting different opinions or changing their minds. As a result, this can lead to conflicts with friends, family members, and co-workers and missed opportunities due to inflexibility.

Pet Peeves

Leos have a penchant for the theatrical and love to be in the spotlight. They strive for perfection and are very loyal friends, but they can be overly critical and often expect high standards from themselves and others. Leos get frustrated with disorganization and indifference, considering them signs of disrespect or laziness. They demand reliability and accuracy and quickly become irritated by careless mistakes. Leo signs to find it difficult to tolerate criticism without feeling insulted or hurt; they prefer constructive rather than hurtful feedback. Indecisiveness is another pet peeve because Leos crave structure, predictability, and stability—all traits commonly associated with their sign.

Ruling Planet

The ruling planet of the Leo zodiac sign is the Sun. The Sun strongly associates power, leadership, and self-expression, making it perfectly suited to those born under this fire sign. For Leos, the Sun symbolizes a shining light of confidence and ambition that encourages them to make healthy decisions and stand out uniquely. It also encourages Leos to increase their knowledge and strive to further understand themselves and those around them. By blazing the trail with its bright energy, the Sun's influence supports Leos in achieving their wildest dreams. With its ruling presence over Leo, this regal star encourages people to respect their own strength, speak up for what's right, and unleash their fiery passions without fear of being judged or criticized.

Leo as a Sun Sign

People born under the Leo sun sign are blessed with many potential and gifts. They are fiercely loyal and inspiring individuals who can lead the way for anyone. Leos have natural charisma and ambition, allowing them to thrive at whatever they put their minds to. They have an innate understanding of the importance of gratitude, making them often very generous in their interactions. These bright personalities often bring joy and optimism wherever they go by using their creativity to make people smile. Leos often find ways to overcome obstacles through determination and hard work, setting a strong example for everyone. All these traits combined make Leos truly amazing individuals, bringing light and love to any situation.

With romantic compatibility, Leo sun signs seemingly have the best of both worlds when they look for potential partners. While some negative combinations of elements can occur, most pairings make for a successful match that can go the distance. Fire signs, such as Aries and Sagittarius, share Leo's enthusiasm for life and their tendency to show appreciation for one another. Air signs like Libra and Aquarius can bring an intellectual balance to the relationship that compliments Leo's leadership tendencies, allowing them to forge strong partnerships without compromise. Earth signs like Virgo might surprise people by bringing out the more organized aspects of Leo's personality.

Leo as a Moon Sign

Having Leo as a moon sign can be quite a unique experience. People with Leo as their moon sign are affectionate, loyal, and have an inner confidence to take on any challenge. They live with a lot of enthusiasm and have a natural flair for leadership. It might not always come naturally, but they can inspire others through their conviction and sheer will. If there's anything they care deeply about, they'll put everything into it. This passion might sometimes be overwhelming or intimidating for others, but it's another testament to their commitment. With these traits in mind, having Leo as a moon sign can open up many possibilities for someone wanting to impact the world.

Leo moon signs are wonderfully compatible with a select few other moon signs, including Libra and Sagittarius. While the risk-taking and bold nature of Leo moon signs allow you to make daring decisions, Libra and Sagittarius bring a more grounded focus to your partnership dynamics. Libra helps you see the value in stable relationships, which help you grow and evolve together. Sagittarius brings their enthusiasm for exploring new ideas, which can spark your creative energies. Combining these three moon signs will guarantee interesting partnerships with plenty of fun-filled activities and meaningful conversations, keeping each other on their toes.

Leo as a Rising Sun Sign

If you have Leo as your rising sun sign, you are associated with vibrancy and joy. People with this sign often bring energy wherever they go, radiating confidence and ambition. They have an unwavering appreciation for the finer things in life and always strive to live up to their fullest potential. Leo's risings seek admiration and love to be admired for their natural intelligence, creativity, and charming personality. With the Sun at its peak in Leo Season, it's a great time to channel their vibrant inner energy - from bolder style choices to stronger career moves - and aim high while achieving dreams.

Leo as a Descendant Sign

Leo is a descendant sign that reflects a person's desire for expression and creativity. Those with strong Leo energy are known for their leadership, strength, warmth, and generosity. They are motivated by love and recognition, so they often seek environments where they can be the center of attention. Leo inhabitants yearn to be admired, respected, and acknowledged for their unique gifts. Individuals with this sign often take the initiative to become active agents of change in the world to reach their desired outcomes. Leos enjoy manifesting the creative power within them into tangible results that bring joy to those around them.

Virgo

Glyph

The glyph for the Virgo zodiac sign is an M with a loop tucked inside it. This shape represents a woman waiting, nay-inquiring — with curiosity and discernment. Mercury, the planet of communication and movement, rules Virgos. So, it makes sense that the glyph symbolizes their anointment as truth seekers, appraising every experience to uncover its deepest kernel of knowledge. The loop in the center implies findings within and without; Virgos are adept at collecting infor-

Virgo.[12]

mation from external sources and introspection. A whole constellation of possibility is represented, patient, curious, and never content with merely scraping the surface.

Dates

August 23 to September 22

Key Phrase

"I Analyze"

The key phrase associated with the Virgo zodiac sign is "I analyze" because Virgos are thoughtful and detail-oriented, always striving to make sense of the world around them. They are highly critical, often taking things apart to understand them fully. This combination of qualities makes it natural for Virgo to melt away complex problems by carefully examining every aspect before coming up with a solution. Virgos usually have an aptitude for logical thinking and analytical problem-solving, making this phrase a great symbolic representation of their personality type.

Strengths

- Organization
- Practicality
- Kindness
- Hard-working
- Loyal
- Resourcefulness

Virgos are extremely organized and efficient. They have an eye for detail, which helps them stay on top of their tasks and keep things in order. They are practical people who appreciate structure and organization, making them great problem solvers.

Despite their tendency to be more analytical than emotional, Virgos are kind-hearted individuals with good empathy toward others.

Virgos will work hard to get the job done right the first time. They take pride in their work and strive for excellence.

They have an incredible sense of loyalty and commitment in relationships with their friends, family, and partners.

Virgos are extremely resourceful and can make the most out of a situation. They know how to utilize their surroundings to get the job done.

These traits make the Virgo zodiac sign one of the most reliable signs in astrology. They always put others before themselves and strive for excellence in everything they do, making them one of the most dependable people you'll ever meet.

Weaknesses

<table>
<tr><td>• Insecurity</td><td>• Overly critical</td></tr>
<tr><td>• Worry</td><td>• Procrastinate</td></tr>
<tr><td>• Perfectionism</td><td>• Expressing Emotion</td></tr>
</table>

Virgos often battle insecurity and self-doubt, leading them to overthink situations and make impulsive decisions without considering the consequences. They are easily overwhelmed with too many tasks or responsibilities and have difficulty meeting deadlines or delivering projects on time.

Virgos worry a lot, especially when something isn't going according to plan or when they encounter unexpected obstacles. This anxiety can be paralyzing and prevent them from taking action even though they know it's necessary.

Due to their perfectionism, Virgos are prone to nitpicking details and missing the bigger picture. It becomes difficult for them to delegate tasks as they feel no one else can do it like them.

Virgos can be overly critical of themselves and others, making them seem judgmental or unapproachable. They find it hard to accept compliments or praise, which could make them feel their efforts are not appreciated.

As much as Virgos try to stay organized, they procrastinate on projects due to their fear of failure. They have difficulty focusing and getting things done timeously.

Virgos struggle to express their emotions openly, causing communication issues in relationships. Open dialogue is important, but Virgos might have difficulty asking for help or support when needed. Virgos need to recognize that it's okay to express their feelings and ask for assistance occasionally.

These are some weaknesses that many Virgo battle with daily. Although they can be difficult to overcome, understanding where these issues stem from helps them become more confident. With enough self-awareness and determination, they can use their strengths to compensate for weaknesses they encounter.

Pet Peeves

Virgo's are one of the most organized and logical zodiac signs, but some things will always set them off. One of the main pet peeves of a Virgo is being disorganized or inefficient. This tendency can lead to frustration as they feel their time is wasted. Virgos are also detail-orientated; it doesn't take much for something to go wrong, and they will quickly lose interest. They can get overwhelmed when someone overcomplicates something with unnecessary sound bites or jargon. They prefer conversations to be kept clear and concise. When things aren't taken seriously enough, it irks Virgo; they enjoy meaningful discussions and debate topics to gain understanding. Virgos might come across as nit-picky on certain issues, but ultimately, they're merely seeking an environment that works in their favor. Everything must have purpose and meaning for Virgo to stay engaged.

Virgo as a Sun Sign

People born with a Virgo Sun Sign are experienced as reliable and organized individuals. They often volunteer their assistance to help those around them and excel in managing daily tasks. They excel at handling their own issues and enjoy helping others achieve success through their expertise and knowledge. Virgos analyze things in extreme detail and aim for perfection in any situation or project. Although they are often criticized for having high expectations, it is part of Virgo's nature to strive for excellence with anything from family dynamics to major life decisions. While having a Virgo as a friend or partner comes with great benefits, this driven sign also needs plenty of support and understanding to reach its fullest potential.

Virgo is generally compatible with other Earth signs in the zodiac, Taurus and Capricorn, who have a lot of commonalities with Virgo, like their grounded and sensible personalities. Virgo also gets along very well with air signs like Aquarius and Libra because they think logically and analyze situations. Virgos mix best with water signs, like Pisces and Cancer, because of the latter's sympathetic, nurturing nature that complements Virgo's pragmatic attitude.

Virgo as a Moon Sign

Being born with a Virgo Moon sign is a blessing. Those with this sign are analytical, hardworking, and overachievers. They are detail-driven and will strive for perfection in everything they do. Having a Virgo moon sign signals that the person has an affinity for the natural world and maintains order since Virgos view the universe with great clarity. Those with a Virgo moon sign appreciate routines and stability and enjoy having clear goals to pursue. This combination of traits makes them deep thinkers who can take on complex challenges.

Compatibility between Virgo moon signs and other moon signs can offer great insight into how two people interact. For instance, Virgo moon signs are detail-oriented, loyal to their partner, and responsible with day-to-day tasks. It makes them an ideal match for fellow analytical and logical signs like Taurus, Capricorn, and Aquarius. Scorpios can also make great companions thanks to their creativity and emotionality, which provide a good balance for the practicality of Virgo moon signs. Aries can appear too impulsive or flamboyant, but Virgos might appreciate someone pushing them out of their comfort zones. When matched with an Earth sign like Virgo, air signs like Gemini or Libra can add spice to the love equation.

Virgo as a Rising Sun

People with Virgo as their rising sun sign are highly analytical and perfectionist in their approach, often using a logical rather than emotional lens when problem-solving. They are known for getting absorbed in details and relying on detailed data to make decisions. While this can make them reliable workers, it also means it's difficult for them to take risks or embrace change. Those with a Virgo rising sign often have strong concentration powers and are very organized in their environment. People who know them value their insight and integrity, as they always look deeply into situations before concluding. Virgos can bring precision and accuracy to any task they put their minds to.

Virgo as a Descendant

A descendant of the Virgo sign has been blessed with a unique sense of purpose. Virgos are renowned for their sharp intelligence and analytical thinking skills while possessing a great eye for detail and an admirable dedication to any task they undertake. These traits are undoubtedly useful in the majority of life pursuits. The Virgo nature allows them to stay focused on goals no matter how difficult situations become and become increasingly curious about discovering new knowledge. Virgos embody many defining aspects of this zodiac sign, such as being organized, reliable, kind, and loyal.

Chapter 8: Libra and Scorpio

Searching to learn more about Libra and Scorpio can cause confusion. A vast array of information is available, making it difficult to sift through. But read further. You will discover everything to know about these zodiac signs. Libra and Scorpio are opposing star signs with characteristics that add balance and harmony to the universe. While they appear similar, their symbolisms differ greatly. Understanding more about each will give insight into their power and influence. With an open mind and some patience, you'll have the knowledge to make sense of these enigmatic figures.

Libra

Glyph

The Libra zodiac sign is represented by the glyph of two lines that interlock in a gentle curve. This symbol, called "The Scales, " symbolizes justice, balance, and fairness. Libra's ruling deity is Aphrodite, the Greek goddess of love, beauty, and harmony. In Ancient Greece, she was associated with scales, ensuring all interactions were fair, even in matters of love. Many

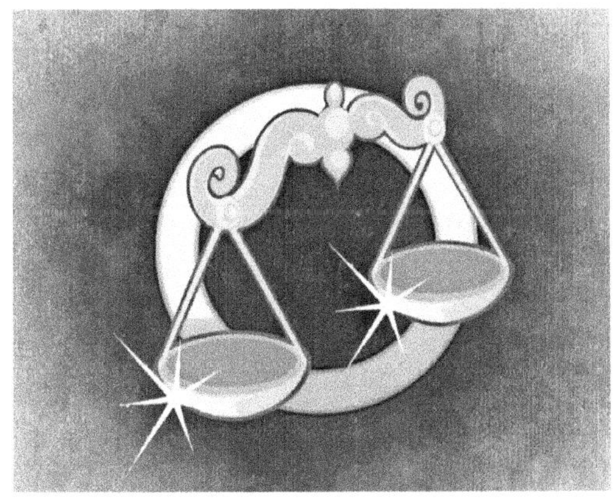

Libra.[18]

people born under Libra strive for balance in their everyday lives. They often seek ways to bring harmony to their relationships and are naturally diplomatic. Being ruled by Aphrodite gives Libra natives an appreciation for beauty, creativity, and sensitivity. These traits help balance any situation.

Date

September 22 to October 23

Key Phrase

"I Balance"

The Key phrase associated with the Libra zodiac sign is "I balance." This phrase speaks to the values and qualities characterizing those born under this sign, specifically the desire for balance and justice. It reflects their need for order and balance, particularly in romantic and friendship relationships. This drive for balance relates to a willingness to sacrifice comfort or stability for fairness and equality. On an emotional level, it speaks to a person's ability to remain open-minded when considering different sides of an argument before deciding, essentially finding a middle ground. It connotes creating alliances with diverse groups of people by empathizing with each other and understanding how they can work together harmoniously. It's highly indicative of the mature and diplomatic personality accompanying those born under Libra.

Strengths

Libra zodiac sign, represented by the symbol of scales, is naturally balanced. People born under this sign have many great qualities that make them stand out from other signs. Here are some traits and characteristics of Libras

- Balanced
- Diplomatic
- Intellectual
- Sociable
- Charming
- Loyal
- Romantic

Libra people are well-known for staying calm and level-headed in even the most challenging situations. They strive for balance, fairness, and justice and always look to create harmony between differing points of view.

Libra people are known for their diplomatic skills; they can easily resolve conflicts while maintaining good relationships with all parties involved. It makes them excellent mediators who can quickly come to an amicable resolution.

Libras are intelligent and can think critically. They process complex information quickly and devise creative solutions that most other signs might miss.

Libra people are sociable; they love meeting new people and making new connections. They are popular among their peers, making everyone feel included and accepted in a group setting.

Libras are very charming and have the natural ability to attract people with their energy and charisma. It is one of their most powerful traits, allowing them to easily garner positive or negative attention from others.

Libras are loyal to those they care about. Once they have formed a connection with someone, it is hard for them to let go and move on.

Libra people are very romantic and enjoy the finer things in life—good food, luxury items, or spending time with their loved ones. They are sensitive in love matters and want nothing more than to make their partner happy.

These traits and characteristics make Libras strong individuals who know how to handle situations life throws at them. They can handle difficult situations gracefully and bring balance and harmony into our lives. They are compassionate, loyal friends with a great sense of humor and can turn even the dullest moments into fun memories. Libras also make excellent partners in crime and as life companions. These qualities make Libras strong and capable individuals who are always ready to take on whatever challenges come their way. With such an impressive list of strengths, it is no wonder that Libras have been successful throughout history.

Weaknesses

- Indecisiveness
- Too Nice
- Easily Manipulated
- Unreliable
- Emotionally Sensitive
- Lack of Passion
- Passive Aggressive

People with the Libra zodiac sign often have difficulty deciding due to their inability to objectively weigh the pros and cons of both sides. They overanalyze situations, causing hesitation and an inability to conclude.

Librans are usually very kind, generous people who go out of their way for someone in need. This attribute is great, but sometimes it can be taken advantage of by others because they don't stand up for themselves or take on too much without considering their well-being.

Due to the inherent trusting nature of Libras, it is easy for others to manipulate them, and they fall prey to emotional blackmail.

Librans can be unreliable because they often put too much on their plate and struggle to prioritize. It is mostly due to their innately agreeable disposition to putting others' needs before theirs, leading to commitments not being fulfilled on time or at all.

Librans are emotionally sensitive and can become overwhelmed by situations quickly, leading them to shut down communication rather than discuss the issue.

Libra people can lack passion when pursuing long-term goals or projects as they have difficulty committing due to indecisiveness.

Due to their shy nature, Librans can be passive-aggressive, expressing themselves without confrontation. This behavior can cause misunderstandings and hurt feelings in relationships.

The Libra zodiac sign's weakness can be managed with proper care and understanding. With time, Librans can learn to cope with their weaknesses and focus on their strengths.

Pet Peeves

Libra zodiac signs often have a long list of pet peeves. One that tops the list is when people don't put in their fair share of effort. Libras are all about balance, so they hate it when someone isn't pulling their weight. They don't handle rudeness well because they prefer diplomatic and composed behavior. Libras expect their significant others to show appreciation for their efforts to make them feel loved; failure will quickly become a pet peeve. Furthermore, a balanced lifestyle is important to Libras, so they despise feeling overwhelmed and tiring themselves out with too much work or commitments. Any unbalanced situation will likely create a pet peeve for the Libra zodiac sign.

Ruling Planet

The ruling planet associated with Libra is Venus, the planet of beauty, love, and harmony. It is significant as it reflects the core qualities attributed to the sign, such as its natural inclination toward balance, diplomacy, and fairness. It also amplifies their urge for harmonious relationships and indicates social awareness. Venus encourages beauty and artistry to be incorporated into every aspect of life. It highlights their need for an aesthetically pleasing environment that radiates positive energy and promotes peaceful experiences. Venus helps bring a level of understanding to this sign, assisting them in creating enjoyable interactions with others.

Libra as a Sun Sign

Those born with the sun in Libra are natural diplomats, excelling at solving conflict and connecting people. They're often well-liked, as they are warm and generous toward others, even if the feeling is not reciprocated. Libras have a heightened sense of fairness and strive for harmony in all aspects of life. Being represented by the scales suggests a need for balance; you'll find that those with this sun sign are diplomatic when handling tense situations and take their time to consider alternative solutions. Due to this, they sometimes appear indecisive; however, they want to do what is right rather than what is popular. People with Libra as their Sun sign will go out of their way to spread kindness and create meaningful and mutually beneficial relationships.

Libras are known for being patient listeners and enjoy having thought-provoking conversations about anything from music to history. Consequently, Libra pairs well with Sagittarius, who have an insatiable thirst for knowledge, and Geminis, who love socializing and having deep conversations. Geminis offer exciting intellectual conversations for Libra's mind, Leo brings contagious energy to Libra's spirit, and Aquarius gives new perspectives on life that help explore their curiosity even further. Libra also complements Pisces, who need understanding and trust to feel safe in relationships. Ultimately, for Libra's compatibility with other sun signs, there are many possibilities in the stars.

Libra as a Moon Sign

Having the moon in Libra can be a unique experience. It focuses heavily on relationships for those lucky enough to possess this sign. Those with their moon in Libra always strive to maintain balance and harmony, which can be difficult when navigating a more turbulent life. They truly appreciate the beauty of life and their surroundings, often having an intense appreciation for art, music, and philosophy. They are often reflective, with a thought-provoking inner monologue constantly internalizing. The degree of selflessness of a moon in Libra is unparalleled. They go above and beyond to ensure everyone is comfortable and happy regardless of the circumstances. Most importantly, Libras take other people's feelings extremely seriously besides their own, and ensuring everyone gets along well with each other is a top priority for those born beneath this sign.

Libra moon signs are typically known for being friendly, sociable, and diplomatic. Their balanced and fair-minded nature often makes Libra moon signs compatible with most, if not all, other moon signs. For example, Libra moon signs get along better with air moon signs like Gemini and Aquarius because they share similar traits, like being light-hearted, curious, and open-minded. Fire moon signs like Aries, Leo, or Sagittarius can bring a Libra's life more joy due to their strong spirit and enthusiasm. Water moon signs like Scorpio and Pisces bring an emotional depth that Libra might not possess, allowing for real connection. Earth moon signs like Taurus and Virgo are practical, and Libra appreciates when decision-making. Libra's easy charm and understanding make it compatible with the rest of the zodiac family.

Libra as a Rising Sign

As a Rising sign, Libra means those born with this astrological placement rely heavily on their intuition for decision-making. Libra risings are often thought of as charming and diplomatic, directly resulting from their ability to maintain balance in all situations. Since they strive for balance, those with Libra rising must constantly assess their environment and carefully consider both sides before making a statement or taking action. They enjoy socializing and find it can bring harmony if both parties respect one another's opinions. By having a Libra rising sign, you have the skill to be persuasive and successful in business and personal settings.

Libra as Descendant Sign

As your descendant sign, Libra can be a blessing in many ways. People with this sign typically have good social skills and quickly make connections with those around them, which can open many doors of opportunity. This outgoing attitude is beneficial in relationships as it often creates a balance between the partners, helping them reach compromises without compromising their needs and values. Moreover, Libras have a keen eye for beauty and aesthetics, making them great at creating art or designing unique spaces that stand out from the crowd. Having a Libra descendant position in the natal chart can add balance to an individual's life by giving them the social skills necessary for success.

Scorpio

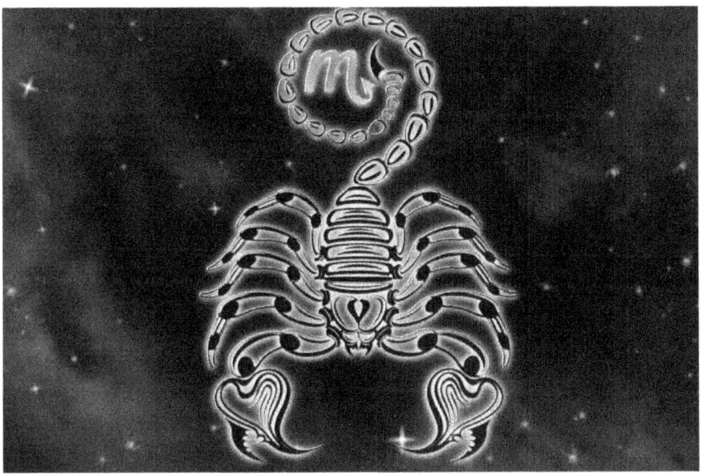

Scorpio. [14]

Glyph

The Scorpio Glyph comprises the letter M and a stylized lowercase s. It's an ancient symbol of death, regeneration, and sexuality. It perfectly represents the Scorpio zodiac sign with its close affinity to transformation and deep insightfulness. In addition, the Scorpio Glyph or "M" closely resembles the spear-shaped weapon the Egyptian sun god Ra used to vanquish his enemies. This glyph symbolizes courage since it takes strength to go through transformative processes connected to Scorpios. Several deities are associated with this zodiac sign, such as Osiris and Isis - two figures in ancient Egyptian mythology devoted to life after death. These symbols associated with Scorpios represent the inner fire of their personality, allowing them to truly understand deeper aspects of life and pursue whatever they set their minds on.

Date

October 23 to November 21

Key Phrase

"I Desire"

The key phrase for the Scorpio zodiac sign is "I Desire." This phrase accurately sums up the motivations and intentions of Scorpio, often driven by a passion and intensity to always seek out new interests and experiences. People with this zodiac sign don't settle for ordinary or mediocre experiences; they want extreme, powerful, and challenging things. They are extremely goal-oriented and determined individuals who will not rest until their desire is fulfilled. This key phrase is crucial in understanding the motivations and unique qualities that Scorpios possess – which can ultimately be self-improvement and reaching desired aspirations.

Strengths

- Loyalty
- Passionate
- Perceptive
- Resilience
- Ambitious
- Intuitive
- Adaptable
- Resourceful

People born under the Scorpio zodiac sign are incredibly loyal and devoted to those they love. They ensure their friends, family, and partners always feel secure in their relationships.

Scorpios have intense passions and strong emotions that drive them forward. They will pour themselves into a career or a charity project enthusiastically and feverishly.

Scorpios are perceptive individuals who can pick up on subtle details and combine seemingly unrelated information to create powerful insights about people or situations.

Scorpios are known for being resilient in adversity. They can bounce back from tough situations and never give up on their goals regardless of the difficulty of the journey.

A Scorpio's ambition is unrivaled by other zodiac signs and can often lead to great success.

People born under Scorpio have a highly developed intuition that helps them decide quickly and accurately in most situations.

Scorpios are incredibly adaptable individuals who can take any challenging situation and find a way to make it work.

Scorpios are extremely resourceful individuals who use their skills and knowledge to get the most out of their situations. They are creative problem solvers who can think quickly on their feet and come up with effective solutions.

Scorpios have many unique strengths that set them apart from other Zodiac signs. They possess loyalty, passion, perception, resilience, ambition, intuition, adaptability, and resourcefulness. These traits make them strong-minded individuals capable of achieving great things. With these qualities working for them, Scorpios can reach any goal they set and achieve anything they put their minds to with a little determination and hard work.

Weaknesses

- Stubbornness
- Suspicion
- Jealousy
- Emotional Intensity

- Stubbornness
- Self-Destructive Tendencies
- Manipulative Behaviors

People with the Scorpio zodiac sign are known to be very stubborn and set in their ways. They often refuse to see other viewpoints or change their opinions, even when convincing evidence suggests otherwise. It makes them seem inflexible and unyielding, a liability in relationships or work scenarios.

Those born under the Scorpio sign can sometimes struggle with trust issues due to their suspicious nature. They question people's motives and probe for hidden agendas, making it difficult for them to open up and let others into their lives.

Scorpios are often plagued by jealousy that can quickly spiral into possessiveness and controlling behavior. They are extremely protective of people and possessions they consider theirs.

Scorpios are known for their intense emotions, often overwhelming to them and those around them. They feel things deeply and experience life passionately, but this causes them moodiness, depression, or anger more frequently than other signs.

People with the Scorpio zodiac sign are very set in their ways. They often refuse to see another point of view or change their opinions, even when presented with convincing evidence suggesting otherwise. They seem inflexible and unyielding, which can be a liability in relationships or work scenarios.

Scorpios often push themselves too hard, leading to negative behavior like overworking, substance abuse, or unhealthy relationships. They can be their own worst enemies due to a deep-rooted need for self-destruction they cannot control.

Scorpios are master manipulators who use any means necessary to get what they want from a situation or person. They might not always realize it, but their tactics are sometimes aggressive and controlling, making it difficult for them to form meaningful relationships. It is especially problematic in romantic relationships, where trust is essential for a healthy connection.

Through hard work and dedication, Scorpios can learn to control their behavior and emotions so that these weaknesses won't ruin important relationships or opportunities. Working on self-awareness and self-improvement helps them become better versions of themselves. With practice, Scorpios can use their strengths to make up for shortcomings and live life to the fullest without letting these weaknesses hold them back from achieving success.

Pet Peeves

Scorpio is a strong, tenacious zodiac sign, but with that comes some less-than-desirable traits. Scorpios are often so independent they need to do everything alone despite being offered help. They are overly critical of their loved ones, expecting too much in return. They hold onto resentments and grudges, leading to difficult relationships and misunderstandings. As highly emotional people, Scorpios can quickly anger and argue when disagreed with or criticized. They are suspicious of others for no reason, making unfair assumptions about people and further straining their relationships.

Ruling Planet

The ruling planets of Scorpio are Mars and Pluto. Mars is associated with passion, determination, and independence and governs the ambitions and desires of Scorpio, fueling them through challenges and encouraging them to take risks. Meanwhile, Pluto represents transformation and regeneration - paralleling the Scorpio's ability to completely reinvent themselves by expelling negative thoughts and behaviors. The combination of these planets gives Scorpio the traits to go deep, persist in their quest for understanding, accept change with courage, and use aggression constructively without sacrificing their drive for knowledge and power.

Scorpio as a Sun Sign

Being a Scorpio with the sun in this part of the zodiac is an exciting adventure. It can be a great source of strength, power, and resilience. Scorpio-born individuals typically have an intense magnetism that draws others to them, often feeling deeply passionate and compassionate toward others. These people possess an investigative mind enabling them to think critically and carefully to decide on complex matters. They are better at analytical tasks and appreciate an atmosphere that rewards insight and intelligence. Furthermore, those with a Scorpio sun sign are tuned into their creativity resulting in great artworks or inventions. Having Scorpio as a sun sign means you are gifted with unique traits and are unique from the rest.

Scorpio sun signs are known for their intensity, loyalty, and passion. Those born under this zodiac sign get along well with other water signs, like Cancer and Pisces. They might find it difficult to connect with air signs like Aquarius or fire signs like Leo and Aries. Scorpios are secretive and can appear intimidating, which isn't always well-received by the more extroverted signs. Conversely, these characteristics draw out the affectionate traits of others, leading to an intense connection between even the most incompatible pairings.

Scorpio as a Moon

Having a Scorpio moon sign brings intense and dramatic emotions. Scorpios often feel their emotions deeply; a person's moon sign speaks to their innermost emotions and amplifies this trait. Since Scorpio is a water sign, those with a Scorpio moon are especially sensitive to their environment and the feelings of others, adding to the passion behind their emotional experiences. People with a Scorpio moon often require alone time to decompress or explore these intense and powerful feelings. They might also enjoy journals, art projects, or other creative outlets that allow them to express themselves freely. They can be fierce defenders of justice and adversaries of oppression, driven by a deep empathy for those who experience injustice firsthand.

Scorpio moon signs are intensely passionate creatures who often look for an intense connection with their romantic partners. Those with an intense sign are most compatible with the likes of Taurus, Pisces, Cancer, and Capricorn moons. Each pairing offers a mutual understanding, warmth, and respect for strong relationships.

Scorpio as a Rising Sign

Those born with Scorpio as their rising sign are strong-minded, passionate individuals. This sign's influence is a heightened sense of resourcefulness and resilience, allowing them to handle situations or challenges. Scorpio-rising folk are ambitious; they know what they want and will strive to get it. In addition to this determination, Scorpio risings display intensity and secrecy qualities. However, Scorpio rising is associated with deep empathy, allowing them always to understand other people's emotions. Scorpio risings have an innate ability to stay firm and unwavering on what is right, even if everything around them tells them otherwise. Having Scorpio as your rising sign means you have the strength of character and tenacity to carry out your goals whenever you set your mind on something.

Scorpio as a Descendant Sign

Scorpio, ruled by Pluto, is a water sign known for its intensity and deep thinking. As the descendant sign, it indicates that while it's important on an inner level, you have difficulty expressing those traits to others. Being in control and expressing power is natural with this Scorpio energy, but sometimes those characteristics must be balanced with kindness and understanding for others. Scorpio risings are easily attracted to strong partners who can help bring out their strengths without shutting them off from the people around you. With Scorpio as a descendant sign, learn to use your intensity to connect with and understand people deeper. It could be crucial in your relationships.

Chapter 9: Sagittarius and Capricorn

Next in line in our journey of exploring zodiac sign compatibility, we come to Sagittarius and Capricorn. Sagittarius is a fire sign, and Capricorn is an earth sign, and both have very different personalities. This chapter explores everything about their strengths, weaknesses, and how compatible they are with other zodiac signs.

Sagittarius

Glyph

The symbol for Sagittarius is an arrow pointing upward. This sign always looks to the future, giving us the energy to reach our dreams. It's an inspirational sign, motivating us to aim high and progress toward our goals. The arrow indicates an energetic, adventurous spirit, and this sign is never content to remain in one place for too long. This symbol reminds us to stay positive and follow our passions, even when life throws

Sagittarius.[15]

us a curveball. Sagittarius is all about aiming for the stars and embracing life's challenges.

Another interpretation for this glyph is a centaur – half man, half horse - symbolizing the ability to adapt to any situation and take on different roles. It speaks to the sign's love of travel and exploration, always seeking new horizons. A centaur symbolizes strength, courage, and freedom – qualities Sagittarians embody.

Ultimately, the glyph for Sagittarius is a reminder to stay focused on our goals, embrace life's adventures, and always keep our eyes on the prize. It encourages us to be brave, take risks, and reach for the stars.

If you're a Sagittarius or know someone who is, then you know they're always energetic and ready to take on whatever life throws them. This symbol captures this spirit perfectly and is an inspiration.

Dates

November 22nd to December 21st.

Key Phrase

"Aim for the stars."

This phrase encapsulates what it means to be a Sagittarius – always looking to the future, being courageous and adventurous, and never settling for anything less than their dreams. It's an inspiring phrase that encourages us to take risks, stay positive even when life throws us a curveball, and reach for our highest potential. Sagittarians have an almost magical ability to make the impossible possible, and this phrase is a great reminder. So, don't be afraid to aim high and reach for the stars – you never know what success awaits.

This phrase is perfect for Sagittarius because it represents their ambition, creativity, and willingness to take risks. The phrase speaks to the sign's passion for exploration and travel, always seeking new horizons. They're curious, open-minded, and always eager to try something new or different. This phrase encourages them to push past their limits and potentially take them further than they ever imagined. They're natural-born leaders and pioneers, and this phrase reminds them they can achieve greatness if they believe in themselves.

Strengths

- Optimistic
- Adventurous
- Courageous
- Outspoken
- Independent
- Wise
- Humorous
- Loyal
- Problem-solvers
- Dynamic
- Open-minded
- Motivated
- Passionate

Sagittarians are known for their optimism, courage, and adventurous nature. They have outspoken personalities and are often independent, wise, and humorous. With a loyal heart, Sagittarians are problem-solvers and take the initiative to get things done. They are also dynamic, open-minded, motivated, and passionate about life.

Sagittarians are independent and adventurous, always looking to explore and experience new things. They're creative problem-solvers with a strong sense of justice. Sagittarians are loyal and humorous, often finding the silver lining when faced with adversity. Additionally, they're wise, motivated, and passionate about life.

Sagittarians are an incredible breed of optimistic people who possess the courage to overcome any obstacle. With their strong sense of justice, loyalty, and problem-solving abilities, they make amazing friends, partners, and colleagues. So, recognize their incredible strengths and appreciate them for all they are.

Weaknesses

- Impulsive
- Stubborn
- Impatient
- Lack of tact
- Risk-taking
- Forgetful

Sagittarians can be impulsive and reckless, often speaking before thinking. They are impatient and can often be too bold and tactless in their approach. But it's not all bad news. Sagittarians are known for taking risks, which often leads them to success and exciting new experiences. They might forget important details from time to time, but their enthusiasm and optimism are greatly appreciated.

Pet Peeves

The pet peeves of a Sagittarius are people who put them in a box and limit their freedom. They can't stand overly pessimistic people or who lack ambition. They're all about adventure, so being bogged down by the details or pessimistic attitudes is not something a Sagittarius can handle. Ultimately, they want to be free and have the space to explore their passions.

Ruling Planet

The ruling planet of Sagittarius is Jupiter, which represents justice and truth. Sagittarians often strive to see the best in others and are very optimistic. They take a pragmatic approach to problem-solving and enjoy using their intellect to explore new ideas and solutions. Sagittarians are known for their curiosity, enthusiasm, and adventurous spirit. They love to learn new things and challenge themselves with enthusiasm and determination.

They are often thought of as courageous and can make great leaders. They tend to be social butterflies and enjoy meeting new people. The planet Jupiter gives Sagittarians a unique combination of strength, intelligence, and social grace.

Sagittarius as a Sun Sign

When this sign is your sun sign, you will likely embody the traits associated with its ruling planet, Jupiter. This sign is associated with a quest for knowledge and exploration, meaning you will be an independent thinker who loves learning new things. Sagittarian Suns are naturally optimistic, generous, and open-minded but might sometimes appear blunt or insensitive. You are philosophical and greatly appreciate freedom, so you value independence highly. You are quite adventurous and willing to take risks to reach your goals. When interacting with other zodiac sun signs, Sagittarius is likely to get along well with Aries, Leo, Aquarius, and Gemini, who are similarly optimistic and independent. With Cancer, Virgo, Libra, Scorpio, Capricorn, and Pisces, however, Sagittarius struggles to connect due to their different outlooks on life. Ultimately, the relationships Sagittarian forms will always be based on their ability to find common ground and mutual understanding.

Sagittarius as a Moon Sign

When the moon is in Sagittarius, you are emotionally independent and can adjust easily to new situations. Your passion for learning and exploring new places, cultures, and ideas is stronger. You are optimistic and enthusiastic about most things in life. You have a strong desire for freedom and independence in relationships and are likely to be open-minded and nonjudgmental of others.

Those with a Sagittarius moon sign will usually have an outgoing, active lifestyle and make many friends along their life journey. So, you can expect a life full of exploration and discovery. You might be drawn to activities or people you wouldn't normally be interested in and appreciate their different perspectives and ideas.

You are drawn to the intellectual side of other zodiac signs and appreciate how they challenge you. Sagittarius Moon Signs like to keep things lighthearted and fun and are often the life of the party. You can be drawn to more spiritual paths, seeking deeper and more meaningful connections with the world around you. Regardless of your sign, if the moon is in Sagittarius, you will have an open and adventurous attitude.

Sagittarius as a Rising Sign

When Sagittarius is your rising sign, you are an enthusiastic, positive go-getter who loves to explore new ideas. You're a natural optimist with a determined attitude, always striving to be better than you were the day before. As an independent spirit, you are inspired by those around you but never tied down by them. Your idealistic outlook and free-spirited nature make you a natural leader who inspires others to reach for the stars. You thrive on adventure and always look for new opportunities to learn and grow. Being part of a larger community or collective is important, as you can find great comfort and satisfaction in connecting deeper with others. With your huge heart, dreams, and curiosity, you always seem to find your way toward an exciting and fulfilling future.

When analyzing rising signs associated with Sagittarius, you'll find that each sign expresses itself differently. Aries will bring fiery enthusiasm and passion to the mix, while Taurus brings a more practical, grounded approach and a greater appreciation for the tangible. Gemini adds an intellectual and social element to the equation, while Cancer adds a nurturing and compassionate side. Leo adds creative energy and strong ambition, and Virgo brings analytical skills and attention to detail. Libra balances and harmonizes the situation, while Scorpio adds intensity and power.

Finally, Capricorn will add a more serious, responsible tone, while Aquarius brings innovative ideas and an individualistic outlook. With each of these combinations, Sagittarius, as your rising sign, can help you find the perfect balance of freedom, growth, and exploration.

Sagittarius as a Descendant

When Sagittarius is your descendant, you are an open-minded and proactive individual. You have a deep connection to the outside world and take on a lot of responsibilities. You might be prone to taking risks, but you also intuitively understand people and situations. Additionally, you have a strong sense of adventure and can take on any challenge with excitement and enthusiasm.

Regarding the other twelve zodiac signs, your Sagittarius descendant can bring a sense of optimism and exploration. You will likely take on a lot of responsibilities, but at the same time, see the bigger picture. Your descendant can enable an understanding of different cultures and encourage you to explore new ideas and concepts. Regarding relationships, your Sagittarius descendant will be a great listener and provide honest and sage advice. Lastly, you might appreciate life's simple pleasures, such as nature and outdoor activities. Having a Sagittarius descendant can bring about a sense of inquisitiveness, adventure, and understanding to your life.

Capricorn

Glyph

The glyph for Capricorn is the sea goat, which symbolizes ambition and drive. It's a sign of hard work and determination, showing that Capricorns are go-getters who strive for excellence. The mountain goat symbolizes ambition and progress, reminding us to never give up on our dreams no matter how hard the journey is. This sign is about slowly and steadily climbing up the mountain of success, never letting obstacles stand in the way. The mountain goat symboliz-es determination and optimism, encouraging us to keep going despite challenges.

Capricorn.[16]

This symbol speaks to the sign's dual nature; one side focuses on its goals, while the other seeks pleasure and leisure. The combination of these energies gives rise to the determined and ambitious spirit of a Capricorn.

Capricorns are extremely ambitious, organized, and responsible. They're goal-oriented, driven individuals with a knack for problem-solving and making things happen. They know how to get the job done, often taking on more than they can handle.

Dates

December 22nd to January 19th.

Key Phrase

The key phrase for Capricorn is "upwardly mobile." Capricorns are driven to create success and never give up in the face of adversity. They are resilient and focused, willing to do whatever it takes to reach their goals. They have the ambition and determination to take on the world and come out on top. With their ambitious attitude, Capricorns always look to move forward and upward in life. They always strive for excellence and strive to reach the next level of success. Capricorns are natural-born leaders who stop at nothing until they achieve their goals. So, when life throws them a curveball, these determined individuals will use it as an opportunity to move even further up the ladder of success. Hence, the key phrase for Capricorn is "upwardly mobile."

Strengths

- Loyal
- Hardworking
- Diligent
- Innovative
- Organized
- Resourceful
- Ambitious
- Independent
- Self-reliant
- Daring
- Adaptable
- Strong-willed
- Energetic

Capricorn is one of the zodiac's most hardworking, ambitious, and driven signs. They are loyal and dependable, always willing to roll up their sleeves to get the job done. Capricorns are methodical and resourceful; they devise creative solutions to difficult problems. They are independent, self-reliant, and don't like to rely on others for help. They are fearless and confident in their judgment, often taking calculated risks and moving forward with their ideas. Capricorns are highly adaptable, often making creative changes on the fly. Moreover, they have a strong will and vitality to see projects through from start to finish. These combined qualities make Capricorn's natural leaders essential for any team.

Weaknesses

- Stubborn
- Overly-serious
- Too proud
- Pessimistic
- Materialistic
- Vain

Capricorns are too serious and stubborn when getting things done. Their perfectionism borders on vanity, and they tend to be overly critical of themselves and others. They're also too proud to ask for help and may feel that their goals are unachievable if they don't reach them alone. Capricorns can also be very materialistic and pessimistic, believing that nothing will ever turn out how they want it to. Pushing themselves too hard with unrealistic expectations only exacerbates this issue. Above all, Capricorns need to learn how to manage their expectations and give themselves some grace when things don't go as planned. With a bit of patience and positivity, they can make their dreams come true.

Pet Peeves

- Incompetence
- Carelessness
- Unreliability

Capricorns can't stand incompetence, carelessness, and unreliability in people. They pride themselves on their hard work, dedication, and responsibility, so when someone fails to take their job seriously, Capricorns can become very frustrated. They must remember that everyone has their strengths and weaknesses, and giving people the benefit of the doubt can help them better understand and appreciate everyone's unique talents.

Ruling Planet

Saturn, the planet of structure and discipline, rules Capricorn. So, Capricorns are focused, hardworking, and take responsibility seriously. They have a strong ambition to reach their goals and value hard work. Capricorns are loyal to those they love and enjoy stability. They are traditionalists and prefer to stick with tried-and-true methods. Capricorns can be hesitant to take risks, but if the challenge is worth it, they are ready to tackle it head-on. This sign is practical, disciplined, and motivated to succeed.

The Capricorn is an Earth sign, so they love comfort in their environment and value quality over quantity. They are quite goal-oriented and can focus on the task at hand with laser-like precision. Capricorns are quite savvy regarding money, ensuring they get the most bang for their buck. They can be quite responsible and reliable, making them a great partner for anyone looking for stability and commitment.

Capricorns have an eye for detail and are willing to put in the time and effort to get things done right. They like to plan and are known for their patience and perseverance, making them ideal for careers requiring dedication and hard work. Capricorns are practical yet optimistic, a combination that can take them far.

Capricorn as a Sun Sign

As a sun sign, Capricorn is associated with the enduring traits of ambition, stability, and responsibility. People born with their sun in Capricorn are usually quite serious and hard workers, driven to reach their goals. They have a strong work ethic, great attention to detail, and often have a knack for money management.

People with Capricorns as their sun sign are reliable, sensible, and traditional. They are loyal to their friends and family, rarely straying far from the path they have set themselves. Capricorns value stability and security, making them strong partners for those seeking committed relationships. They can be quite stubborn and sometimes need to learn to compromise, but the rewards are worth it once they do.

Capricorn's energy can accomplish great things when focused and working hard. Capricorn reminds us there is power in dedication and consistency; we can achieve anything with a little hard work and commitment.

Capricorn as a Moon Sign

As a moon sign, Capricorns are associated with structure and stability traits. People with their moon in Capricorn are very organized and detail-oriented. They love routines, plans, and structure and usually have a strong work ethic.

Capricorns with moon signs are cautious and practical but also ambitious. They love rules and regulations but can occasionally be too rigid and inflexible. They are loyal to those they love but can sometimes be too serious and need to lighten up a bit.

As a moon sign, Capricorn teaches us the importance of structure and routine. It reminds us to plan, be organized, and take responsibility for our actions. With some hard work and dedication, Capricorns can make things happen and succeed.

Capricorn as a Rising Sign

As a rising sign, Capricorn is all about order, discipline, and organization. Capricorns are very detail-oriented and often take on a lot of responsibility in their lives. When a Capricorn is your rising sign, you are the person who always takes charge and is the leader in any situation. This sign loves a good challenge and loves to be in charge. With Capricorn as your rising sign, you can expect strong determination and ambition as you reach your goals. Your clear-headedness and practicality will be your greatest asset as you strive for success. Capricorn's rising signs are loyal and committed partners who will always make a relationship work.

Capricorn as a Descendant Sign

As a descendant of Capricorn, you might struggle to let go and relax. You will be the person who strives for balance and stability in life but might sometimes feel overwhelmed. You are likely to take on a lot of responsibility regarding relationships and feel guilty or resentful if something doesn't go your way. With Capricorn as your descendant, it's important to learn to set boundaries and be assertive. This sign teaches you the importance of planning and self-discipline, but you must learn to let go of some worries and relax.

Capricorn, as a descendant, reminds you to stay organized and practical in your approach to life and know when it's time to step back and give yourself a break. When you take the time to rest, it helps you feel rejuvenated so that you can take on the world again. Additionally, with Capricorn as your descendant, you feel overwhelmed, so it's important to take the time to practice self-care. Learning to prioritize your time and goals will go a long way in helping you stay balanced and grounded.

Chapter 10: Aquarius and Pisces

Aquarians and Pisceans are the most mysterious signs in the zodiac. They have a highly imaginative, intuitive, and creative nature that can be hard to pin down. They often have a unique approach to life and prefer independence and autonomy over traditional structures. Let's explore Aquarius and Pisces in greater depth to better understand people with these signs.

Aquarius

Glyph

Aquarius is represented by the glyph of a wave, symbolizing fluidity and continuous flux. This sign has been associated with intellectual progress, originality, and innovation since ancient times. It is linked to social justice and humanitarianism, as Aquarians are known for their generosity and compassion toward others.

This sign is connected to independence and autonomy. It reflects the rebellious streak that can be seen in many of its

Aquarius.[17]

representatives. The presence of air in Aquarius's symbolism suggests a creative spirit that values strong relationships with others. Aquarians have an innate curiosity and appreciation for knowledge, making them highly analytical individuals, always challenging themselves intellectually.

The traits associated with this sign include a friendly, sociable nature and a strong sense of individuality. Aquarians are independent thinkers, often progressive and unwilling to conform to traditional norms. They possess a strong intellect and have an original and creative way of viewing the world.

Dates

January 20 to February 18.

Key Phrase

"I know"

This phrase reflects Aquarian's need for knowledge and understanding of complex ideas. Aquarians have a unique perspective on life largely based on their expansive knowledge. They are always looking for new ways to expand their knowledge and stay informed. This phrase indicates Aquarians' ability to think independently and approach life from a creative perspective while remaining grounded in facts and logical analysis.

Aquarius is one of the most intellectually curious and open-minded signs, so they thrive on learning new things and being exposed to new perspectives. Hence, "I know" is a key phrase accurately reflecting Aquarians' desire for intellectual exploration.

Strengths

* Curiosity
* Openness
* Optimism
* Imagination
* Friendliness
* Compassion
* Fun
* Innovative
* Generosity
* Unconventionality
* Originality
* Independence
* Humanitarianism

Aquarians are true visionaries with high standards and an eye for detail. They can remain cool and collected, even in stressful situations. They are extremely independent and prefer to stay out of the spotlight. Instead, they work behind the scenes, creating tangible results that speak for themselves. They are often seen as forward-thinking and humanitarian, constantly looking for ways to innovate.

Aquarians become passionate about causes they believe in, making them passionate and fun-loving. They appear zany, with an intellectual wit uniquely its own. These characteristics make Aquarius one of the most powerful signs regarding cooperation and problem-solving.

Aquarians shine when working with others. They bring enthusiasm and creativity into any situation to quickly break down barriers between people so everyone can work together efficiently and effectively toward common goals. They are excellent communicators and can be persuasive in their arguments without resorting to aggressive tactics.

Aquarians seem cold and indifferent to the world but are quite emotional. They can be very sensitive and compassionate toward others when they open up, which makes them great friends and allies. Aquarians are incredibly loyal and supportive of their friends, family, and co-workers, providing a listening ear regardless of the situation. They are quite generous, often willing to go above and beyond for anyone in need. These qualities make them great team players and allow them to form meaningful connections easily with others.

Weaknesses

• Unconventional	• Detachment
• Impatience	• Stubbornness
• Rebelliousness	• Aloofness
• Bluntness	• Isolationism
• Indecisiveness	• Mysteriousness

The main weakness of Aquarians is that they often lack the emotional depth to invest in relationships. They are extremely outgoing, social, and friendly – yet struggle with understanding or forming deep connections with others. It leads to misunderstandings and difficulties in their personal and professional lives.

Thoughtful and philosophical, Aquarians often get stuck in their head. Despite the incredible insight they can provide on difficult topics, this deep thinking can lead to many second-guessing themselves and ruminating in circles over every tiny detail. Aquarians don't like it when people try to control or manipulate their decisions into something they don't want to do. They hate being constrained by rules and regulations -

it's about doing what feels right instead of conforming to the expectations of others.

Their emotional detachment can sometimes be detrimental. They need help to connect with people or understand the emotions of others due to their analytical approach. Aquarians take things too far in their quest for freedom and isolate themselves from everyone else in a bid for personal autonomy. Aquarians can be unpredictable in their behavior and responses, leaving those around them bewildered by their mysteriousness.

Pet Peeves

Stubbornness is a pet peeve for Aquarius; if someone argues with them on a point that was made clear from the start, it can lead to frustration. They can be uncompromising with issues they feel strongly about and often find themselves in heated debates with those who think differently. Aquarius get irked by superficial conversations lacking substance or meaning - they prefer deep discussions over small talk and lighthearted banter.

Aquarius has a love-hate relationship with change - while something is thrilling about the unknown, they don't like disrupting their routines or being suddenly surprised. Sometimes change is necessary for growth, but if it's too abrupt, it can cause Aquarius to become overwhelmed.

Ruling Planet

The ruling planets of Aquarius are Saturn and Uranus, which infuses the sign with an air of unpredictability. The influence of this duo gives Aquarius a unique mix of traits, from being deeply analytical and introspective to inventive and independent. This combination creates a forward-thinking individual who values their independence above all else.

They are goal-driven people who challenge themselves to break from traditional conventions to reach new heights that most never dare tread. These two planets standing guard over the sign create an atmosphere of creative exploration and a willingness to take risks to achieve success. Aquarians display intellect, wit, and innovation that can only be found in those under this constellation's influence; it is unique to the sign.

Aquarius as a Sun Sign

As a Sun Sign, Aquarius carries the power of an independent spirit and the drive to pursue their goals with no restraints. Those born under this sign are curious, always seeking new experiences to grow. Despite their obstacles, they have a "big picture" approach to life, as they never lose sight of the larger goal.

Their ability to remain level-headed and driven often leads them to success. Aquarians are highly inventive and bring unconventional thinking to the table, which can lead to creative solutions no one else would have thought of. They often put collective needs before their own, always considering the feelings of others when decision-making.

As a sun sign, Aquarius is a romantic, generous, and compassionate energy deeply connected with friendship and the collective. With their naturally empathetic nature, Aquarians always seek to connect with others and give them an understanding of the world beyond their worldview. Regarding relationships between each of the twelve zodiac signs as sun signs, Aquarians can bring a unique perspective by giving insight into different cultures, beliefs, and ideologies.

Each sign has traits benefiting from this connection with an Aquarian—for instance, Aries can gain empathy. Gemini could use their curiosity to explore new ways of thinking. Aquarius's ability to look at things objectively can help Virgo and Scorpio to find balance in any situation. Aquarian energy is a great way to bring out the best aspects of every sign and enrich their lives with new perspectives. In other words, when analyzing each sign's compatibility based on the sun signs, an Aquarian can connect them all.

Aquarius as a Moon Sign

As a Moon sign, Aquarius has an inner sensitivity that is often more closely guarded. They retreat from expressing intense emotions and instead focus on intellectual pursuits like literature, science, or art. This can come across as aloofness, but it's simply their way of protecting themselves emotionally—they prefer to keep their innermost feelings private.

Those born under the influence of the Aquarius moon have the innate ability to connect with people deeply by understanding them beyond what's visible on the surface. Their natural empathy makes them excellent listeners who remain nonjudgmental no matter how difficult the conversation gets.

Aquarius moon possesses a mental and emotional depth allowing them to understand the complexity of each situation, giving them the capacity to find resolution even in the most difficult circumstances. They have a distinct sense of justice that compels them to do what's right, and their passion for helping others is unparalleled.

Aquarius gets along best with the Gemini and Sagittarius moons. They have similar personalities and a natural curiosity about life, creating an easy rapport between them. However, Aquarians should watch out for too much emotional overload when dealing with the Cancer or Pisces moons, as these signs express their feelings more openly than others.

Aquarius as a Rising Sign

An Aquarius rising sign is a trendsetter. They have an innovative, one-of-a-kind approach to life beyond the mainstream and are not afraid to express it. An Aquarius rising can be assured their ideas are unique and interesting enough to draw attention. It makes them the perfect social catalyst, inspiring others with their forward-thinking outlook.

Having an Aquarius as a rising sign can be very beneficial when examining compatibility between signs. The combination of independence and creativity ensures relationships remain stimulating, irrespective of how long you've been together. With an Aquarius at the helm, conversations become lively debates about current trends or topics of philosophy instead of repeating the same tired routine.

But, the real kicker with an Aquarius rising is they're not bound by norms - which can often be seen as eccentric or even strange. Whether wild fashion choices or a novel approach to problem-solving, an Aquarius rising is always pushing boundaries and coming up with new ideas.

An Aquarius rising sign is well-suited for all twelve zodiac signs. With Aquarius at the helm, each sign can find new and exciting ways to express themselves in relationships and work pursuits. For example, an Aries with Aquarius as a rising sign will be more open-minded and willing to try new things — something an Aries isn't always known for. Similarly, a Taurus with Aquarius as a rising sign will take calculated risks and step outside its comfort zone regarding business endeavors or creative projects. Other signs like Gemini, Libra, and Sagittarius benefit similarly. These signs bring a balance of intellect and emotion, making them the perfect partners for Aquarian risings who need both.

Aquarius as a Descendant Sign

People with Aquarius as their descendant sign are social butterflies. They love meeting diverse people and having interesting conversations, regardless of the situation. Their independent nature allows them to look for relationships that give them a sense of freedom and adventure, so they're drawn toward those who can keep up with their lively spirit and dynamic lifestyle.

This air sign is most compatible with Gemini, Libra, Aries, and Sagittarius. With these signs, Aquarians find a perfect balance between intellectual conversations, freedom of expression, and creative exploration. They feel supported by their partners and can experience profound growth together.

On the other hand, Aquarians experience tension when interacting with Taurus, Scorpio, or Capricorn, as they often want different things from relationships.

Pisces

Pisces. [18]

Glyph

The glyph of Pisces is represented by two fish swimming in opposite directions, connected by a band. This band symbolizes the connection between Pisces and the preceding sign, Aries, which marks the beginning of the zodiac wheel. The two fish represent transitioning from one stage of life to another while staying connected to past experiences as we move forward. The Pisces sign stands for sensitivity, emotionality, and compassion - essential for understanding ourselves and others.

This sign brings an increased awareness of emotions, which can be comforting when dealing with difficult situations. Those born under this sign have natural creativity and imagination, making them particularly insightful when looking at things from different perspectives. In relationships, they bring an emotional depth that helps foster strong bonds and lasting connections. Ultimately, Pisces is a sign of transformation and renewal - perfect for those looking to embrace change and find new ways of expressing themselves.

Dates

February 19 to March 20.

It is the time of year when the sun shines brightest, bringing warmth and a sense of optimism.

Key Phrase

"I believe"

The phrase "I believe" speaks to the sign's ability to trust their instincts and have faith in themselves, even when uncertain. Pisces are notoriously open-minded, believing that anything is possible if we keep searching for it. This phrase encapsulates their never-ending curiosity and willingness to explore new paths and ideas.

They aren't afraid of dreaming big or taking risks - they know anything can be achieved with a little hard work and dedication. Pisces value their opinions and perspectives, stand firm in their beliefs, and never waver from their convictions. Ultimately, this phrase represents Pisces' desire to create, explore, and believe in themselves, regardless of their challenges.

Strengths

- Versatile
- Empathetic
- Compassionate
- Intuitive
- Creative
- Imaginative
- Generous
- Romantic
- Dreamy
- Sensitive

Pisces are known for their unique ability to look at the world differently. They have a profound understanding of life. Their intuitive nature allows them to tap into emotions, dreams, and imagination others cannot. Pisces are some of the most compassionate people you'll ever meet, always looking out for those who cannot care for themselves. They are generous with their time and energy, often going above and beyond what is asked of them.

If you're looking for romance, Pisces will sweep you off your feet with their passionate relationships filled with intimacy and connection. Dreamers at heart, Pisces never tire of exploring the depths of their imagination. From creating creative solutions to expressing themselves through art and writing, they always look for new ways to express themselves.

Weaknesses

- Impulsive
- Shy
- Easily hurt
- Overly trusting
- Escapist tendencies
- Prone to depression
- Indecisive
- Ill-disciplined
- Cynical

Pisces are known for their impulsive nature, which can lead them into some tricky situations. They are shy and easily hurt by criticism or negative energy. They have an overly trusting nature, making them vulnerable to manipulation and exploitation. Pisces possess escapist tendencies, making it hard for them to stay in the present moment. They are prone to depression due to their sensitive disposition, leaving them overwhelmed by negative thought patterns that can affect their mental health.

Pisceans are incredibly indecisive when making essential life decisions, often needing help to think ahead or foresee the potential consequences of their actions. They struggle with self-discipline in certain areas of their lives - leading to a careless and sometimes rash approach with damaging results. Pisces is known for its cynical outlook on life. They are easily suspicious of people who give them too many compliments or do something nice without wanting anything in return. This attitude can lead them to push away potential friends and loved ones, making it difficult for them to form meaningful relationships.

Pet Peeves

Pisces dislikes anything that could be more structured or packed. They feel restricted and confined in an environment that lacks creativity or spontaneity, finding it hard to express themselves authentically.

They dislike too much noise and chaos, preferring quiet and solitude for moments of thoughtful reflection. Pisces cannot stand dishonesty or manipulation from others. They have a strong sense of justice and fairness and will not tolerate any form of unjust treatment.

Ruling Planet

Pisces is ruled by the planet Neptune, which reinforces its creative and dreamy personality. This celestial body governs creativity, imagination, and spirituality, inspiring Pisceans to explore their boundless imaginations.

With an affinity for daydreaming and introspection, they have a deep love of art and music that resonates with their soulful nature.

Neptune oversees illusion and escapism. It makes Pisceans overly trusting of others or have difficulty staying in the present moment. When taken too far, their escapist tendencies can create a barrier from reality and make it difficult for them to establish healthy boundaries around themselves.

At its best, Neptune adds an element of magic to Pisces's life. They can use their inner power and intuitive gifts to overcome obstacles and find true contentment.

Pisces as a Sun Sign

The Pisces sun sign is characterized by dreamy and imaginative energy. Those born under this sign possess an intuitive and spiritual nature that seeks creative outlets for self-expression. They have an intense inner world and often see things from a different perspective than their peers. With an affinity for daydreaming and escapism, they prefer to spend time alone in thought or exploring the mysteries of life on their terms.

Pisces are highly sensitive to emotion - theirs and those around them. This heightened sensitivity can sometimes lead them into difficult situations if they become too trusting or fall prey to manipulation. Conversely, when used positively, Pisceans can use its intuition and empathy to connect with others on a spiritual level. These kind souls are at their best when they can express their unique passions and help others.

Pisces sun signs often pair well with water signs, such as Cancer and Scorpio, who share similar qualities of sensitivity and understanding. Passion for life and creativity make them compatible with fire signs like Aries or Leo. Air signs like Libra or Aquarius can balance Piscean relationships, while fellow Earth sign Taurus provides stability. Regardless of the sign, it's ultimately up to the individuals to make any relationship work - something Pisceans understands better than most.

Pisces as a Moon Sign

If Pisces is your moon sign, water governs you, and you're likely to be extremely sensitive and dreamy. You have a strong intuition that guides you through life and can sense when something's amiss before it happens. Emotions run deep for you, making it difficult to express yourself sometimes. It leads to isolation from others, who might not understand the depths of what you're feeling. At its best, having Pisces as your moon sign enables you to sympathize deeply with others and dedicate generous time to helping them when in need.

People with Pisces as their moon sign are most compatible with other Pisces, Cancer, Scorpio, Virgo, and Capricorn Moons. Those with Virgo or Libra Moon signs have the closest affinities, as they can relate to and understand your emotional depths. Moon sign Pisces generally gets along well with any other sign, regardless of their other sign.

Pisces as a Rising Sign

Pisces rising shows compassion, kind-heartedness, and being in tune with the spiritual realms. Those born with Pisces as their rising sign have an ethereal air around them, making them appear gentle and often quite dreamy. They are prone to feeling sensitive and easily influenced by the energy around them, getting lost in their world of imagination. Pisces rising is a highly imaginative, creative sign that loves to explore all possibilities.

These people have an almost limitless capacity for understanding different perspectives and views. They can be idealistic and even naive sometimes, but this helps them see what others often don't.

Pisces is most compatible with Cancer, Virgo, and Scorpio. Those born under these signs resonate deeply with the intuitive energy that radiates from Pisces individuals; there's an immediate understanding between them even when they meet for the first time. It creates powerful connections that bring out their unique strengths if nurtured correctly.

Pisces as a Descendant Sign

Having Pisces as your descendant sign means that you are a creative and compassionate individual who is always looking for ways to help those around you. You have an intuitive sense of understanding people, their emotions, and how to make them feel better.

Pisces are naturally drawn to artistic endeavors like painting, music, or writing. You are likely a romantic individual who enjoys spending time with your partner or loved one to make them feel special. The most compatible zodiac signs for Pisces as a descendant sign include Sagittarius, Gemini, Scorpio, Cancer, and Virgo. These signs have the potential to complement each other and create harmony in relationships.

Conclusion

People don't come with handbooks. You never know what to expect from someone until you interact with them. Fortunately, astrological compatibility lets you know beforehand whether you will get along with someone. It is a guide to understanding your and other people's personality.

One main reason people are interested in astrology is relationships and finding out if they are compatible with their partners. The book began by explaining the concepts of astrology and compatibility and then explained synastry and its role in evaluating your relationships with others.

You can't fully understand something without first learning about its history, which is why we took a trip back in time to uncover the significance of compatibility in Western, Vedic, and Chinese astrology.

Some people are skeptical about astrology. However, this book challenged these thoughts by providing psychiatrist Cal Jung's study on synastry and astrology and how they led to his theory of Synchronicity. The book proved that astrology is more than an entertaining topic; it can also help you in many areas of your life. The first chapter ended with the many benefits of using astrology in your interpersonal relationships for healthy interactions with others.

Most beginners believe that your star sign is the sole determiner of your compatibility with others. However, your moon and rising signs are significantly relevant. The book explained the different signs in detail. First, we presented the twelve zodiac signs and then explained how they manifest in your sun, moon, and rising signs. Each sign reveals a different aspect of your personality. The book explained these aspects and provided tips on calculating each sign.

It isn't only your sign that is significant in synastry; it is also the planet's position when you were born and your astrological house. We explained the role of each planet, including the Moon and Sun, in astrology and provided detailed information and analysis about each. The book explained astrological houses and described the significance of lunar houses in astrological compatibility.

You can understand the basics of reading your synastry chart. The book defined the concept of a synastry chart and provided tips on calculating your chart. We presented step-by-step instructions on how to read your chart.

The second part of the book covered each of the twelve zodiac signs in detail by presenting their main characteristics, strengths, weaknesses, and other significant information to explore their compatibility with the other signs.

This informative book answered all your questions about astrological compatibility and can act as your guide as you navigate the world of astrology and its impact on your relationships.

Part 2: Tarot Spreads

A Self-Care Guide with Tarot Spreads for Love, Spirituality, Career, and More for Beginners, Including Everything from the Celtic Cross to the Zodiac Spread

Introduction

Albeit a little more challenging to use than other divination forms, Tarot cards can reveal an immense amount of information about your past, present, and future. It takes time and practice, but using the cards can teach you how to access the information you can use to improve your life. No, they won't reveal your exact future. Most of the information you'll gain already exists in your subconscious; the cards are only a tool you use to access knowledge. However, because Tarot readings rely heavily on intuition, they can also be an excellent form of self-care. By developing your intuition through Tarot readings, you're becoming more aware of your desires and needs. You'll be able to reflect on these and plan your next moves.

You'll your intuition to the cards to achieve all of the above. to achieve all of the above. This book provides thorough guidance on choosing the right deck, which is the first step in working with Tarot cards. You'll be introduced to the most common deck types available today, including the Rider-Waite deck, on which most popular variants are based. The subsequent chapter is a detailed guide on the cards of the Major and Minor Arcanas, which are the two subcategories in each Tarot deck.

Once you've understood the meaning and symbolism of the cards, you'll be ready for a few lessons on tapping into your intuition when working with the cards. Having mastered listening to your gut, you can move on to the following chapters that detail the steps you need to take to read the cards properly. This is a crucial step, as you'll only get accurate answers to your questions if you know how to interpret the messages from the cards. Make sure to refer to the tips and tricks provided in the relevant chapter, as they're designed to make this learning process easier for you.

After learning how to use your intuition to its fullest during the readings, you can move on to the chapters that list all the different spreads you can try. Whether you seek information regarding love, self-care, spiritual development, or work, you'll be able to find the perfect layout for you. Or, you can try some popular spreads that use a specific number. Some of these are suitable particularly for beginners and are great for practicing daily readings. They all come with a practical step-by-step guide, difficulty rating, and tips for modification to ensure your success. Lastly, you'll be encouraged to create your own spreads. You'll receive plenty of practical advice on how to do that. So, if you're ready to delve into the amazing world of Tarot spreads, keep reading.

Chapter 1: Introduction to Tarot

This first chapter will introduce you to the historical and cultural background of Tarot, including its origins, what it was used for, and how its application has changed through time. It will also look into the most common deck types used today, such as the Rider-Waite, Thoth, and Marseille. You'll also learn about the structure of the cards and the similarities and differences between each.

The earliest reference to tarot cards goes all the way back to the 1440s.[19]

History of Tarot

The earliest historical reference to Tarot cards originates from 1440s Europe. However, due to the intricate nature of its use at that time, it is believed that Tarot was created a couple of centuries before its European reference. At first, the cards the European artists made were used for games. These decks had 4 suits similar to the Cups, Swords, Discs, and Wands still in use today. Soon after, artists from Venice, Milan, Florence, and Urbino began creating more cards with different illustrations and added them to the decks. These cards were called triumph (trump) cards and were often commissioned by distinguished members of the society. Sometimes the order even dictated that a unique set of cards be created for a noble family featuring members of that family on the trump cards. Since not everyone could afford to hire artists to create customized cards for them, Tarot cards were typically reserved for the privileged until mass printing became available.

By the 18th century, Tarot had spread from Italy to France and gained a new purpose. Users began to attach different meanings to each card, turning it from a fun parlor game to a divinatory tool. According to historical records, Tarot has been used for prophecy from the late 16th century or the early 17th century, albeit in a more simplified way than it's done today. The cards got even more specific meanings a century later, and spreads were created. At the same time, people also learned that Tarot card symbolism is heavily linked to the esoteric teachings of Egyptian religious practices. Some meanings of the Tarot cards have been associated with the ancient lore of the Egyptian gods Osiris and Isis. According to Antoine Court de Gebelin, a French Freemason, the Egyptian teachings made their way to Rome, where the Catholic Church tried (unsuccessfully) to keep them away from the public. While there isn't much historical evidence to support this theory, we know people accepted it. In fact, some of the oldest Tarot decks used today, like the Marseille Tarot, were designed based on Gebelin's theory.

The initial Tarot deck for divination was created in 1791 by French occultist Jean-Baptiste Alliette. He was among the first whose interest in the occult led to the creation of Kabbalah-based art, including Tarot cards linked to hermetic mystics. In the Victorian Era, even upper-class families used Tarot as a parlor game by holding reading séances. A little over a century later, the Rider-Waite Tarot deck was born. Also featuring Kabbalistic symbolism, this deck was the first one with characters to depict the symbolism of the lower cards. Not only were there the customary Swords, Coins, Wands, and Cups, but the creators also used human figures to symbolize the meaning of each card. Due to this, the Original Rider-Waite Tarot deck (also known as the Waite-Smith deck) has become the most widely used deck in history and is still heavily used today.

Since reading methods have evolved since the creation of the first Tarot cards, they are now available in a broad range of designs. And more importantly, Tarot is known and accessible to anyone who wants to learn how to use them for divinatory, spiritual, and many other purposes. And while the cards themselves haven't changed much, the intricate nature of their use made it possible for readers to add their own spin to the traditional meanings of a layout.

Tarot Decks Used Today

Several different Tarot decks are in use today, each with its own theme and symbolism. Here are some of the most popular ones.

Rider-Waite

The Rider-Waite suit was assembled by Arthur Edward White and illustrated by Pamela Coleman Smith in 1909. It has similar interpretations of the Major Arcana and Minor Arcana cards as its classical predecessor did in the 18th and 19th centuries. However, its illustration is much more colorful, giving way to vibrant imagery, which users often find helpful for intuitive readings. Due to their classical imagery, most people find learning how to use these cards pretty straightforward. The images have origins in Paganism, beliefs that existed in the medieval eras, and even Christianity. You'll learn more about the symbolism of the Rider-Waite cards later in the book.

Thoth

Aleister Crowley – a famous English occultist and rival of White – designed another set of cards, the Thoth deck. The cards in this deck were painted by Frieda Harries and depicted a slightly different symbolism for Tarot cards. Crowley and Harries got ideas for the card imagery from several spiritual systems, the occult, and Crowley's own unique spiritual views.

When compared to the Rider-Waite deck, the Thoth deck shows several distinctive differences. Moving away from intuitive imagery, Crowley opted for less-classical design. For example, the Fool card in the

Thoth deck is depicted as the Green Man, the universal symbol of life, birth, and rebirth. Meanwhile, this card portrays a young man facing a life-changing journey in the Rider-Waite deck. This and similar changes give readers a fresh perspective on the classical Tarot card symbolism and conjure new ideas and messages when reading the cards.

Crowley also changed the names of some of the cards. For example, the Strength card in the Major Arcana is called Naked Lust in the Thoth. The Pentacles are named *Discs*, and the numerical and astrological correspondences of several cards have changed. These features allow readers to interpret the cards in a new and unique way.

Marseille

One of the oldest Tarot decks still used today is the Marseille deck. The Marseille deck is a true classic created by François Gassman in Geneva, Switzerland. Despite featuring the same Major Arcana and Minor Arcana cards as many contemporary decks, this one has traditional baroque-style imagery. It has several variations, but most cards have kept their primary French names. Not only that, but when it comes to the four suits, the creator stayed true to the original naming traditions, leaving them as Cups (Coupes), Swords (Épées), Coins (Deniers), and Clubs (Bâtons).

The Cards

Most Tarot decks (Rider-Waite, Thoth, and Marseille) have 78 cards, although some artists can create one or two unique additions to the standard pack, making decks with 79 or 80 cards. Each card has its own symbolism and meaning, which can be used in single-card readings. However, when reading spreads, the meaning of the cards can differ, depending on their combination in the layout. The cards are divided into two categories based on their meanings and symbolism. These categories include the Major Arcana (22 cards depicting a journey, also known as the bigger picture showing the answer you're seeking) and the Minor Arcana (56 cards revealing the minor nuances affecting the answer).

Not only do different Tarot decks have different names (after the artists that created them), but the cards in these decks can have names and several symbols that vary greatly depending on the deck's purpose. Some cards have numbers (in Roman numerals) and names, while others will have only one of the two. Either way, having a name and/or number helps familiarize new readers with cards and their meanings. The number of cards typically stays the same (78). However, the artists might change the order of their numbering to represent a slightly different theme. Other artists will only provide symbolic images to the cards in their deck without naming or numbering them. These are typically used by those who prefer to rely on intuitive readings and not traditional card meanings.

The Best Deck for Beginners

Being the first mass-distributed Tarot decks in history, the original Rider-Waite deck is the most widely researched one that you can find. Because there is no shortage of information about the symbolism and use of this deck, it's the most recommended Tarot deck for beginners. The standard description makes it easy to familiarize yourself with the essential functions and incorporate them into your daily practices. As one of the most popular versions of the original Rider-Waite tarot deck, the Radiant Rider-Waite deck is also recommended to beginners due to its similarity with its predecessor. If you find these too esoteric, you can always try your luck with the Classical Tarot. This deck captures symbols you can interpret intuitively, which many find easier.

How to Choose the Right Tarot Deck

Most Tarot decks you'll find today are Rider-Waite derivatives, which is why this book will focus only on this deck. You're free to choose whichever Tarot decks you wish to work with. Below are some tips on finding the right deck for beginners.

Look for Intuitive Connections with the Cards

The best way to find the right deck is to choose the one you are drawn to. While you can get recommendations for specific decks, you should never go by other people's experiences. Look at the recommended decks, but if you don't feel a personal connection to them, it means that they simply aren't suitable for you and your personality. However, if your gut tells you to learn more about a deck (or certain cards in the deck), you should explore them more deeply. Because of this, it's always better to buy your first Tarot deck in person. Feel free to touch the cards and contemplate the type of energy you pick up from them. You should feel a personal connection with at least one or more cards in the deck. Whether you're getting it from a bookstore or a new-age shop, you'll get a much better picture of your reaction to the cards than if you were to buy them online. That said, if your only option for buying a Tarot deck is purchasing them online, explore the cards they contain beforehand. A quick Google search of the deck you're considering should provide you with enough imagery to decide whether you can connect to the cards.

Explore the Imagery of the Cards

Even if you're buying them in a store, doing a little research on the imagery of the cards is always a good idea. Make sure to go through the cards individually, stopping at each to check your response to them. You'll have a different reaction to the decks. For example, some people are drawn to intricate patterns, while others like vivid colors. Some people can't take their eyes off the images, while others will pick up on specific pieces of the artwork. You should also check different variations of the same deck to see if your reaction is the same to all of them. For example, some feel a much stronger connection to the Radiant Rider-Waite deck than to the traditional Rider-Waite deck simply because it uses more vivid imagery.

While exploring, you should look at the meaning of the cards too. If you can pick up the essence of the cards intuitively, it's a sure sign that you've found the right deck. Look at all the Major Arcana and Minor Arcana cards to see if you find most of them visually appealing. Some decks have significant differences in the illustrations, and some readers find non-traditional depictions extremely unappealing.

Consider Your Experience Level

Beginners often prefer learning the basics of Tarot with straightforward symbolism, like the one used on the Rider-Waite deck. Others like a more minimalist design and will choose the likes of the Everyday Tarot Deck, which allows a more practical approach to connecting with the imagery. On the other hand, those with some experience with Tarot prefer more challenging and complex decks, like the Thoth deck. Make sure to match your experience level with your connection with the cards. Whether you find it easier to work with the classical Rider-Waite deck becomes irrelevant if you can't form an intuitive link with them.

Determine if You Want a Traditional or Modern Deck

Some people are instinctively drawn to contemporary imagery, often created by independent artists with a unique view of Tarot symbols. They find these more relevant to our times and come in handy for resolving modern issues. Others are intrigued by the classical decks like the Marseille and the Rider-Waite deck, with their fascinating, European-style imagery. These are better suited for answering age-old questions and looking at the bigger picture in every situation. That said, if you feel a stronger connection with a contemporary design, you can still use them to reveal more in-depth information about the outcome you're interested in exploring. You'll just need to listen to your intuition, and you'll be able to work with any deck.

Check Out the Literature

Most Tarot card artists include a booklet explaining the meaning of the cards in the deck they've created. You can also learn about the cards' symbolism and other helpful information from this small guide. If the deck you've purchased or are about to buy doesn't come with a complementary guide or the latter lacks the information you're looking for, don't worry; you can still learn about the cards (including whether you'll be able to work with them) by looking them up online. Look for reviews from other users, guides on them, or e-books explaining how to work with the particular deck. On the other hand, if you prefer to rely solely on your gut, you can find the lack of predefined symbolism refreshing. Not having preconceived notions about the cards encourages you to hone your intuition even more.

Find the Right Size

Tarot cards come in many sizes; you can pick the one that best fits your needs and purposes. For example, if you do small daily rituals to practice your craft but travel a lot, you should choose mini Tarot cards. These fit perfectly into any bag, so you can take them anywhere. If you prefer to do readings in the privacy of your home, any regular-sized deck will work as long as you can bond with its energy. On the other hand, if you plan to do group readings with family or friends, you'll find giant Tarot decks handy. Ensure you're getting the size you and whoever else will be using the cards are comfortable handling when shuffling and making the spread.

Consider How You Want to Use the Tarot Cards

The purpose of the Tarot cards will also have a bearing on your decision. Some decks are better suited for answering questions about finding peace and harmony in your life. Others are better for intuitive readings or connecting to your spiritual desires. If your practice includes earth-based rituals and spells, choose a deck that accommodates this. There are Tarot decks with versatile backgrounds and symbolism that can accommodate a range of purposes. If you have several uses for your cards, get one that fits all your needs and desires. Experienced readers have several decks on hand. However, for beginners, it's recommended to have only one to learn the basics and develop your intuition enough for it to connect to the cards at all times.

Pay Attention to Quality

The quality of the cards also matters as you'll need something you can use for years and possibly daily. Unfortunately, many inexpensive decks are not quality cards and will tear or get damaged only after a few uses. If you plan to use your cards regularly, investing a little more in a good-quality deck is better than buying something that will fall apart after a couple of uses.

Buy Your Tarot Cards

Some still believe that Tarot cards should only be gifted and not bought by oneself, but this deprives you of the opportunity to check if you'll have a connection with them. No matter how good the gifter's intentions were when they purchased the deck for you, if you can't connect to the cards, you'll have no use for them. Of course, if you have a close friend or a loved one whom you can hint about the deck to which you feel drawn, feel free to do so.

The Benefits of Practicing Tarot Reading

Practicing Tarot reading has many benefits, regardless of which decks you use. Some of these benefits are listed below.

You'll Gain Clarity in Life

Tarot card readings are great for gaining insight into different life situations. Getting clarity on some difficult matters can help you make the next step. The cards also give you a fresh perspective on concerns you mistakenly believed resolved but which were stopping you from reaching your full potential.

You Can Focus on Improving Certain Areas of Life

Tarot cards can also give a better understanding of your personality. For example, if you have a trait that negatively impacts your ability to grow personally, the cards can highlight it. Once you've been made aware of the negative quality, you can start improving it. Remember, no matter how prosperous your life is, there is always room for self-improvement. Tarot cards are the ideal tools for picking up the areas that you still need to work on.

You Can Find Peace and Harmony

Sometimes, your own negativity will hold you back the most, and the cards can point this out. They can also highlight the positive aspects of life you should focus on instead of obsessing over the negative experiences. This can give you the peace of mind you need, alleviating anxiety and creating harmony between the different aspects of your life.

You'll Make Better Decisions

If you're at a crossroads in life and have trouble deciding how to move forward, consulting the Tarot cards can help you make the right decision. The cards will not predict the exact future or tell you how to make decisions. However, they will give you the necessary insight to make the best decision.

You Can Make Improvements to Your Life

If you're looking to transform your life, Tarot card reading is a perfect way to do this. The cards can highlight new talents you can nurture, skills to discover and hone, and any aspects of your personality you need to focus on to become a better version of yourself.

You Can Nurture Your Relationships

Because they help you replace negative influences with positive ones, Tarot cards often prompt people to take a risk they wouldn't otherwise take. One of the greatest (and most rewarding) risks you can take is to open yourself up in your relationships. Tarot readings can give the reassurance you need when taking risks to establish a loving and harmonious relationship with your loved ones. Having created these, you'll become much happier, enabling you to appreciate the positive aspects even more and inspiring you to work on the negative ones.

Chapter 2: The Major Arcana

The Rider-Waite tarot deck is split into two sub-groups, The Major Arcana and The Minor Arcana. Each soul is on a journey to learn lessons and reach enlightenment. The Major Arcana cards, also called The Trump cards, represent the archetypal themes and karmic influences that affect your journey. Each card holds a beautiful, deep, and complex meaning, but this is part of what makes them fascinating. Understanding these cards will give you the keys to uncovering your consciousness and learning all life's lessons.

The Major Arcana.[20]

There are twenty-one numbered Major Arcana cards and one unnumbered which is called "The Fool card." The Fool is the most significant card and the star of the story. He takes a life-altering journey through all the Major Arcana cards. He meets different characters along the way, and each one has a lesson to teach him until he finishes his journey in the last card, "The World card." The only way to understand the Major Arcana cards is to explore and learn about the *Fool's journey.*

The Fool's Journey

The Fool

Number

Zero

Element

Air

Corresponding Planet

Uranus

Zodiac Sign

Aquarius

Upright Meaning (if the card appears upright, not upside-down)

Free spirit, spontaneity, innocence, new beginnings, adventure, faith, freedom, eccentricity, impulsiveness, purity, originality, and courage.

The Fool upward card represents new opportunities and beginnings. Like the

The fool.[21]

Fool, you are embarking on a new journey into the unknown. You don't need a destination; you are following your heart and committing to the path. It can seem like a crazy or risky adventure, but you take a leap of faith and trust that the Universe will guide you. The Fool will encourage you to open your heart and mind to what's coming. Let go of your worries and fear and step into the unknown. Whatever happens, happens, you're not the one in control, but you have faith in the Universe's plan for you. You are experiencing a new world where you will learn new lessons and grow.

Reversed Meanings (if the card appears upside-down)

Lacking adventure, stupidity, restrictions, not thinking things through, playing it safe, chaos, naivety, lack of direction, being gullible, and poor judgment.

The Fool reversed means that you have a new project or idea but aren't ready to share it with the world. You don't have faith in yourself and are questioning your abilities, or you feel that this isn't the right time. Something is standing in your way, and you allow it to hold you back from reaching your full potential. You choose to wait because you are afraid to take a risk. You are standing still, refusing to take any new steps. However, if you have been reckless recently, the reverse Fool card reminds you to slow down and consider the consequences of your actions.

The story begins with the Fool feeling inspired and excited as he embarks on his new journey. However, there is so much that he still needs to learn. He is naive as this is his first adventure, so he is unaware that he is about to walk off a cliff. Yet, he is very enthusiastic, and his heart is in the right place. He is extremely hopeful and feels that anything is possible. He takes a moment and prepares himself to get into a different mindset than his own, the mindset of the Magician.

The Magician

Number

One

Element

Air

Corresponding Planet

Mercury

Zodiac Sign

Gemini

Upright Meaning

Creativity, visualization, action, manifesting desire, power, willpower, smooth-talking, inspiration, skill, self-employment, resourcefulness, and communication.

The magician.[23]

The upward Magician card represents magic, transformation, healing, and willpower. He uses the power of the elements to inspire a strong will and a desire for change in the fool. He is the link between above and below or heaven and Earth. The Magician understands that the world and the human mind aren't different from one another. In fact, one is a reflection of the other. This means that if one uses their inner power, they can create a beautiful world inside of them which will reflect on their external world. The Magician inspires you to dig deep and reach your full potential. Whether it's a new relationship, a job, or a career, it pushes you to act now and make the necessary changes. Some opportunities come once in a lifetime; if you miss them, there is no going back.

Reversed Meaning

Bad intentions, deceit, manipulation, lying, feeling out of your depth, poor communication skills, creativity block, and abuse of power.

The reversed Magician card means that you aren't tapping into your creativity. Maybe you feel that the world isn't ready for your ideas, or you don't have the confidence to share your creativity with others. It can also mean that you lack leadership skills.

As the Fool goes into the Magician's mindset, he harnesses his inner power to make his dreams come true. He believes in the power of magic and that he can perform miracles if he works with the universe. While the fool is discovering his metaphysical gifts, he encounters the High Priestess.

The High Priestess

Number

Two

Element

Water

Corresponding Planet

The Moon

Zodiac Sign

Cancer

Upright Meaning

Divine femininity, mystery, inner voice, sensuality, intuition, desire, high power, unattainability, thirst for knowledge, fertility, subconscious, mind, and creativity.

The high priestess.[28]

The High Priestess's upright card signifies that you should trust your instincts and make the right choices for yourself. Listen to your gut and ignore what everyone tells you. The Universe is on your side, helping you and sending you signs. It is working with you to achieve your dreams. The card can also mean that the knowledge you seek is deep inside you. Your inner divine female is ready to guide you and give you the answers you seek. The High Priestess encourages you to accomplish anything you set your mind to and provides you with answers. She wants you to protect your heart and mind from negative thoughts and better understand your abilities and skills so you can go far in life.

Reversed Meaning

Silence, secrets, sexual tension, poor psychic abilities, superficiality, fertility issues, hidden motives, angry outbursts, confusion, repressed intuition, withdrawal, and unwanted attention.

The card suggests that although looking inward will grant you the wisdom you seek, you will struggle with indecisiveness and a wandering mind. You will ignore your goals and dreams and focus on your drama. It can also mean that no one really knows you as you don't share your true self with the world. You lack self-confidence and constantly question yourself. You also live in denial and aren't aware of your inner abilities. Your glass is half empty as you are focused on the negative things in life.

The Fool meets the High Priestess as he prepares to expand his powers and develops a better understanding of the spiritual and physical worlds. She stands as a guard to the human's intuition and invites the Fool to join her in a world of Divine wisdom and knowledge. She becomes his teacher.

The fool wonders if he is in the right direction, and this is when his mother, The Empress, appears.

The Empress

Number

Three

Element

Fire

Corresponding Planet

Venus

Zodiac Sign

Taurus

Upright Meaning

The empress."

Fertility, nurturing, femininity, abundance, sensuality, safety, divine figure, security, beauty, creation, peacefulness, motherhood, harmony, pregnancy, success, and connection with nature.

The Empress represents connecting with your feminine side, which includes nurturing, sensuality, elegance, and fertility. Connecting with your femininity is necessary as it creates a balance between men and women and invites beauty into your life. The Empress urges you to connect with your five senses and experience all life's pleasures through them. Tap into your creative mind and express yourself through art or music. She wants to show you that you are growing and are about to achieve all your dreams. The Empress reminds you to be grateful because you have everything you need to be happy.

Reversed Meaning

Smothering, insecurity, inability to move forward, infertility, lack of progress, negligence, low self-confidence, and disharmony.

The reversed Empress card reminds you to take care of yourself because you have been ignoring your needs for so long. You have been focusing on people's feelings and neglecting your own. You give others power and let them influence your actions and decisions. The reversed Empress wants to show you that giving your time and effort to others is affecting your well-being. The card can also mean you are experiencing a creativity block and need to connect with nature.

The Empress represents nurturing and fertility and reminds the fool to connect with Mother Nature. Then his father, The Emperor, appears.

The Emperor

Number

Four

Element

Fire

Corresponding Planet

Mars

Zodiac Sign

Aries

Upright Meaning

Leadership, stability, logic, structure, practicality, protection, providing, authority, safety, dependability, maturity, and fatherhood.

The emperor.[25]

This card is a symbol of a father figure. Whether you are a man or woman, it represents your role as a protector and provider of your family. You bring stability to your loved ones; they depend on you and see you as a role model. The Emperor reflects your position and the respect that comes with it. You are a leader who desires power; you know what you want and are prepared to go after it. As a leader, you are firm but fair and always open to hearing others' input, but you end up doing what you believe is right.

Reversed Meaning

Tyranny, abuse of power, domineering, controlling, father issues, overbearing, lack of control, overpowering, stubbornness, and manipulative.

The Reversed Emperor reminds you that you are abusing your power and can be too controlling. The card invites you to assess your leadership style, look within yourself, and evaluate how you treat others.

When The Emperor meets the Fool, he provides him with specific rules that he must follow to guarantee that his journey is safe and prosperous. The Emperor reminds the Fool that he should carry his traditions in his heart because they will keep him level-headed and grounded as he experiences a spiritual awakening. The Fool wants to explore spirituality and hopes to find an experienced teacher to guide him. This is when The Hierophant appears.

The Hierophant

Number

Five

Element

Earth

Corresponding Planet

Venus

Zodiac Sign

Taurus

Upright Meaning

Teamwork, religion, safety, belief, education, commitment, spiritual wisdom, traditions, marriage, conformity, and sharing knowledge.

This card reminds you to embrace traditional ideas and thoughts. Even when you are tempted to experience the unconventional parts of life, set some boundaries so you don't compromise your beliefs. It also means that you are a follower, not a leader, and prefer to stay with the conventional rather than try something new.

The hierophant.[26]

Reversed Meaning

Peer pressure, freedom, non-conformity, personal belief, rebellion, challenging traditions, new methods, and ignorance.

The reversed Hierophant tarot represents rebelling and breaking the rules. It invites you to let go of the old rules that have been governing your life. Challenge social norms and ask yourself if they are worth following or not.

The Hierophant influences the Fool to learn the traditions and beliefs of his culture and conform to social norms.

Now the Fool begins to experience loneliness and yearns for a sexual partnership and hopes to find his soulmate and experience The Lovers.

The Lovers

Number

Six

Element

Air

Corresponding Planet

Mercury

Zodiac Sign

Gemini

Upright Meaning

Soulmates, relationships, love, sexual bonds, passion, connection, and physical attraction.

This card represents the union and harmony between a couple. When you meet your soulmate, what you feel is beyond physical attraction; it is a divine feeling that only true lovers experience. It is a pure relationship built on trust, closeness, and honesty.

The lovers.[27]

Reverse Meaning

Impulsive choices, trust issues, conflicts, lack of intimacy, broken promises, detachment, and coldness.

The reversed Lovers card represents challenges in a relationship. You and your partner are unable to communicate, and the time has come to go your separate ways.

The Lovers teach the Fool cooperation and balance his feminine and masculine sides. Now, he feels that he has learned enough to succeed in life, so he rides The Chariot to take a journey to achieve his goals.

The Chariot

Number

Seven

Element

Water

Corresponding Planet

The Moon

Zodiac Sign

Cancer

Upward Meaning

Action, direction, strength, control, ambition, tenacity, determination, motivation, and success.

This card means you are ready to apply what you have learned, make the right decisions, and take action. The Chariot encourages you to harness your inner power to achieve the goals you have set for yourself.

The chariot.[38]

Reversed Meaning

Hostility, lack of direction, helplessness, and loss of control.

The Chariot reversed tells you you need to change your plan or direction because whatever project or task you are working on won't help you achieve your goals. If you are working on something and feel stuck, assess the situation, and consider changing directions.

The Fool has acquired Strength through his journey that tames the fiery ambition he experienced on The Chariot. He now understands that some goals take longer to achieve, which leads him to experience maturity and growth.

The Strength

Number

Eight

Element

Fire

Corresponding Planet

The Sun

Zodiac Sign

Leo

Upright Meaning

Courage, health, bravery, inner power, boldness, kindness, and compassion.

This card symbolizes the inner strength that drives you to overcome any challenges you face. You are calm, patient, mature, and composed. You have a quiet presence that influences those around you. You have the courage to achieve anything, even if you are afraid.

Strength.[29]

Reversed Meaning

Self-doubt, disbelief, vulnerability, weakness, insecurity, anxiety, and low self-esteem.

This card means that you are experiencing setbacks and losing your confidence. Tap into your inner strength and let it empower you.

The Fool needs to reflect on everything he has learned so far, so he spends some time by himself and becomes The Hermit. As The Hermit, he tries to make sense of the world. This leads him to discover that there are no coincidences and everything is going according to the Universe's plan.

The Hermit

Number

Nine

Element

Earth

Corresponding Planet

Mercury

Zodiac Sign

Virgo

Upright Meaning

Guidance, contemplation, meditation, self-discovery, retreat, introspection, and solitude.

This card represents taking a break from your social life and spending time alone to focus on your inner self. Search deep into your soul to find that the truth and knowledge you seek are within you.

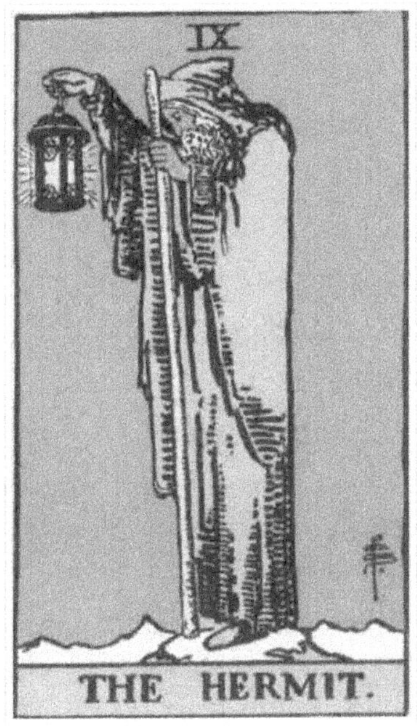

The hermit.[80]

Reversed Meaning

Withdrawal, seclusion, loneliness, restriction, rejection, paranoia, and isolation.

This card has two meanings: either you are too focused on your inner self or not at all. It reminds you to spend some time nurturing your spiritual side by meditating and rebuilding yourself. However, if you spend too much time on self-reflection, this card suggests that you have isolated yourself and become a hermit. Remember the value of personal relationships and connecting with others.

The Fool is introduced to The Wheel of Fortune, where he learns about the concept of Fate. Everything happens for a reason and at the right time.

The Wheel of Fortune

Number

Ten

Element

Fire

Corresponding Planet

Jupiter

Zodiac Sign

Capricorn

Upright Meaning

Chance, good luck, the cycle of life, destiny, decisive moments, karma, and soulmates.

This card reminds you that life is constantly moving and changing. No matter how bad things are now, they will get better. You will experience good fortune sooner or later. However, if things are going well, this can also change. Life is an ongoing cycle, so enjoy what you have now because you don't know what the future will bring,

Wheel of fortune.[81]

Reversed Meaning

Setbacks, bad luck, delays, disorder, disruptions, and unwelcome change.

This reversed card indicates bad luck. You will find your life changing for the worst, and you can do nothing to fix it. However, taking responsibility for your actions and believing you are in control can change your destiny.

The Fool then learns that there is justice and consequences for his actions.

Justice

Number

Eleven

Element

Air

Corresponding Planet

Venus

Zodiac Sign

Libra

Upright Meaning

Justice, law, karma, consequences, truth, fairness, and honesty.

This card reminds you that you will pay the price for your actions. If you live an honest life without harming others, you are safe. However, you will be held accountable for your mistakes if you haven't.

Justice.[89]

Reversed Meaning

Injustice, dishonesty, corruption, and lack of responsibility.

This card means you made a mistake but are afraid to admit it. So, you either keep it hidden or confess and make things right. It also means you refuse to take responsibility for your mistakes and blame others for them.

The Fool now becomes The Hanged Man and sets out to discover the world.

The Hanged Man

Number

Twelve

Element

Earth

Corresponding Planet

Venus

Zodiac Sign

Taurus

Upright Meaning

Letting go, giving up, sacrificing, thoughts, waiting, and perspective.

This card wants you to let go of your old way of thinking, change your perspective, and see the world differently. The appearance of this card in a reading means that the projects you are working on will suddenly stop. Take this time to reassess your direction. The Universe has paused your projects because something better is coming along.

The hanged man.[38]

Reversed Meaning

Delays, indecision, stagnation, resistance, apathy, and avoidance.

This card means you are keeping yourself busy because you don't want to confront your issues. Your mind and body want you to slow down and pay attention to them.

The Fool now experiences Death as his old self fades away, and he is a new man embarking on the next chapter in his life.

Death

Number

Thirteen

Element

Water

Corresponding Planet

Pluto

Zodiac Sign

Scorpio

Upright Meaning

Release, transformation, letting go, endings, and transitions.

The Death card doesn't hold a negative meaning. It represents letting go of a life that no longer serves you and freeing space for something that will add value and meaning to your life. Release the past and welcome new opportunities. Transformation allows you to let go of the old and welcome the new.

Death.[34]

Reversed Meaning

Decay, fear of change, and stagnation.

Reversed Death card indicates that you are resisting change. You still hold on to old perspectives that no longer serve you. As a result, you feel stuck and experience periods of stagnation.

Now, as the Fool lets go of the past, he is at peace. He is much wiser and more patient as he is able to find balance with Temperance. He understands that not everything needs to happen right away.

Temperance

Number

Fourteen

Element

Fire

Corresponding Planet

Jupiter

Zodiac Sign

Sagittarius

Upward Meaning

Balance, serenity, harmony, peace, tranquility, patience, and moderation.

This card reminds you to stay calm, especially when life is getting hectic or stressful. Remain level-headed and in control of your emotions, and don't allow anything to ruin your day. It invites you to welcome people with different perspectives and accept them instead of being stubborn.

Temperance.[85]

Reversed Meaning

Imbalance, hastiness, recklessness, excess, and discord.

This card reminds you to let go of excess and embrace moderation. It also indicates that things aren't going right for you. Assess your life, make the necessary adjustments, and bring back the flow.

The Fool tries to move forward, but he is still stuck in the past and unable to let go. The Devil shows up and encourages him to look at the parts of his past that prevent him from moving forward.

The Devil

Number

Fifteen

Element

Earth

Corresponding Planet

Saturn

Zodiac Sign

Capricorn

Upward Meaning

Obsession, secrecy, adultery, dependency, and mental illness.

This card shows your dark side and the negativity within you that prevents you from growing. Whether it's a toxic relationship, addiction, or negative thoughts, you feel trapped. You choose instant gratification over your well-being and long-term goals.

The devil.[36]

Reversed Meaning

Detachment, realization, independence, revelation, and regaining control.

This card appears when you are about to make a discovery. But you are held back by your unhealthy lifestyle or attachments. You must let go of your darkness before embracing a new and better version of yourself.

The Fool gets help from The Tower by forcing him to let go of the shackles of the past. Although this can feel scary, it's for his own good and can free him.

The Tower

Number

Sixteen

Element

Fire

Corresponding Planet

Mars

Zodiac Sign

Aries

Upright Meaning

Disaster, chaos, destruction, and trauma.

When this card appears, expect your life to take a turn for the worse. Chaos and destruction will bring a great change into your life. This can be a health issue, divorce, financial troubles, losing your job, or the death of a loved one.

The tower.[87]

Reversed Meaning

Averting distance, resisting change, and delaying the inevitable.

This also indicates change, but unlike the upright Tower where things are beyond your control, you are the one making the changes. You are questioning everything, like your purpose and life's meaning, which will lead you to experience a spiritual awakening.

The Star shows up to light his way, guides him, and gives him hope. The Fool feels its inspiration as he shows his truest self.

The Star

Number
Seventeen

Element
Air

Corresponding Planet
Uranus

Zodiac Sign
Aquarius

Upright Meaning
Hope, positivity, inspiration, healing, creativity, and renewal.

The Star brings hope after the destruction caused by The Tower. After everything you have been through, you now know who you truly are. You are one with the universe and can handle anything life throws at you. This is a new chapter where you will experience peace and mental stability.

The star.[88]

Reversed Meaning
Despair, boredom, negativity, and hopelessness.

This indicates that you have stopped believing in your connection with the universe. You feel the Divine isn't on your side and are questioning everything happening to you, "Why is this happening to me?"

The Moon represents the Fool's fears that interfere with his peace of mind. His old anxicties and the things he put behind him are returning to haunt him.

The Moon

Number

Eighteen

Element

Water

Corresponding Planet

Neptune

Zodiac Sign

Pisces

Upright Meaning

Deception, confusion, fear, and insecurity.

This card represents letting your fear interfere with your present and future. This can be the result of suppressing your emotions and not dealing with them. It also indicates a state of illusion, so refrain from making decisions when this card appears.

Reversed Meaning

Insomnia, bad dress, and unhappiness.

The reversed Moon means that you understand the impact of your fears and anxieties on your life and the steps you need to take to make the necessary changes.

Now the Fool has overcome his anxieties and fears and has transformed into The Sun. He has become a new man -aware of his purpose in life. He is sharing his truest self with the world and is guiding others to do the same.

The moon.[89]

The Sun

Number

Nineteen

Element

Fire

Corresponding Planet

The Sun

Zodiac Sign

Leo

Upright Meaning

Enlightenment, vitality, joy, marriage, and success.

The sun.[40]

The Sun reminds you of your positivity and optimism. People enjoy your warm personality and ability to see the silver lining in everything. Your sunny attitude will give you the strength to handle whatever comes your way. The Sun also reminds you that things will always get better.

Reversed Meaning

Lack of clarity, sadness, and false impressions.

This card is saying that you have been taking life seriously, and it's time to reach into your inner child and have fun. It is OK to take a break every once in a while and to enjoy yourself. The card also reminds you to look on the bright side.

The Fool is now aware of his true purpose and knows his destiny. Everything is real. There are no lies or illusions left, similar to a final Judgment.

Judgment

Number

Twenty

Element

Fire

Corresponding Planet

Pluto

Zodiac Sign

None

Upright Meaning

Awakening, transition, renewal, and redemption.

Judgment.[41]

This card means that you are finally aware of your purpose in life. You are answering your spiritual calling as you shed your old self and embrace the real you. This card appears when everything in your life has fallen into place and you are ready to enter a significant chapter in your life.

Reversed Meaning

Poor decisions, self-doubt, and stagnation.

Pay attention if you see this card because the Universe is sending you a message. Something big is about to happen in your life, but you aren't hearing the Universe's call or seeing the signs.

The Fool has completed his journey and has grasped everything The World is trying to teach him. He has learned many lessons and is celebrating his accomplishments.

The World

Number

Twenty-One

Element

Earth

Corresponding Planet

Saturn

Zodiac Sign

None

Upright Meaning

Achievement, success, possibility, and fulfillment.

The world.⁰

If you see the World card, you should be proud of yourself. You have achieved one of your biggest goals and are reveling in your success, like getting a promotion, marrying your soulmate, having a child, or graduating college. You have made your dream a reality. Take a moment to reflect on your journey and the lessons you have learned, and be grateful for everything you have accomplished.

Reversed Meaning

Failed plans, stagnation, and delayed success.

This card indicates your desire for closure. You have to accept that things have changed so you can move on from the past. It can also mean you want to achieve a big goal and aren't prepared for it.

The Fool's journey mirrors each person's path in life. You begin it naive and inexperienced but learn through experiences and taking risks. Life is the best teacher one can ask for; just pay attention to what it's trying to teach you.

Chapter 3: The Minor Arcana

The Minor Arcana tarot is the second subgroup of cards in the Rider-Waite tarot deck. There are fifty-six cards, each symbolizing the adversity and affliction of the human experience. Although these cards are referred to as "minor," they are no less significant or influential than the Major Arcana cards. They provide you with insight into your day-to-day life and shed light on the changes you need to make to achieve your goals.

Minor arcana.[48]

Unlike the Major Arcana cards that focus on your longer-term experiences, the Minor Arcana have a temporary impact as they represent what goes on in your life in the present moment. The Minor Arcana Cards are categorized into four different suits.

1. Cups

2. Swords

3. Pentacles

4. Wands

Each consists of ten numbered cards and four court cards: the King, Queen, Knight, and Page. Each suit focuses on various parts of your life.

The Suit of Cups

Keywords: Intuition, emotions, relationships, and feelings.

Element: Water

Alternative Names: Chalices, goblets, or vessels.

Jungian Function: Feeling

The Suit of Cups represents your emotions, feelings, and the daily energy that flows inside you. It shows your behavior and interactions with the people in your life. These cards also reflect how you connect with yourself and your loved ones. When the suit of Cup cards is strong, they symbolize your compassionate, kind-hearted, caring, creative, and empathetic nature. You can put yourself in other people's shoes and relate to them. It also means that you are extremely intuitive, and some call you psychic.

When these cards are weak, you live in a fantasy world, and you don't listen to reason or facts.

Ace of Suits

Element: Water

Corresponding Planet: Mercury

Zodiac Sign: Capricorn

Upright Meaning

Happiness, creativity, new beginnings, relationships, fulfillment, love, pregnancy, new connections, fertility, socializing, joy, and festivities.

Reversed Meaning

End of relationships, self-love, anguish, repressed emotions, bad news, intuition, infertility, unrequited love, miscarriages, breakups, and sadness.

Two of Cups

Element: Water

Corresponding Planet: Venus

Zodiac Sign: Cancer

Upright Meaning

Love, mutual attraction, happiness, partnerships, relationships, unified love, connection, mutual respect, peace, marriage, engagements, proposals, soulmates, fairness, alignment, compatibility, and passion.

Reversed Meaning

Disharmony, arguments, distrust, anguish, self-love, strained relationships, breakups, separations, divorces, bullying, discord, dominance, abuse, ending friendships, inequity, fights, and unhappy marriages.

Three of Cups

Element: Water

Corresponding Planet: Mercury

Zodiac Sign: Cancer

Upward Meaning

Friendships, happiness, joy, celebration, creativity, good conversation, collaboration, happy times, meetings, graduation, social gatherings, engagement parties, weddings, enjoyments, indulgences, and festivals.

Reversed Meaning

Cheating, independence, frustration, alone time, gossiping, extreme partying, lack of excitement, overindulgence, isolation, loneliness, lack of social life, freedom, affairs, and termination.

Four of Cups

Element: Water

Corresponding Planet: Moon

Zodiac Sign: Cancer

Upward Meaning

Depression, meditation, feeling stuck, apathy, missed opportunities, re-evaluation, turning down offers, regrets, contemplation, self-absorption, negativity, boredom, disillusion, nostalgia, apathy, remorse, stagnation, frustration, and missed opportunities.

Reversed Meaning

Passion, withdrawal, taking action, enthusiasm, moving forward, retreat, being proactive, getting over regrets, interest, gratitude, focus, motivation, self-awareness, end of stagnation, optimism, and seizing the moment.

Five of Cups

Element: Water

Corresponding Planet: Pluto

Zodiac Sign: Scorpio

Upward Meaning

Pessimism, loss, regret, failure, sadness, disappointment, grief, trauma, remorse, sorrow, guilt, tragedy, rejection, unwanted change, despair, missed opportunities, emotional immaturity, misery, and negativity.

Reversed Meaning

Acceptance, moving on, forgiveness, overcoming sorrow, peace, healing, setbacks, releasing emotions, accepting help, getting over hopelessness, moving forward, trauma recovery, and being sociable.

Six of Cups

Element: Water

Corresponding Planet: The Sun

Zodiac Sign: Scorpio

Upward Meaning

Innocence, carefree, playful, nostalgic, innocence, joyful, childhood memories, reunions, children, memories, freshness, melancholy, purity, longing, creativity, the impact of the past, protection, compassion, support, goodwill, family, simplicity, gifts, sharing, childhood, and immaturity.

Reversed Meaning

Forgiveness, independence, maturity, boredom, leaving home, living in the past, immobility, lack of playfulness, childhood issues, growing up, monotony, and a lack of imagination.

Seven of Cups

Element: Water

Corresponding Planet: Pluto

Zodiac Sign: Scorpio

Upward Meaning

Multiple options, meditation, illusions, fantasy, opportunities, choices, wishful thinking, decisions, hallucinations, possibilities, procrastination, imagination, and dreaming.

Reversed Meaning

Acceptance, reality, alignment, forgiveness, finding peace, overwhelming options, bad choices, clarity, healing, personal values, shallowness, reality, lost opportunities, sobriety, decisiveness, being trapped, and a lack of spiritual growth.

Eight of Cups

Element: Water

Corresponding Planet: Neptune

Zodiac Sign: Pisces

Upward Meaning

Fatigue, escapism, traveling, introspection, abandonment, letting go, disappointment, disconnecting, withdrawal, cowardice, self-analysis, letting go, and reaching your limit.

Reversed Meaning

Stagnation, unreal happiness, fear of the unknown, inability to move on, trying, drifting aimlessly, indecision, clinginess, living in toxicity, monotony, staying, self-doubt, and lack of self-awareness.

Nine of Cups

Element: Water

Corresponding Planet: Neptune

Zodiac Sign: Pisces

Upward Meaning

Joy, happiness, rewards, making dreams come true, accomplishments, fulfilling wishes, prosperity, positivity, gratitude, satisfaction, contentment, abundance, cheer, success, and optimism.

Reversed Meaning

Pain, pessimism, nightmares, grief, broken dreams, failure, destruction, indulgence, disadvantage, lack of accomplishment, materialism, dissatisfaction, misery, low self-confidence, negativity, disappointment, and unsatisfied feelings.

Ten of Cups

Element: Water

Corresponding Planet: Neptune

Zodiac Sign: Pisces

Upright Meaning

Harmony, joy, marriage, imagination, happiness, children, partnerships, family, karma, prosperity, reunions, domestic bliss, alignment, divine love, security, fulfilling relationships, stability, abundance, playfulness, compassion, happy endings, best friends, and good fortune.

Reversed Meaning

Conflict, disagreements, infertility, despair, separation, divorce, incompatibility, broken family, dissociation, difficult relationships, broken values, unconventional families, instability, and toxic families.

Page of Cups

Element: Water

Corresponding Planet: Moon

Zodiac Sign: Cancer

Upright Meaning

Possibilities, loyalty, dreams, idealism, kindness, naivety, curiosity, inner voice, happy news, feeling young, emotional maturity, kids, creativity, intuition, opportunities, sensitivity, inner child, loyalty, and engagements.

Reversed Meaning

Immaturity, attention seeking, vulnerability, ideas, unfulfilled dreams, childhood issues, sexuality, jealousy, obsession, bad news, childishness, creativity block, ignoring your gut, and seduction.

Knight of Cups

Element: Water

Corresponding Planet: Neptune

Zodiac Sign: Pisces

Upright Meaning

Beauty, grace, offers, romance, chivalry, invitations, negotiation, charm, gentleness, listening to your heart, tact, imagination, creativity, idealism, action, and peacefulness.

Reversed Meaning

Heartbreak, obsession, envy, cheating, deception, jealousy, disappointment, mood swings, overactive imagination, turmoil, unrealistic, undiplomatic, superficiality, irritability, and procrastination.

Queen of Cups

Element: Water

Corresponding Planet: Neptune

Zodiac Sign: Cancer

Upright Meaning

Warmth, maturity, caring, shyness, female instinct, kindness, comfort, sensitivity, empathy, femininity, loyalty, love, womanhood, compassion, stability, intuition, safety, healing, joy, beauty, courage, respect, giving advice, nurturing.

Reversed Meaning

Superficiality, lack of trust, neediness, weakness, insecurity, untrustworthy, melancholy, co-dependent, self-love, immaturity, over-sensitivity, and smothering.

King of Cups

Element: Water

Corresponding Planet: Neptune

Zodiac Sign: Pisces

Upright Meaning

Creativity, loyalty, compassion, faithfulness, wisdom, sympathy, tolerance, consideration, dependability, harmony, diplomacy, emotional balance, passion, and simplicity.

Reverse Meaning

Bad advice, controlling, intolerance, unfriendly, emotional, unreliable, stress, unproductive, naivety, nervousness, manipulation, indifference, mood swings, depression, withdrawal, and instability.

Suit of Swords

Keywords: Communication, intellect, ideas, logic.

Element: Air

Alternative Names: Spades

Jungian Function: Thinking

The Suit of Swords tarot focuses on your intellect, mind, and thoughts. They represent logical thinking, communication skills, and applying reason to any situation. When these cards are strong in your reading, they influence your communication skills and self-expression. However, when they are weak, they make you confused, cold, and aggressive.

Ace of Swords

Element: Air

Corresponding Planet: Venus

Zodiac Sign: Libra

Upright Meaning

Clarity, triumph, focus, breakthrough, force, opportunities, intensity, success, intellect, concentration, excitement, new ideas, beginnings, and communication.

Reverse Meaning

Lack of productivity, misunderstandings, injustice, frustration, destruction, creativity block, insults, lost opportunities, inability to focus, poor communication skills, forgetfulness, and failures.

Two of Swords

Element: Air

Corresponding Planet: Venus

Zodiac Sign: Libra

Upright Meaning

Avoidance, resistance, struggling with making decisions, feeling concerned, and reconciliation.

Reverse Meaning

Indecision, anger, disruptions, deception, cancellations, emotional detachment, anxiety, work overload, confusion, tension, and caution.

Three of Swords

Element: Air

Corresponding Planet: Venus

Zodiac Sign: Libra

Upright Meaning

Loss, separation, treason, heartbreak, withdrawal, sadness, absence, pain, division, loss, isolation, depression, misery, sadness, grief, confusion, and distraction.

Reverse Meaning

Negative inner voice, moving on, forgiveness, optimism, letting go of pain, suppressing feelings, overcoming adversity, and compromising.

Four of Swords

Element: Air

Corresponding Planet: Venus

Zodiac Sign: Libra

Upright Meaning

Planning for the future, relaxation, introspection, making good decisions, retreat, worry, meditation, opportunities, stress, clarity, anxiety, breakthrough, rest, contemplation, need for solitude, recovery, peacefulness, and frustration.

Reverse Meaning

Renewal, rising, exhaustion, irrationality, peace, restlessness, destruction, lack of productivity, healing, stagnation, loss of faith, and coming out of isolation.

Five of Swords

Element: Air

Corresponding Planet: Pluto

Zodiac Sign: Scorpio

Upright Meaning

Arguments, failure, battle, transformation, defeat, conflict, competition, deception, aggression, winning, lying, and bullying.

Reverse Meaning

Compromising, communicating, getting in trouble, solutions, paying for mistakes, sacrifices, violence, moving on, vengeance, reconciliation, fixing mistakes, risky behavior, and reducing stress.

Six of Swords

Element: Air

Corresponding Planet: Mercury

Zodiac Sign: Aquarius

Upright Meaning

Making peace, transition, healing, travel, escapism, moving on, change, improvement, stability, trips, and overcoming hardships.

Reverse Meaning

Feeling trapped, recovering, overwhelmed, unable to change, and lacking progress.

Seven of Swords

Element: Air

Corresponding Planet: Uranus

Zodiac Sign: Aquarius

Upright Meaning

Lying, strategy, betrayal, manipulation, deceit, stealing, cheating, spying, escaping responsibility, trickery, adaptability, and taking risks.

Reverse Meaning

Being accountable, confessing, starting over, deceiving yourself, being a secret keeper, turning over a new leaf, making plans, and taking action.

Eight of Swords

Element: Air

Corresponding Planet: Jupiter

Zodiac Sign: Gemini

Upright Meaning

Unproductive, fear, imprisonment, negativity, drama, feeling stuck, difficulty, restrictions, feeling powerless, emergency, hopelessness, victim mentality, losing your voice, weakness, and anxiety.

Reverse Meaning

Escapism, hope, being in control, new perspectives, freedom, negative inner voice, surviving trauma, honesty, empowerment, productivity, letting go of negativity, healing, letting go of anxiety, confronting your fears, and believing in yourself.

Nine of Swords

Element: Air

Corresponding Planet: Mars

Zodiac Sign: Gemini

Upright Meaning

Despair, nightmares, regret, panic, anxiety, worry, remorse, negativity, overreaction, dissatisfaction, feeling overwhelmed, hopelessness, fears, burden, and guilt.

Reverse Meaning

Clarity, improvement, secrets, optimism, recovery, overcoming fears, turmoil, coping mechanisms, helping others, and conflict.

Ten of Swords

Element: Air

Corresponding Planet: Mars

Zodiac Sign: Gemini

Upright Meaning

Financial problems, laziness, backstabbing, resentment, sad endings, failing, wounds, enemies, betrayal, complaining, loss, breakdowns, crises, disasters, and hitting rock bottom.

Reverse Meaning

Perseverance, overcoming trauma, rebirth, starting something new, new coping mechanisms, improvement, and learning from your mistakes.

Page of Swords

Element: Air

Corresponding Planet: Mercury

Zodiac Sign: Gemini

Upright Meaning

Inspiration, planning, high self-esteem, caution, justice, youthfulness, protection, communication skills, curiosity, ideas, knowledge, and thinking.

Reverse Meaning

Lack of productivity, living in a fantasy world, manipulation, paranoia, silliness, defensiveness, burnout, mind games, expressing oneself, being in a rush, and not taking action.

Knight of Swords

Element: Air

Corresponding Planet: Mercury

Zodiac Sign: Libra

Upright Meaning

Changes, focus, courage, bravery, accomplishment, rebellion, persistence, adventure, honesty, impulsiveness, intelligence, wit, ambition, success, taking action, impatient, and seizing opportunities.

Reverse Meaning

Self-doubt, aggression, restfulness, stagnation, cruelty, laziness, lost opportunities, lack of focus, exhaustion, loss of control, poor manners, assertiveness, and danger.

Queen of Swords

Element: Air

Corresponding Planet: Uranus

Zodiac Sign: Libra

Upright Meaning

Support, honesty, empathy, justice, protection, strength, talkative, funny, morals, independence, boundaries, communication skills, unbiased judgment, wit, solving problems, and sadness.

Reverse Meaning

Carelessness, pessimism, cruelty, gossip, danger, manipulation, cold heart, resentment, emotions, vengefulness, dishonesty, and cheating.

King of Swords

Element: Air

Corresponding Planet: Saturn

Zodiac Sign: Aquarius

Upright Meaning

Fatherhood, honesty, structure, authority, routine, leadership, intelligence, logic, clarity, truth, conversation, power, strength, integrity, and morals.

Reverse Meaning

Behaving irrationally, tyranny, abuse of power, brutality, immorality, aggression, manipulation, violence, power, lack of discipline, and cynicism.

The Suit of Pentacles

Keywords: Stability, materialism, nature, and physical body.

Element: Earth

Alternative Names: Discs and coins

Jungian Function: Sensation

The suit of pentacles cards focuses on one's perception of the world around them and how one shapes their reality. The cards represent your ego and self-esteem. When these cards are strong, they represent your strength and optimism during adversity. When they are weak, they reflect laziness and stubbornness.

Ace of Pentacles

Element: Earth

Corresponding Planet: Saturn

Zodiac Sign: Capricorn

Upright Meaning

Gaining money, abundance, investments, prosperity, manifestation, stability, beginnings, new opportunities, new career, and comfort.

Reverse Meaning

Negativity, greed, frustration, instability, missed opportunities, insecurity, and inability to plan.

Two of Pentacles

Element: Earth

Corresponding Planet: Saturn

Zodiac Sign: Capricorn

Upright Meaning

Balance, flexibility, adaptability, perseverance, resourcefulness, multi-tasking, and time management.

Reverse Meaning

Imbalance, chaos, bad organization skills, messiness, over-commitment, and feeling overwhelmed.

Three of Pentacles

Element: Earth

Corresponding Planet: Saturn

Zodiac Sign: Capricorn

Upright Meaning

Growth, common goals, teamwork, learning, recognition, collaboration, and effort.

Reverse Meaning

Lack of motivation, ego, disharmony, conflict, lack of ambition, apathy, working solo, and competition.

Four of Pentacles

Element: Earth

Corresponding Planet: Saturn

Zodiac Sign: Capricorn

Upright Meaning

Desire for control, possessiveness, security, materialism, saving, inability to change, boundaries, stability, acting conservatively, control, and wealth.

Reverse Meaning

Generosity, greed, acceptance, letting go of the past, relinquishing control, openness, overspending, and giving.

Five of Pentacles

Element: Earth

Corresponding Planet: Venus

Zodiac Sign: Taurus

Upright Meaning

Financial troubles, loss, anxiety, lack of faith, abandonment, solitude, illness, poverty, adversity, rejection, struggling, hardships, disgrace, and unemployment.

Reverse Meaning

Victory, luck, health, financial gain, recovery, positive changes, forgiveness, and overcoming adversity.

Six of Pentacles

Element: Earth

Corresponding Planet: Venus

Zodiac Sign: Taurus

Upright Meaning

Generosity, support, charity, balance, giving, prosperity, gratitude, receiving, and community.

Reverse Meaning

Debt, desperation, self-care, extortion, and inequality.

Seven of Pentacles

Element: Earth

Corresponding Planet: Venus

Zodiac Sign: Taurus

Upright Meaning

Hard work, patience, investment, harvest, success, results, perseverance, rewards, progress, planning, and growth.

Reverse Meaning

Impatience, waste, delay, laziness, setbacks, poor planning, procrastination, and lack of growth.

Eight of Pentacles

Element: Earth

Corresponding Planet: Mercury

Zodiac Sign: Virgo

Upright Meaning

Ambition, quality, perfection, expertise, talent, commitment, developing skills, accomplishment, dedication, repeating tasks, and high standards.

Reverse Meaning

Bad reputation, workaholic, development, laziness, and lack of motivation.

Nine of Pentacles

Element: Earth

Corresponding Planet: Mercury

Zodiac Sign: Virgo

Upright Meaning

Independence, rewards, abundance, success, comfort, achievement, luxury, leisure, prosperity, and financial security.

Reverse Meaning

Feeling stuck, shallowness, success, pride, reckless spending, self-worth, over-investment, and financial instability.

Ten of Pentacles

Element: Earth

Corresponding Planet: Mercury

Zodiac Sign: Virgo

Upright Meaning

Inheritance, wealth, tradition, legacy, success, ancestry, family, foundations, contribution, financial security, privilege, and stability.

Financial troubles, bankruptcy, family issues, instability, separation, limitation, loss, debt, and breaking traditions.

Page of Pentacles

Element: Earth

Corresponding Planet: Venus

Zodiac Sign: Taurus

Upright Meaning

Faithfulness, ambition, manifestation, planning, accomplishing your goals, practicality, consistency, and developing skills.

Reverse Meaning

Procrastination, irresponsibility, immaturity, unattainable goals, lack of progress, foolishness, and underachieving.

Knight of Pentacles

Element: Earth

Corresponding Planet: Mercury

Zodiac Sign: Virgo

Upright Meaning

Improvement, routine, consistency, efficiency, hard work, strong will, patience, productivity, and commitment.

Reverse Meaning

Laziness, irresponsibility, perfection, stubbornness, boredom, trapped, dullness, gambling, and possessiveness.

Queen of Pentacles

Element: Earth

Corresponding Planet: Saturn

Zodiac Sign: Capricorn

Upright Meaning

Down to earth, generosity, comfort, caretaker, healing, nurturing, security, sensible, success, and prosperity.

Reverse Meaning

Self-care, smothering, dependence, envy, intolerant, selfishness, jealousy, greed, and insecurity.

King of Pentacles

Element: Earth

Corresponding Planet: Saturn

Zodiac Sign: Capricorn

Upright Meaning

Security, reliability, wealth, sensuality, feeling grounded, provider, business, protection, stability, abundance, and discipline.

Reverse Meaning

Instability, gambling, corruption, possessiveness, materialism, greed, stubbornness, and bad financial decisions.

Suit of Wands

Keywords: Power, willpower, drive, creativity, and energy.

Element: Fire

Alternative Names: Scepters, clubs, or rods

Jungian Function

Intuition

The suit of wand cards represents your day-to-day activities. When they are strong, they fill you with passion and courage and drive you to take action. However, when the cards are weak, you become reckless, dangerous, and destructive.

Ace of Wands

Element: Fire

Corresponding Planet: Mars

Zodiac Sign: Aries

Upright Meaning

Breakthrough, growth, challenge, new beginnings, potential, great ideas, inspiration, fertility, creativity, action, good news, enthusiasm, travel, and boldness.

Reverse Meaning

Abuse of power, disappointment, delays, predictability, hesitation, irrationality, distractions, boredom, infertility, lack of morals, lack of direction, and lost opportunity.

Two of Wands

Element: Fire

Corresponding Planet: Mars

Zodiac Sign: Aries

Upright Meaning

Decisions, anticipation, discovery, waiting, power, restlessness, progress, withdrawal, partnership, detachment, choices, and planning for the future.

Reverse Meaning

Sudden change, indecisiveness, fear of the unknown, uncertainty, goals, poor planning, and limitation.

Three of Wands

Element: Fire

Corresponding Planet: Sun

Zodiac Sign: Aries

Upright Meaning

Exploration, success, progress, leadership skills, freedom, foresight, moving on, traveling, self-esteem, planning for the future, growth, and living life to the fullest.

Reverse Meaning

Regret, self-doubt, poor planning, lack of foresight, inability to grow, restrictions, bad choices, being haunted by the past, and low self-esteem.

Four of Wands

Element: Fire

Corresponding Planet: Venus

Zodiac Sign: Aries

Upright Meaning

Celebration, joy, reunion, homecoming, gathering, excitement, stability, teamwork, security, weddings, success, harmony, events, relaxation, belonging, pride, and surprises.

Reverse Meaning

Walking away, insecurity, transition, cancellations, sad family life, conflict, loneliness, and instability.

Five of Wands

Element: Fire

Corresponding Planet: Saturn

Zodiac Sign: Leo

Upright Meaning

Challenges, struggle, conflict, fighting, disagreements, battle, tension, rivalry, diversity, arguments, aggression, opposition, petty, chaos.

Reverse Meaning

Compromise, peace, avoiding conflict, harmony, truce, teamwork, solutions, releasing tension, focus, and shyness.

Six of Wands

Element: Fire

Corresponding Planet: Jupiter

Zodiac Sign: Leo

Upright Meaning

Victory, pride, progress, triumph, rewards, winning, fame, self-esteem, praise, recognition, acclaim, success, accomplishments, support, and goodwill,

Reverse Meaning

Failure, disgrace, weakness, broken promises, betrayal, ego, lack of support, arrogance, low self-esteem, disappointment, bad intentions, and lack of achievement.

Seven of Wands

Element: Fire

Corresponding Planet: Mars

Zodiac Sign: Leo

Upright Meaning

Conviction, challenge, determination, competition, defiance, protection, strong will, assertiveness, self-defense, stamina, and dominance.

Reverse Meaning

Burnout, compromise, solutions, teamwork, feeling overwhelmed, weakness, surrender, defeat, and lack of respect.

Eight of Wands

Element: Fire

Corresponding Planet: Mercury

Zodiac Sign: Sagittarius

Upright Meaning

Excitement, speed, taking action, making fast decisions, travel, thrill, excitement, movement, quick changes, progress, freedom, and solutions.

Reverse Meaning

Limitations, impatience, frustration, negativity, delays, slow progress, inability to change, and lost opportunities.

Nine of Wands

Element: Fire

Corresponding Planet: Moon

Zodiac Sign: Sagittarius

Upright Meaning

Perseverance, grit, protection, exhaustion, bravery, battle, resilience, boundaries, persistence, resilience, and being easily hurt.

Reverse Meaning

Inability to compromise, retreat, struggle, withdraw, feel overwhelmed, give up, paranoia, defensiveness, and stubbornness.

Ten of Wands

Element: Fire

Corresponding Planet: Saturn

Zodiac Sign: Sagittarius

Upright Meaning

Struggle, obligation, hard work, duty, responsibility, restriction, burden, delays, completion, and resistance.

Reverse Meaning

Stress, breakdowns, problems, release, delegation, and challenges.

Page of Wands

Element: Fire

Corresponding Planet: Jupiter

Zodiac Sign: Sagittarius

Upright Meaning

Cheerfulness, positive thoughts, free spirit, confidence, ideas, good news, inspiration, fearlessness, extroversion, discovery, energy, excitement, creativity, potential, adventure, optimism, intelligence, and playfulness.

Reverse Meaning

Ill intentions, naivety, impatience, new ideas, spiritual path, haste, laziness, low energy, outbursts, low self-esteem, boredom, and fearfulness.

Knight of Wands

Element: Fire

Corresponding Planet: Jupiter

Zodiac Sign: Sagittarius

Upright Meaning

Charm, bravery, passion, heroism, confidence, hot temper, independence, rebellion, free spirit, impulsiveness, warmth, adventure, confidence, energy, and open-mindedness.

Reverse Meaning

Arrogance, controlling, shallowness, passive, restlessness, impatience, frustrations, abuse, competition, delays, aggression, haste, violence, recklessness, enthusiasm.

Queen of Wands

Element: Fire

Corresponding Planet: Mars

Zodiac Sign: Aries

Upright Meaning

Attraction, energy, bravery, humor, passion, cheerfulness, confidence, friendliness, wholeheartedness, charisma, optimism, independence, social, strength, determination, and motherhood.

Reverse Meaning

Volatility, infertility, self-respect, deception, jealousy, unfaithfulness, introversion, spite, selfishness, manipulation, insecurity, vengeance, and self-righteousness.

King of Wands

Element: Fire

Corresponding Planet: Mars

Zodiac Sign: Leo

Upright Meaning

Protection, optimism, honor, experience, innovation, excitement, vision, confidence, inspiration, charm, entrepreneur, friendliness, energy, fear, responsibility, leadership skills, taking action, magnetism, control, and loyalty.

Reverse Meaning

Selfishness, control, force, manipulation, extremism, poor manners, bullying, impulsiveness, abuse, broken promises, expectations, ruthlessness, domination, and flirting.

The Minor Arcana tarot cards are significant in your reading as they can open your eyes to issues that impact your daily life. Pay attention to them when you get them in your reading, as there is always a useful message to be had.

Chapter 4: Connecting with the Cards

Through their powerful images and symbols, tarot cards help us gain insight and understanding into our lives. However, many people find it difficult or don't understand how necessary it is to connect with their spread and use their full potential. Connecting with the cards leads to deeper insights and more accurate readings. With practice, you can learn how to trust your intuition and better understand the messages they reveal. This chapter will provide tips on establishing a deeper affinity with your tarot cards. You will learn how to cleanse the cards to reinstate energy and how to attune your spread for divination and readings.

It is important to connect with your cards to have a successful reading."

What Does a Strong Connection Feel Like?

A strong connection with your tarot cards can be likened to a relationship with a partner, friends, or family. When you first start speaking with a new friend, you might need help expressing yourself. As you continue the conversation, you become more comfortable, and your words flow more naturally. Similarly, connecting with your tarot cards will make you more confident and fluent in their language, energy, and messages. You will also feel more confident interpreting your cards to maximize their wisdom and guidance. And sure enough, a strong connection will feel exactly like the one you have with someone you respect and admire.

How to Connect Your Intuition to the Deck

In order to fully connect with your tarot cards, you must bridge your conscious and unconscious mind. One of the best ways to do this is to spend time with them. Bring the images and symbols of the spread to life by holding them in your hands, running your fingers along their edges, and feeling their weight. Actively visualize yourself in the scenes you see to weave your own interpretation into your readings. For example, suppose you get the Five of Wands (conflict and change), and it brings up feelings of frustration. In that case, you can weave an experience from your life into your reading to connect to the card. Perhaps you have felt frustrated with an assignment at work or school. By weaving your memories and emotions into each card, you connect them with your own life experiences, activating their power.

Spend Quality Time with Them

By sleeping with the cards close to you, you will be able to focus more deeply on the meanings behind their messages. This will also help you open yourself up to the power and possibilities the cards reveal. You can leave them next to you (wherever you leave your phone) or keep them under your pillow. Before going to sleep, take a few moments to meditate and focus on the cards. If one comes to mind, go with the thought, and try to imagine the specifics of the card. Specifics include color, shapes, and message. This will allow you to be open to the messages that they give you. Then when you wake up in the morning, take a few moments to reflect on any messages you received while sleeping. And consider why these messages relate to the cards.

Examine Each Card

Examining the cards in a tarot deck can be both a thrilling and daunting experience. To ensure that you become attuned to your spread, take time to examine each card thoroughly. Be aware of any feelings, thoughts, or images that come to your mind.

1. Start by looking at the artwork on the card.

2. Note any symbols, colors, people, and animals that appear in the image.

3. Then, read the card's description and associated keywords.

4. Spend some time meditating on the card, allowing yourself to draw connections between the artwork and the meaning.

5. To deepen your understanding of the card, journal your thoughts and feelings on the card.

These days, most spreads come with an accompanying booklet describing the nuances of each card. And although they can be useful for beginners to understand what the cards are supposed to mean, once you connect with them, they might start saying more to you. If this happens, this is a good sign. It means the spread is speaking to you.

As you examine each card, ask yourself the following question to establish a connection and alignment with them:

- Are there any recurring symbols or motifs? If so, how does this recurrence make you feel? And why do you think that is?

- Do they have different names from other decks you've seen? If so, does this bring a new meaning to them? Make them unique to you?

- Is there a color theme? If so, do these colors resonate with you, and why?

- Are there any cards you like or dislike more than others? If so, why?

Remember that there is no right or wrong answer to these questions. The aim is for you to establish feelings about the spread themselves. This will help you to connect with them more. Like when we meet someone we like, we can't stop thinking about them, and it makes us feel closer to them.

Shuffle the Spread

Flip through a new tarot spread, and you'll feel a sense of anticipation and excitement. As you shuffle them, pay attention to how they look and feel in your hands. It's best to do this while sitting down. If you haven't shuffled before or aren't very good at it, as the cards fall, they will fall close to you, not to the floor. Don't feel pressured to get this right on your first attempt. As you practice and get to know the cards, shuffling them will become easier for you.

- A deck of tarot cards can be quite substantial, with a luxurious feel
- They have a texture that is both soft and inviting yet firm and sturdy
- Their artwork can be beautiful and carefully designed to convey the various meanings in the spread
- When you flip through the cards, notice symbols, archetypes, and images that you are familiar with
- Each card has its own unique meaning and can often evoke intense feelings and subtle energies
- As you hold the cards in your hands, take note of the power of the symbols and artwork.

You might also be drawn to some of the cards depending on the tarot spread. As you go through them, you might find that some cards have more meaning for you than others, and this can be a clue for how you can use the deck to harness their powers.

A sense of energy or calm might also come from the spread as a whole, which can be very calming and meditative as you explore its depths.

The Interview Spread

The Interview Spread is a popular technique used by tarot readers to gain insight into their tarot spread. Because every card in the spread has a unique meaning and interpretation, spend time familiarizing yourself with the individual personalities of each one. Not just visually, as you have done so far, but emotionally. Interviewing the spread is a fun yet insightful way to do this. Treat this as though you were talking to a new friend. What can you ask that will make you know your friends (spreads) intentions towards you?

You can lay the cards out however you want. Lay them out in a spread of six (like a diamond shape) or keep them in a pile and pick one at a time. Go through each card and ask the following questions. It will also be useful for you to write down what answers you get. This will help to formalize your thoughts, as well as track your learning process. You'll find you get more answers the more you do this method.

1. What is your defining characteristic?
2. What are your strengths?
3. What are your limitations?
4. What work can we do together?
5. What can you teach me?

Care for Them

Taking the time to properly care for your cards helps to show your appreciation for the power of tarot and the insights they can provide. They are powerful tools of divination and so should be treated with reverence. To show your respect and appreciation, take the time to properly store and care for your spread. Storing your cards with respect is essential to keep them in the best condition and ensure they are as effective as possible when using them. The best way to store them is to keep them in a special box or pouch designed for this purpose. It should be lined with cloth or velvet and have a lid to keep out dust and debris. The cards should be placed in the box in a meaningful way; some practitioners like to arrange them by suit, others by color. If you use a pouch, you should ensure it is large enough for all the cards and closed securely to keep them from slipping out.

Use Them

As you become familiar with each card's personality, don't forget to use the deck as a whole. While each offers something different, the deck as a whole provides guidance, advice, and spiritual insight that can be used as a tool for self-discovery and personal growth. Try giving yourself a personal reading. Choose a spread that you feel comfortable with, then draw the cards relevant to the situation you would like guidance on. You can then interpret the cards and their meanings to gain insight.

How to Cleanse Your Cards

Cleansing your tarot cards is essential to maintaining their energy and keeping them in good condition. They hold many of our secrets, insights, and intuitions, and keeping them strong and clean is vital. Tarot card cleansing can be a simple yet meaningful ritual that helps you connect with your cards and create a sacred space for them. There are various methods for cleansing tarot cards, from using crystals to visualization and affirmations. Each method can have powerful psychic results; choose the one that resonates with you the most.

What Does It Mean to Cleanse?

The act of cleansing involves ritually clearing space and removing energy from your cards so you can use them with a clean slate. With each new reading, you are adding your imprint on the cards. They become infused with both your energy and the energy of the people for whom you are doing the reading. But cleansing can help you remove any unwanted energy, so you can create a clean space for your cards and a fresh start for each new reading. Cleansing your cards can be done at any point and isn't just necessary before a reading. You can also use cleansing to connect to your cards and create a sacred space for them. This can be a meaningful, spiritual experience that will help you to develop an even stronger bond with your cards.

Why Is Cleansing Necessary?

As you invoke the act of divination for readings, you are adding your imprint on your cards, but this can also make them less pure and less connected to your intuition. Over time, your cards can become weighed down by your energy, impatience, and other emotions, which can make them less effective for future readings. Cleansing your cards helps you to clear any negative energy that might be weighing them down so you can create a fresh space for divine reading. It also helps you connect to your intuition and strengthens your bond with your cards. This can help you to trust your readings more and use them in a much more intuitive and confident way.

Cleansing Methods

There are many ways to cleanse your cards that will fit your way of life. Some methods are more focused than others, so take time to choose the one that's right for you and where you are in your journey. With the right method, you can create a powerful divination experience that will leave a lasting impact on your cards and your readings.

Sage Smoke

One of the most common cleansing methods is to use the smoke from burning sage to remove energy from your cards. You can use a smudge stick, incense, or a sage bowl to burn the sage and then use the smoke to gently wave the cards around. As the smoke wafts around your cards, it will cleanse any negative energy and leave your cards refreshed and ready for a new reading.

Visualization and Affirmations

This method is a great choice if you are new to cleansing and would like to try something simple and effective.

1. Hold your deck in your hands, close your eyes, and visualize a sweeping gesture that erases the cards' energies.

2. Another way to do this visually is to imagine yourself pulling the energy away from the deck of cards and throwing it up in the air.

3. For affirmations, there is no hard and fast rule for this. Remember that these cards are now a part of you, so you need to tell them something reassuring as well as firm for them to know that they need to start afresh.

Crystals

Using crystals to cleanse your tarot cards can be a great way to combine cleansing and other rituals you might already be doing. You can use crystals to cleanse your cards when you are doing a reading or at any other time when you want to clean them. Hold the crystals in your hands, and then gently pass the cards through the energy of the crystals. You can also place the crystals on top of or beside the cards for an added boost of energy. Cleansing crystals include:

- Amethyst

- Rose Quartz

- Selenite

- Black Obsidian

When selecting a cleansing method, don't forget to choose one that resonates with you and to which you feel connected. Cleansing can be a very meaningful and spiritual experience, so choosing a method that helps you reach that higher level of connection and spirituality is essential.

How to Attune Your Cards for Divination

Attuning your deck is an essential step in the divination process and can help you to get the most out of your readings. Attuning is a simple process that requires you to create a connection between yourself and your tarot deck. You can think of it as a way of "tuning in" to the vibrations of your deck and "adjusting" your energy to align with the energy of the cards. It can be done with an intention, a ritual, or a blessing, depending on what feels right for you. When you attune your deck, you create a safe and sacred space for your readings and allow yourself to be more open to the messages the cards offer. Attuning also creates a deeper understanding of the cards, allowing you to further explore their meanings. So, if you want to get the most out of your tarot readings, attuning your deck is a must!

Preparation for Attunement

The first step in attuning your tarot deck is to prepare yourself. You can do this in your room, at your altar, or somewhere else that feels right for you.

1. First, you will want to be away from any noise and distractions. Ensure you are in a quiet environment where you will be free from interruptions.

2. Next, make sure that you have enough space for you to feel comfortable and relaxed.

3. You can also create a sacred space by burning incense, lighting candles, or meditating.

4. Then prepare yourself before you begin the attunement process by deciding on an intention for your deck.

An *intention* is something that you would like to bring out of your deck and into your life. It can be something you wish to improve on, something that you would like more of in your life, or the wishes of someone you are reading for. This can be anything from a wish for financial prosperity to the desire to feel more confident in social situations, so the possibilities are endless! You can also choose to create a ritual or use a blessing for your deck if that feels more appropriate for you.

Energy Method

When you are ready to begin, hold the card in your hand and sense the energy coming from it. What do you feel? How does it feel against your hand? What sounds, smells, or sights can you pick up from the card? Once you have identified the energy that is coming from the card, use your intention to attune the rest of your deck.

Focus Method

This method is a bit more involved but can be very helpful if you are having difficulty connecting with your deck. When you are ready, focus on the card and try to feel what is coming from it. Visualize the card and try to see it in your mind's eye. This can be difficult at first, but it will get easier with practice. Once you have seen the card, try to focus on the feelings that you are receiving from it. Again, what do you feel? What emotions are coming from the card? What sensations are you picking up from it? Then, use your intention to attune your deck.

Connecting with your tarot cards is essential to understanding and interpreting their meanings. While the cards themselves are only a small part of the overall journey of self-discovery, they can provide powerful insight into our lives and can assist us in gaining clarity and understanding. With regular use and practice, you, too, will develop an intuitive understanding of the cards and how they relate to your life. By connecting with the cards and asking questions, you'll understand how different forces impact you and gain clarity on difficult decisions. Now, connect to access the wisdom of your higher self and unlock access to insights to positively shape your life.

Chapter 5: How to Read the Cards

Every Tarot reading is a journey, like reading a book or peeking into a reality you have not lived. Tarot readings give you insight, inform you of blessings, and give you warnings at times.

It is common for beginners to feel overwhelmed at first. This is a normal reaction, given the amount of knowledge that they have to learn before they can read for themselves as others. However, the beautiful thing about tarot reading is that one gets better with practice and time.

There are several factors to take into consideration before you start a reading."

In this chapter, you will find everything you need to read Tarot cards. Not only will you know how to prepare yourself for a reading, but you will also learn how to interpret the cards and what different cards combination mean together.

Intuition

One of the vital tools that you will use while reading the cards is your intuition. Studying Tarot is one thing, and integrating your intuition with reading cards is another. For instance, you can have each card memorized, but this does not make you a tarot reader. A tarot reader integrates their intuition with the reading.

Intuition is often referred to as "gut feeling." It is a voice that emits from your being, and the more you attune yourself to it, the louder and clearer you can hear it. Every human has intuition, but not everyone makes use of it.

How Can You Enhance Your Intuition?

Frequent meditation can help you sharpen your intuition. The more you meditate and pay attention to your body and emotions, the more you can listen to your intuition. Find a quiet place in your house and sit in a comfortable position. Close your eyes and relax your muscles and bones. Regulate your breathing and imagine that your third eye is opening. Tell yourself that you are attuned to your intuition and that you can hear it loud and clear. Repeat your affirmations with every breath that is coming and exiting your body.

What Role Does Intuition Play in Tarot Readings?

Your intuition will be your guide and compass in any given reading. For instance, your intuition will tell you which cards you should pick up and whether a card should be upright or reversed. More importantly, this powerful tool will add to your insight. The cards will communicate what they mean, but your intuition will give you depth to your understanding and interpretation.

Sacred Space

Meditation is necessary, but it is not essential for tarot reading. It is a way to sharpen your intuition, but it does not prepare you for reading. There are other ways to prepare yourself for a reading, like grounding techniques. Grounding looks and feels different for everyone, but if you have not tried any grounding techniques before, then try multiple ones until you find one that works for you.

Take a walk in nature. Embrace the sun on your skin and observe how the plants glisten in the sun. When you are done with your walk, sit on the ground and touch any plants around you. Connect with the earth and take deep breaths. This clears your mind and calms your spirit. You can also swim or take a shower. Connecting with water cleanses you and grounds you.

Grounding feels like establishing a connection or planting yourself in something that is much greater than you. You will feel calm, relaxed, and refreshed when you are done.

Reading Setup

Setting yourself and your environment up for a tarot reading is almost like a ritual. There are several tasks that you need to do before getting into the reading. You will learn how to build an environment that will allow a safe space for smooth and clear readings.

Cleansing

Your space, deck, and self must be cleaned before you begin and end a reading. There are several tools that you can use to cleanse everything, but the best tool that you can use is sage. Sage can cleanse anything it meets, unlike crystals. While crystals can cleanse a deck, they cannot cleanse you. So, before reading tarot, use sage to cleanse your space, energy, and deck. When you end the reading, use sage again. Cleansing the space before and after the reading is crucial.

Techniques

You can use various techniques before you begin reading the cards. Every reader has their own style, and eventually, you will have a style you are comfortable with.

Some readers tap or knock on the cards three times before they shuffle. The knock is seen as a way to cleanse and refresh the cards. It is like hitting the refresh icon on a frozen page. After the three knocks, the readers begin to shuffle. You can shuffle the cards however you like; you can shuffle a Tarot deck the same way you would shuffle any pack of cards. Some readers like to cut the deck and then shuffle, while others do not. Try both and see what you are comfortable with, shuffling-wise. Lastly, questions play an important role in Tarot reading. This means that your questions must be precise and clear before you lay out the cards.

You can ask questions the more you delve into the reading, so you do not have to limit yourself to one question per reading.

Tarot and Symbolism

Intuition is one of many tools that you will use when interpreting the cards. Remember that Tarot cards are not just mundane pictures on paper. On the contrary, they are one of the most effective and precise divination tools that are available for human use. This is not to say that your intuition is not powerful enough to understand Tarot.

Imagine that you are learning a second language. As a student, you need to attune your ears to the language and its music. On your learning journey, you will eventually memorize its letters and understand basic sentence structure. The more you practice and dedicate enough time and effort, the more you will acquire knowledge and become fluent.

It will be helpful to always look at Tarot cards through the same lens. You are a student, and Tarot is a foreign language that piques your interest. This divination tool does not communicate through letters and sentences; it speaks to you through symbols. This means that you will need to understand each symbol alone, then understand how each symbol gives a different meaning when it is around another symbol.

For instance, picture yourself shuffling your deck, and the Sun card flies out of the deck. The Sun card signifies universal harmony that is coming into your life, a joyful new beginning, and entering a successful path. Pulling out this card in a one-card reading means that you are on your way to a happy beginning or a new joyful beginning is very close.

Now, let's say that you pulled the Sun card with the Tower card. The Tower means transformation through failure or painful events. These two cards are almost the complete opposite of each other. It might be disturbing to see these two cards together, but the closer you look, you will find that they are trying to tell you that you will receive a blessing in disguise.

In other words, the cards warn you not to dismiss your coming blessing because it will not look like a blessing at first but will serve you the more you give it time. This can look like losing a job – only to find yourself available for a much better opportunity or ending a relationship because the person you were involved with was not good for you.

You can use several methods to understand the different combinations you will see. This means that you must clearly understand the card's elements, numerology, keywords, court cards, and Major and Minor Arcana.

1. Elements

If you are familiar with astrology's four main elements, you will also easily understand their meaning in tarot readings. The Minor Arcana represents the four elements of fire, earth, air, and water. These elements hide behind certain symbols in Tarot. This means that you need to make a connection between a certain image and one of the elements.

- **Suit of Wands**

  The suit of Wands represents fire in Tarot. As an element, fire in Tarot signifies several ideas, so use your discernment when interpreting a suit of Wands card.

  The suit of wands signifies masculine energy. This means that the card refers to someone who operates from divine masculine energy. It also means Aries, Leo, and Sagittarius. The cards could refer to a person with significant fire energies in their astrological chart. This element also means strength, passion, creativity, drive, and ambition.

- **Suit of Pentacles**

  The suit of Pentacles represents the earth in Tarot. Earth, or Pentacles, symbolizes feminine energy. This suit could also signify someone with a Taurus, Virgo, or Capricorn placement.

  Think of material earthly items and goals when you see the suit of Pentacles. In other words, any Pentacles card could mean riches, authority, taxes, career path, high or low status, winning or losing money, beauty, or receiving a gift.

- **Suit of Swords**

  The suit of Swords represents air in Tarot. As an element, air represents masculine energy. The suit of Swords represents people with air energy, like Gemini, Libra, or Aquarius.

  The suit of Swords means communication, swift action or change, knowledge, innovation, social skills, flaky energy, intelligence, and intellect.

- **Suit of Cups**

  The suit of Cups represents water in Tarot. Like earth, water is feminine energy as well. This suit could be referring to individuals with a Cancer, Scorpio, or Pisces placement in their chart.

The suit of Cups means emotions, feelings, intuition, psychic abilities, deep knowing or knowledge, spirituality, fantasy, imagination, relationships, love, and connections.

Application

Seven of Cups and Ten of Pentacles

Possible meaning: You will receive many riches (Ten of Pentacles), but your imagination (Seven of Cups) is tricking you into thinking that you must tend to several things simultaneously. To manifest the Ten of Pentacles in your life, you must first focus on the Cups, then gradually tend to the rest later.

Nine of Wands and Four of Swords

Possible meaning: You are juggling many things at the moment (Nine of Wands). You are running out of strength and willpower at the moment. This is why you need to make time for rest, even if it does not feel possible at the moment (Four of Swords). Together, these two cards tell you this is the time to rest. You do not need to rest indefinitely, but you need to find short times in the day to rest, breathe, and relax.

2. Numerology

Numerology tells us that every number has a certain meaning. You can apply numerology to your interpretation of the cards. Every card in the Tarot deck has a number. The Major and Minor Arcana have a number on the top of the cards. The court cards do not have a number on top, but you can interpret them as the "number one."

- 0-3

  Meaning: new beginnings, new cycles, or early stages.

- 4-6

  Meaning: progress or in the middle of the cycle.

- 7-10

  Meaning: endings, mature stages, or at the end of the cycle.

Now, what if you get a Major Arcana with two digits? For instance, the moon card has "18" on top. One way to interpret two-digit numbers is to add them together, so 1 + 8 = 9. What if you have the Hierophant and the two wands? Numerologically, you can add 5 and 2 together, and it will give you 7.

Remember that numerology is one part of your interpretation, do not solely depend on it for full interpretations.

Application

The Lovers and Two of Cups

The lover's card has "6" on top, and the two cups card has "2" Depending on the reading, you can add or interpret the numbers alone. For instance, adding the numbers will give you the number "8." This means that the relationship you are reading about is in a mature stage. These cards can also signify a union between two people. The Two of Cups card tells us that this union will be new for the Lovers. Meaning that the "2" will be a new beginning for the "6" on top of the Lovers card.

The Moon and the Two of Wands

The Moon card has "18" on top, and the two of Wands card has "2." Add 1+8=9, then add 9+2= 11, then finally, add 1+1=2. These two cards together imply that anxiety and fears are hindering your progress in the world. This means that you are in a new stage in your life, but your fears are holding you back from your progress.

3. Keywords

When studying Tarot cards, you will find that each has a set of keywords. For instance, upright, the three of Cups card's keywords are friendship, celebration, and creativity. When this card is in reverse, its keywords change, so think isolation and alone time.

Every card has two sets of keywords, a set for the upright card and another for the reversed card. This means that you will need to study and memorize all of the keywords so that you understand the overall meaning.

Application

The High Priestess and the Seven of Swords

Together, these two cards mean that you must use your intuition to understand a situation or a person you are dealing with. Why? Let's break these cards down. The Seven of Swords signifies a situation is not what it seems. It signifies a person deceiving you or a situation where you need to act strategically. The High Priestess means intuition and sacred knowledge. The cards could also mean you must use logic and intuition when making your next move. Your question will determine what the cards mean.

The Queen of Pentacles and Judgement

The Queen of Pentacles' keywords is a homely, motherly figure, representing security and practicality. The judgment's keywords are forgiveness, rebirth, judgment, and inner calling. The meaning of these two cards together will differ depending on the question asked. However, possible meanings could be that you are entering a new phase of your life that will be more secure and homely, or you need to be more motherly with yourself or others.

4. Court Cards

The court cards are the Page, Knight, Queen, and King. The court cards do not have any numbers on them, and the person on the card will be holding one item. For instance, the Queen of Cups holds one cup, and the Knight of Swords holds one sword. You can draw many inferences based on the arrangement that you have.

Application

The Queen of Wands and Page of Swords

These two cards describe a person with a lot of energy and determination. The page of Swords confirms that this person will be able to achieve the goals of the Queen of Wands.

The Knight of Pentacles and Page of Cups

Together, these two cards describe a goal-oriented individual, and while this is a good trait that will aid him in his quest, he also needs to listen to his heart as he strives to attain this goal. It also warns the person to adjust his ever-changing mood because it can hinder his quest.

5. Major and Minor Arcana

Generally, the Major and Minor Arcana signify two different situations. Major Arcana describes a karmic situation, while Minor Arcana refers to a temporary situation. For instance, the Tower card means destruction and transformation, while the Six of Wands card means victory and self-confidence. These two cards signify a karmic event that will change you in this phase of your life.

Application

The Tower and the Six Wands:

The Tower is a karmic event, while the Six of Wands card refers to a temporary phase. Together these two cards are telling you that you will go through a needed transformation phase that you cannot stop. This transformation period might be painful at first. Still, you will come out victorious and a much more confident individual after it.

The Devil and Ace of Pentacles

These two cards tell you that your negative narrative about yourself is getting in the way of new opportunities and creativity. The Devil refers to restriction and shadow self. The Ace of Pentacles symbolizes new opportunities and prosperity. If you see these two cards together, you are being told that your shadow self is getting in the way of your blessings. This means you need to do shadow work to receive the blessings meant for you.

Ending a Reading Session

Every Tarot reading feels like a journey. When you are done reading for yourself, thank the cards and cleanse them with sage. Then cleanse yourself and your space. If you are reading for another person, then make sure that all of their questions are answered. Of course, if you feel drained, apologize to the person and tell them you will continue this reading later if you can. Proceed with cleansing yourself, the client, the space, and the cards after you end the reading session rest. Resting is vital here; you do not want to exhaust yourself by doing demanding activities after a tarot session.

FAQ

1. Can I do multiple readings?

It depends on your energy levels. If you feel like you can do another reading, then proceed. However, you must cleanse your space, yourself, and your cards before you begin another reading.

2. Why do I need to cleanse everything before and after reading?

This is a highly spiritual activity. This means that while using your intuition, you are also dealing with multiple energies. The nature of these energies is irrelevant. Whether they are heavy or light, you need to cleanse your space, yourself, and your environment from this energy. Also, energies from a previous Tarot reading can mix with another, hence the importance of cleansing before and after reading.

3. What if my interpretation is wrong?

It is necessary to practice with yourself before reading for others. If you are reading for yourself and you are questioning your interpretations, then ask the cards for a confirmation card. If the card confirms what you understood, then you were not wrong. If you are wrong, reassemble the cards, cleanse, meditate, knock on the cards, and read again.

Tarot reading is a beautiful step in your spiritual journey. This is no mundane activity. Tarot readings will bless you with rich insight and deep knowledge. The more you practice, the sharper your intuition will be. The readings you do for yourself will answer any questions you have. Eventually, you will be able to read for others and help them receive answers they could not access. However, before you reach this stage, you must study and practice to have accurate readings. Good luck and happy Tarot readings!

Chapter 6: 7 Key Card Spreads

Tarot card spreads are an incredibly powerful tool for gaining insight into any situation. Whether you are a beginner looking to learn the basics or an experienced reader wanting to explore a new type of spread, there is literally something for everyone. Knowing the different spreads available as a Tarot reader will help you understand the cards and their meanings better and help you interpret your readings more accurately. From an easy-to-learn one, two, and three-card spread to the classic Celtic cross, this chapter will have beginners and advanced readers well on their way to a great foundation for learning the Tarot.

What Is a Tarot Card Spread?

A spread is a configuration of cards laid out across a table, floor, or another surface.

Each spread is unique, but most incorporate a variety of cards that are selected and placed in a specific order. Spreads can be simple, such as three cards in a line, or more complex, such as a ten-card layout. The purpose of a Tarot card spread is to offer insight into a particular situation or question. While a single card reading can give you a general sense of the energy surrounding a situation, a Tarot card spread allows you to explore the situation from various perspectives. The idea is to get a more in-depth look at the situation and reveal a better idea of what is coming up in the future.

In general, a Tarot spread will consist of one card laid face up in the middle of the spread and a number of cards laid out around it. The positions of the cards laid out around the other cards indicate how they are related to the central card. For example, a three-card spread might consist of the central card flanked by two other cards, with each of the other cards showing one possible outcome for the central card.

Benefits of Tarot Card Spreads

While a single card can reveal valuable information, a card spread allows you to explore a situation from various perspectives.

- A single card can often be misleading or unclear. A card spread gives you more information

- Through a card spread, you'll have insight into the situation, your emotions, and the people involved

- A spread is a great foundation for learning how to read the Tarot by practicing

- It allows for a more in-depth analysis of the situation.

- It is easier to focus on one situation or question at a time when using a card spread

- A card spread can be for any situation or question

Even advanced readers should try out different spreads to see which ones they prefer. This helps you become more comfortable with the cards and become better at reading them and the situation you've been questioning. Once you have become more familiar with the cards, you will be able to use Tarot spreads to improve your understanding and the accuracy of your readings. Using a specific layout will also help you focus. This is because each different layout highlights different aspects of a reading that might otherwise not come across as clearly. For example, a relationship spread can point out both positive and negative aspects of the relationship.

How Do Beginner Tarot Readers Get Started?

It is true that some Tarot readers choose to start with a different type of spread immediately. However, beginners should start with the one-card spread. Why? The purpose of a spread is to enlighten your mind about a situation or question that you have. The one-card spread is one of the most basic spreads, so it's perfect for newbies to practice on. Once you're comfortable with the one-card spread, you can start branching out and trying other arrangements. But for now, the one-card spread is also one of the easiest to understand and interpret. It's also a great way to learn about cards and their meanings. As you practice with one card, you'll start to recognize patterns and discover meanings that fit your situation best. You'll also start to see how the cards relate to each other and how their messages interact. Let's begin with the easiest spread first and work our way up to more advanced spreads. Having this knowledge will help you deal with multiple cards and their meanings more effectively.

One Card Spread (Beginners)

One-card spreads provide you with an interpretation of a single card. Since it's one of the easiest spreads to understand and use, it's often a good place for beginner Tarot readers. For example, say you want to know what to do about a strained friendship. Then you ask a question regarding this situation and pick up a card. This card will be your answer.

1. One-Card Tarot Spread

The reading for a one-card spread is pretty straightforward.

1. Simply pull a card from the top of the deck pile, or shuffle the cards and take the first one that drops out.

2. Then, read the card and determine what it means.

For example, suppose you set the intention to draw relationship advice. In that case, the card you choose will signify that relationship reading for you.

2. Yes or No Spread

The Yes or No spread is a simple yet powerful way to get an answer to a specific issue. This spread requires only using a single Tarot card. An upright card means yes, while an upside-down card means no. To get the reading right, the trick is to ensure the deck has the same number of upright cards as upside-down cards.

1. First, focus on the question you want the cards to answer, keeping your mind clear, and then select a Tarot card.

2. Once the card is chosen, consider the card's symbolism and overall meaning. You can then interpret the card and its message concerning the question you asked.

Three-Card Spreads (Easy)

The three-card spread is a very common spread. It's one of the easiest spreads to interpret and gives you a rich, detailed perspective. Because it's such a common spread, there are multiple variations. In fact, there are so many variations of the three-card spread that you could almost call it a choose-your-own-adventure type spread. You can use a three-card spread to focus on a specific situation, explore options, or do a general reading.

3 card spread.[46]

3.Sequence Spread

These spreads follow a sequence of events, are used to point out conflict, and are spread in a linear style. Basically, you line up three cards next to each other. The types of reading you get from a sequence spread include:

- Situation – Obstacle - Outcome

- Situation – Obstacle - Advice

- Aspiration – Progress - Idea

- Your potential - Your path - You

- Partner – Relationship - You

These spreads will offer a deeper understanding of a situation than the one-card spread and help you explore the best ways to move forward. The way to read them is like this:

1. Going from left to right, turn over each of the cards.

2. As a whole, this spread indicates a suggested path or outcome.

3. Past-Present-Future Spread

The Past-Present-Future Tarot spread is a classic three-card spread that provides an overview of a person's life. This spread is an excellent choice for someone looking for a general idea of what is going on in their life. It can also be used to make decisions or to clarify a particular issue. The spread consists of three cards laid out in a row, with the first card representing the past, the second representing the present, and the third card representing the future.

1. To begin the spread, shuffle the cards and then lay them out in the three-card spread

2. Then focus on the first card (left to right), which represents the past. This card will shed light on the events and experiences that have led to the current situation.

3. The second card, representing the present, will reveal details about the current situation and how it will likely evolve.

4. The third card, representing the future, will give insight into what could happen if the current situation continues.

4. Seven-Card Spread: The Horseshoe (Easy-Advanced)

The Horseshoe spread is one any self-respecting Tarot reader should have in their arsenal. And luckily, it's one of the easiest to learn. When arranged, this spread looks exactly like a Horseshoe, hence the name. It works best for open-ended questions and uncomplicated readings.

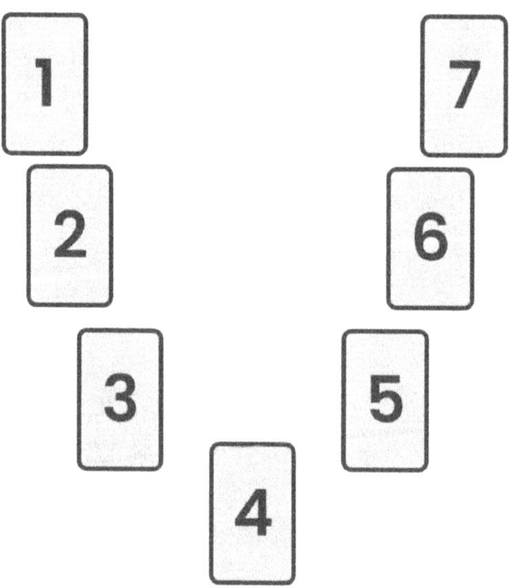

To begin the Horseshoe Tarot reading, determine what issue or question you want to answer. Focus on this as you shuffle the deck. In the next step, select seven cards and arrange them like this:

- **1st card:** Place this card down in front of you. This represents the past influences on the question or situation.

- **2nd card:** This card goes directly below the first card. It symbolizes the current circumstances surrounding the question or situation.

- **3rd card:** Then take a third card, and place it below the second card. This refers to internal conflicts of the subject of the reading.

- **4th card:** Place this card to the right of the third one. In some readings, this is the first card turned over because it symbolizes the client themselves.

- **5th card:** Now, place your fifth card to the right of the fourth card. This represents external factors such as other events or people.

- **6th card:** Place your sixth card directly above your first card. There is where you'll notice the horseshoe's shape beginning to form. This card shows the solution.

- **7th card:** Then lastly, the seventh card goes above the sixth one. This one symbolizes the outcome.

5. Ten Card Spread: The Celtic Cross (Intermediate)

The Celtic Cross spread is one of the most popular Tarot card spreads used today. It is a complex spread showing a comprehensive overview of a topic. This spread is made up of ten cards arranged in a cross pattern. The cards are laid out in a specific order to represent a particular question or theme. The layout is as follows:

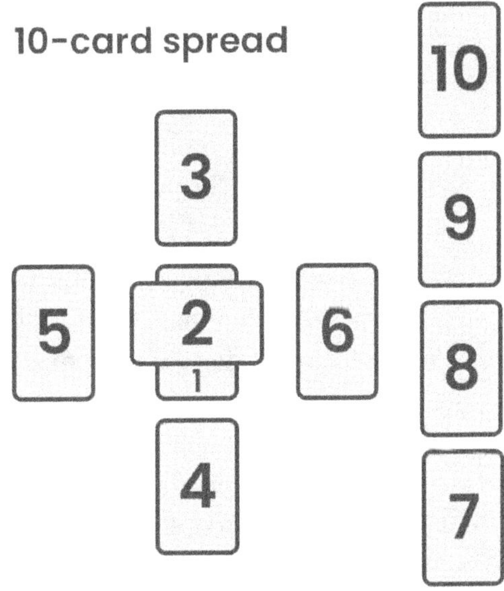

- **1st card:** Place your first card from the deck in the center. This card is typically interpreted as the main focus of the reading because it represents the subject of the reading.

- **2nd card:** Then place your second card directly (at an angle) on top of the first card. This one is interpreted as the main challenge or obstacle.

- **3rd card:** The third card goes to the left of cards one and two. This represents the past's influence.

- **4th card:** The fourth card goes to the right of cards one and two. This symbolizes the future's influence.

- **5th card:** The fifth card goes directly above the first card. This refers to goals and aspirations - things that the subject needs to achieve to resolve their issue.

- **6th card:** The sixth card goes directly below the first card and is placed to the left of the fifth. This card is interpreted as the unconscious fears associated with the situation.

By now, you should have a cross-like shape formed by one card on each side of the first card. Now arrange the cards like this:

- **7th card:** Place the seventh card to the bottom right, away from the cross shape. The card illustrates the subject's approach to overcoming adversity.

- **8th card:** The eighth card goes directly above the seventh card. This details the external influences or events that affect the reading as a whole.

- **9th card:** The ninth card goes directly above the eighth card. It symbolizes the hopes and fears of the subject.

- **10th card:** The last card is directly above the ninth card (the seventh to eighth cards should be in a vertical line). This last card represents the outcome of a situation.

6. Twelve Card Spread: The Zodiac Tarot Spread (Advanced)

This 12-card Tarot spread is based on the 12 signs of the zodiac and is designed to reveal key aspects of the questioner's life. Using the Tarot cards to explore the energies associated with each sign, start by gathering a set of Tarot cards and laying them out in a circle. Each card represents the twelve signs of the zodiac. There are a few variations of this spread, but the one here is the most basic form and best for beginners just starting. This spread works best with those already familiar with the zodiac signs. But anyone can learn to use it.

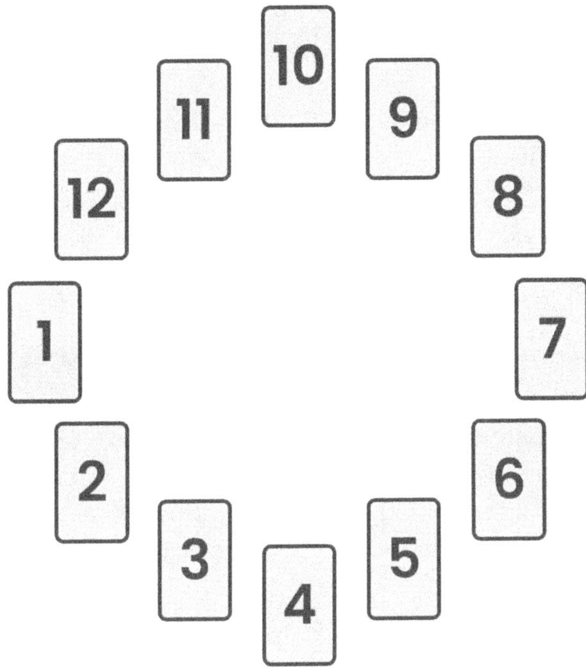

Shuffle the deck and place 12 cards in a circle. The first one is at the 9 o'clock position, with the rest following in an anti-clockwise position. This pattern should be followed until all twelve cards have been placed.

To interpret the Zodiac Tarot, you must know what each card symbolizes.

- **1st card:** Aries, The House of Aspirations - image
- **2nd card:** Taurus, The House of Security - the material
- **3rd card:** Gemini, The House of Thought - communication
- **4th card:** Cancer, The House of Emotion - family, home
- **5th card:** Leo, The House of Persona - creativity
- **6th card:** Virgo, The House of Detail - day-to-day habits
- **7th card:** Libra, The House of Balance - relationships
- **8th card:** Scorpio, The House of Intensity - secrets

- **9th card:** Sagittarius, The House of Philosophy - growth
- **10th card:** Capricorn, The House of Pragmatism - career
- **11th card:** Aquarius, The House of Originality - community
- **12th card:** Pisces, The House of Intuition - the unconscious mind

Turn each card over one by one, and consider how each card relates to the sign it represents.

Then, interpret the whole spread. Think about how each card in the spread relates to the other cards. How do they combine to form a cohesive message?

Tips for Reading Spreads

When it comes to reading Tarot spreads, a few tips guarantee a successful experience. To begin with, make sure that you select a spread appropriate for the issue or questions being addressed. There are many different types of spreads available. And another great thing about Tarot reading is that it is possible to repurpose the spreads to your desired question or situation. Other things to remember:

- Remember that Tarot card spreads do not guarantee a specific outcome. Although the cards can shed light on a situation, interpretation is always possible

- Always work with a clear mind. Before you read the cards, make sure that you are in a calm and clear state of mind

- Always shuffle the cards before a reading. Be sure to shuffle the cards to attune and connect with the deck

- Pay attention to how the cards feel. This is because each card has a specific energy associated with it. By paying attention to how the cards feel, the meaning of the card will become clearer to you

- Remember that you will get what you put into reading. If you are reading with the intention of receiving guidance, the cards will give you guidance. If you are reading with the intention of receiving insight, the cards will give you insight

- Consider the connection between each card. A complete reading involves studying the spread as a whole. Don't be afraid to think outside the box.

Adapting Tarot Spreads

Altering a Tarot spread to your needs is crucial to reading Tarot cards. By doing this, you can concentrate on certain aspects of your life while expanding your knowledge about different areas. Whether you are a beginner or an experienced Tarot reader, here are a few ways to change a spread for the best results.

1. Determine the purpose of the spread. Is it for guidance, insight, or a simple yes or no answer? Knowing your purpose will help you choose the right cards and how many cards to use.

2. Don't be afraid to open your mind to the multitude of possibilities each card brings as you draw them into the overall reading. Consider the different meanings of each card and choose the ones that will best answer your question or offer guidance.

3. Decide how many cards to use. A spread with too few cards won't give enough detail, while a spread with too many cards will be overwhelming, especially for beginners. Consider your purpose and the situation's complexity to determine the right number of cards to use.

4. Play around with the placement of the cards. Changing the order in which you turn the cards over will benefit you as you learn, give you a different perspective, and reveal more information. Think about how the cards relate to each other and how the order of the cards reveals more than what is simply in front of you. Get inventive with your imagination.

5. Finally, take your time. Don't rush the process of modifying a Tarot spread to your particular needs. Take the time to consider the different aspects of your life and how the cards might relate to each other. This will help you learn more in the long run.

Learning Tarot card spreads is a great way to understand yourself better and develop a higher awareness of yourself and your surroundings. They reveal powerful guidance and support in all areas of your life, from relationships to careers to spiritual growth. By starting with the essentials, you'll tap into your intuition and uncover hidden aspects of yourself and others while you learn. Through this journey of self-discovery, you'll be clearer on your life path and confidently make decisions. Tarot card spreads also create a sense of connection with the divine, allowing you to receive messages from the universe and access deeper levels of your inner wisdom. And if you are interested in Tarot reading as a career, education is the key. Understanding the different spreads gives you a highly sought-after skill many of your clients will appreciate. Learning key Tarot card spreads will also increase your knowledge and confidence in your abilities. Just remember to take your time. Tarot reading is an exciting and fulfilling process, and ensuring you learn correctly will only benefit you in the future.

Chapter 7: Spreads for Love and Self-Care

One of the worst feelings in the world is having your love life stuck in limbo with no knowledge of the future and no one to guide you forward. Fortunately, Tarot cards provide a comprehensive interpretation of your love life. Many people are attracted to Tarot reading with questions about love. The powerful messages revealed in a reading can shed light on the present, past, and future romantic events in your life. Questions like "What does my future with my partner look like?" Will I ever find my soulmate?" or "What can I expect for the future of my marriage?" are the most common in Tarot love readings. The meanings and implications of the cards are interpreted by considering the meaningful interactions between the cards. Therefore, considering the order and position of each card is an essential step in interpreting the readings. So, the intuitive insight from Tarot readings can give you all the advice you need to move forward, whether you're in love, out of love, or hoping to find love.

General Love Spread

Difficulty Rating: ★★☆☆☆

This General Love Spread is one you can practice regularly to keep track of how your love life is faring. It's a pretty simple yet insightful spread that doesn't require a lot of experience or practice to get accurate results. You can reflect on your current relationship, including your partner's and your own feelings. Consisting of just three Tarot cards, the layout is simple to interpret and explain. You can perform this reading as often as once a day to tune into the energy of the day. Once you get into the habit of performing this reading daily, you can identify any problems, conflicts, disputes, and concerns before they escalate or plan dates and surprises for the most suitable times.

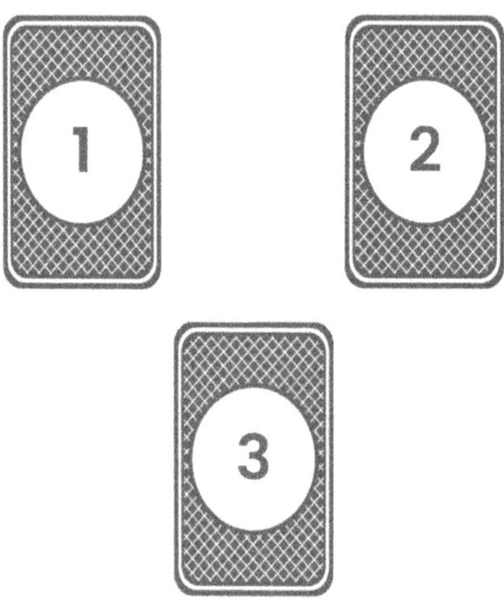

Casting the Cards

- Place the first card in the left corner, in a vertical position. This card represents you in the relationship.

- Place the second card in the right corner, in a vertical position. This position represents your partner in the relationship.

- Place the third card between the first two cards in a horizontal position. This card represents the current state of the relationship.

Interpretation

The first card represents your feelings, including happiness, sadness, thoughts, insecurities, or doubts regarding your relationship and partner. Similarly, the second card represents your partner's feelings about the relationship. Finally, the third card signifies your current state or potential together. For instance, imagine you've placed the following cards in order:

1. The Temperance
2. The High Priestess
3. The Hierophant

According to the Temperance card, your personality is reflected in the relationship as secure and balanced. If you're single, this would be a good time to welcome a new romantic interest into your life. If you're in a relationship, this card suggests that the relationship helps you become a better version of yourself by constantly evolving, developing, and accessing new parts of yourself. On the other hand, the High Priestess reflects your partner's creativity, spirituality, and, most of all, love for your relationship. Finally, the third card, the Hierophant, signifies a structured union. The appearance of this card could suggest a literal marriage, or it could reflect that the relationship is publicly recognized and will last a long time.

Past, Present, and Future Love Spread

Difficulty Rating: ★★★☆☆

This Tarot spread connects your relationship's past, present, and future situations and helps you understand where it is headed. This is an ideal spread to read when you want to figure out what lies ahead for you and your partner. It also helps you understand how events in the past relating to your romantic life connect with and influence your present and future love lives. The present moment card will give you insight into how you're balancing past and future circumstances. The future card will predict how your relationship will move forward. If the future card is something you're not hoping for, you can always change the predicted outcome in your present moment because it's not set in stone.

1. Past
2. Present
3. Future

Casting the Cards

- Place the first card in the left corner, in a vertical position. This card represents your own self in the relationship.

- Place the second card in the right corner, in a vertical position. This position represents your partner in the relationship.

- Place the third card between the first two cards in a horizontal position. This card represents the current state of the relationship.

- Place the fourth card below the third card in a vertical position. This card represents your past.

- Finally, place the fifth card above the third card, in a vertical position, in alignment with the fourth card. This card represents your future.

Interpretation

Like the interpretation described above, the first card reflects your feelings about the relationship and your partner. The second card suggests your partner's feelings about you, and the third represents your relationship's current potential. The fourth card shows how your past connects with your present and how it has shaped it. Finally, the fifth card will predict how your future will be shaped in connection with your present and past circumstances. Let's take the same example for the first three cards, while the remaining two can be assumed to be:

1. The Temperance
2. The High Priestess
3. The Hierophant
4. Ace of Wands
5. Three of Pentacles

Imagine that this is a person you have just met. In this case, the first three cards might make little sense to you. After all, why has the Hierophant card shown up for someone you haven't known for long? However, once you consider the past and future cards, the Tarot spread will start making a lot more sense. For instance, the Ace could reflect that this person is someone you've had feelings for longer than you think, and now, they have started to develop into something stronger. The Three of Pentacles card can hint at a future collaboration with this person. A reading like this can also suggest that you will be excellent creative partners with this person but not necessarily romantic partners, which means you would be better off as friends.

Stay or Go Spread

Difficulty Rating: ★★★☆☆

Although it's difficult to consider letting go of a person, even when things aren't working, doing so may be for your own good. However, letting go of them is especially challenging if you truly care about them. Deciding whether to stay in a relationship or end it is a serious decision that has life-altering consequences for both of you.

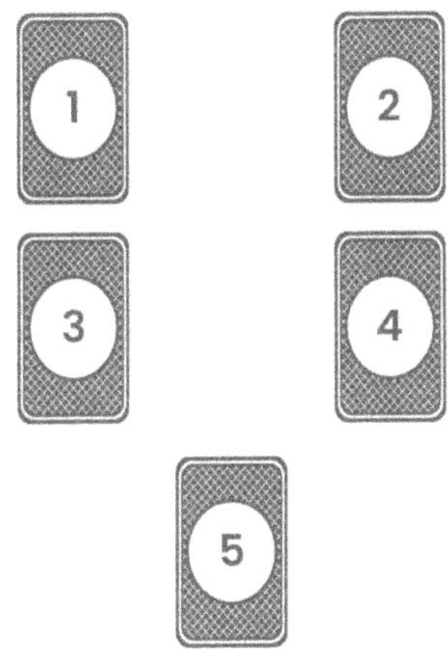

1 = Future with my partner if I remain in the relationship

2 = My future if I remain in this relationship

3 = Future with my partner if I leave it

4 = My future if I leave this relationship

5 = Advice to consider

Making a decision about whether you should continue or end a relationship is not easy. There will always be consequences either way for you and your partner. Luckily, what you can do is turn to Tarot reading to help guide you and make the decision-making process much easier. This Stay or Go Spread will provide insight regarding either future or the path you decide to take.

Casting the Cards

- Place the first card in the left corner, in a vertical position. This card will suggest changes that need to be made if you stay.

- Place the second card next to the first one in a vertical direction. This card will represent how you must act if you stay in the relationship.

- The third card should be placed next to the second one but slightly above it. This card will help you decide whether to stay in or leave the relationship.

- Place the fourth card to the right of the third card, in a vertical position and in alignment with the first and second cards. This card will define the purpose of the relationship if you decide to leave.

- Place the fifth card in the right corner, in a vertical position. This card will suggest how you must let go of the relationship.

Interpretation

The first card represents the changes needed to make your relationship whole again. This will give you the insight you need regarding changing your and your partner's attitudes concerning the relationship. The second card will suggest how you need to act with your partner once you decide to stay. The third card will help you make your final decision regarding the relationship. The fourth card will explain the relationship's purpose or meaning if you decide to leave. This will give you closure and let you move on from the relationship in a calm way. Finally, the fifth card will suggest how you move on from the relationship. Let's consider an example reading with the following tarot cards:

1. The Hanged Man
2. The Queen of Swords
3. The Lovers
4. Seven of Pentacles
5. Three of Cups

Before observing any of the other four Tarot cards in this spread, you will need to consider the third card, as it will help you make your final decision. In this case, the third card, the Lovers, suggests that your relationship will go much deeper. This means that you can decide to stay. Next, consider the cards placed on the left side of the spread. The

Hanged Man suggests that you must stop being so passive and accommodating. You need to bring this change to your relationship to improve it. The Queen of Sword advises you to speak your heart and be assertive to better navigate your relationship. If the third card signaled your decision to be "no," the Seven of Pentacles would reflect that your relationship taught you patience. The Three of Cups would suggest that you celebrate the good friendships you have and leave the past behind.

Love Compatibility Spread

Difficulty Rating: ★★★☆☆

This spread is a variation of the five-card Tarot Love Spread, which helps you determine if you are compatible with a new romantic interest. This is a fun spread to try out when you start dating someone new, as it will not only help determine your compatibility but also reveal the intentions you and your partner have for each other. As a result, both of you will have an open understanding of each other's desires, leaving little to no room for misunderstandings or unmet expectations. This reading will also show your likes, dislikes, common interests, and similarities. All of these factors will be helpful when starting a new relationship.

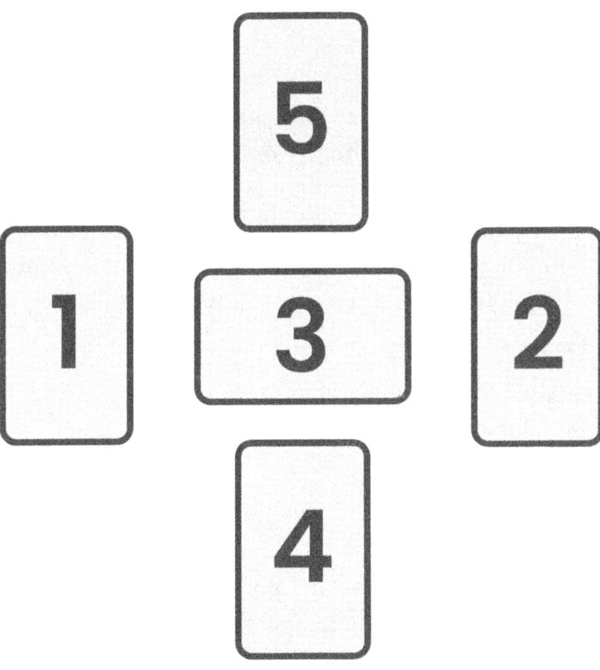

Casting the Cards

- Place the first card at the left-hand corner of the table in a vertical position. This card represents your feelings about the person.

- Place the second card at the right side of the spread, again, in a vertical direction. This card will represent your partner's feelings towards you.

- The third card will need to be placed between the first two cards in a horizontal position. This card will determine the dominant feature of the relationship.

- The fourth card should be placed below the third card in a vertical direction. This card will represent the challenges or conflicts that you might face in the relationship.

- Finally, the fifth card should be aligned with the fourth card, right above the third (center) card. This card will indicate the potential of the relationship.

Interpretation

In this Love Tarot Spread, the first and second cards represent your feelings and your partner's feelings, respectively. They will tell you how well you and your partner are connected or aligned. The third card may be the most important one in this spread. It will dictate the tone or major characteristic of your relationship. Sometimes the third card might not reflect the overall relationship status. Still, something unique might be influencing it at the moment, which might be reflected. The fourth and fifth cards provide insight into the relationship dynamics. They will predict any conflicting situations or the strong potential of your relationship. The overall reading will also provide insight into how this relationship might affect your life. Let's consider an example with the following tarot spread:

- The Three of Wands
- The King of Pentacles
- The Six of Pentacles
- The Five of Wands
- The Two of Pentacles

The Three of Wands indicates that your feelings have a strong base but require effort to deepen. The King of Pentacles shows how stable and secure your partner feels in your relationship. The Six of Pentacles represents union, which is also the main theme of your relationship. Moving further, the Five of Wands suggests that the relationship will have opposing ideas, and neither party will be willing to compromise. Finally, the fifth card, the Two of Pentacles, suggests that a balance should be maintained for the relationship to succeed, and each of you needs to adapt to the other's expectations.

The Soul Mate Spread

Difficulty Rating: ★★★★☆

Many people believe in the concept of soulmates. Some believe we can have multiple soulmates, while others argue that one person can only have a single soulmate for life. Wherever your beliefs are, this Soulmate Tarot Spread can help determine whether a person is or isn't your soulmate. This helpful spread can help you get the guidance you seek and identify if someone really is your soulmate. The difficulty level of this spread is a bit higher than others because of the complicated interpretation it requires.

Casting the Cards

- Place the first card at the top-middle of the spread in a vertical position. This card represents the characteristics of your soulmate.

- Place the second card in the right corner, in a vertical position. This position represents your partner in the relationship.

- Place the third card between the first two cards in a horizontal position. This card represents the current state of the relationship.

Interpretation

The first card reflects an aspect of your soulmate's personality. It can either point towards physical or emotional characteristics in your soulmate. The second card represents the circumstances in which you will meet. These could include a trend, a personality, or an external force. The third card will suggest the actions you can take to make the meeting possible. The fourth card depicts any obstacles possibly preventing your meeting with your soulmate. The final position represents an overall assessment of the reading. This is something you should be mindful of.

1. The Queen of Wands
2. The Two of Swords

3. The Six of Pentacles

4. The Sun

5. The Seven of Cups

Your soulmate is a master of social skills. They have good social aptitude, determination, and confidence. Although their social skills come easily to them, this is not the true source of their power. The situation in which you meet your soulmate may involve you having to make a difficult decision. The Two of Swords reflects that you should pay attention to your heart and your intuition in this situation. The Six of Pentacles card suggests being selfless and kind during this situation. Make a just decision, no matter how hard it is. When making this decision, remember that the roles could be reversed. The Sun reflects that there will be no obstacles in your meeting with your soulmate. An inverted Seven of Cups card indicates that caution is to be exercised when making this decision; often, things aren't as they seem.

Although all relationships bring you a share of happiness and joy, the right one will prove to be immensely rewarding. At the same time, relationships also bring conflict, sorrow, hardship, and transformation. All relationships can be considered to be a journey of love. No matter your stage, it's crucial to put in the effort and make time for your loved one. Uncertainties are also a common part of relationships, whether you're at the beginning of a new relationship or deeply in love with a person. Various Tarot spreads can help reveal important lessons, courses of action, and useful insight that can be used to improve your relationship. By tuning into the wisdom of these Tarot spreads, you will have full access to knowledge about the best course of action moving forward.

Chapter 8: Spreads for Spiritual Development

Like the previous one, this chapter also lists several helpful Tarot spreads, this time for spiritual development. Developing a close relationship between your intuition, the cards, and yourself can be incredibly beneficial for spiritual growth and personal development. It is another form of self-care that inspires you to learn about yourself. The best thing about spreads for spiritual development is that you can include them regardless of your religious and cultural background. The Tarot card layouts described here have different difficulty ratings, so you can decide whether they're suitable for your experience level.

Tree of Life Spread

Difficulty Rating: ★★★★☆

The Tree of Life is a powerful symbol in several belief systems, from Norse mythology to Kabbalah to Celtic practices. The following spread has taken inspiration from all of these religious traditions, yet it enables you to incorporate parts of your own spiritual beliefs. It's also great for self-discovery and reflecting on what you can do to change your life.

Tree of Life Spread

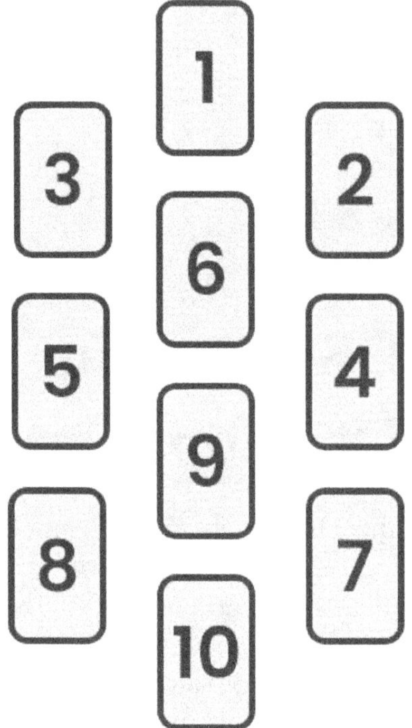

Casting the Cards

This spread uses 10 cards which you will arrange in a tree shape. Cards 1-4 should be laid down in the middle, cards 5-7 on the left, and cards 8-10 on the right. The stem of the Tree of Life reflects your personality. The branches to the left represent your connection to nature and the universe. The branches towards the right symbolize your future and the path you'll be taking based on your current actions. More specifically:

- The first card represents your spiritual state

- The second card denotes your traits and personality

- The third card indicates knowledge hidden in your subconscious

- The fourth card represents your home and your relationship with your family

- The fifth card reveals your connection to your ancestors

- The sixth card symbolizes the link you have to your past

- The seventh card reveals your connection to all the other realms
- The eighth card symbolizes the wisdom you've gathered throughout your life
- The ninth card indicates personal growth and spiritual development
- The tenth card embodies renewal and rebirth

Interpretation

As an example, let's say that you have the following cards in your spread:

1. Wheel of Fortune
2. King of Swords
3. Queen of Cups
4. Ace of Pentacles
5. The Fool
6. The Hierophant
7. The Moon
8. Eight of Wands
9. The World
10. Seven of Wands

Your first card is the Wheel of Fortune. It symbolizes things you can't control. Since it came up in the spirituality position, you can see it as a reminder that you'll need to trust the universe that your spiritual development will be favorable. You need to allow the wheel to take you wherever it wants to because it's moving in the right direction. Pulling the King of Swords in your personal card means you're a strong person who thinks logically. At the same time, drawing the Queen of Cups in your subconscious card suggests that deep down, you're a sensitive individual; you are just repressing this part of yourself. You've received the Ace of Pentacles in your family card, which indicates that you value financial stability. Then, you have The Fool in your ancestral card. This card is about taking a huge leap into the unknown. If you're in a situation where you need to take risks, this card encourages you to do so. The past card revealed The Hierophant, a card denoting traditions and conventions you've lived by in the past. Consider whether they still affect you in your present life. Your connection with the other worlds unveiled The Moon, indicating that you're probably confused about what lies in those realms. The Eight of Wands symbolizes progress, and if you have received the wisdom card, you're on the right path toward personal growth. This is reinforced by your growth card, which is The World. In this context, this card indicates that you have achieved much of what you have been working on for so long. And finally, you've received the Seven of Wands in your rebirth card. According to this, you're ready to take on your next challenge. As long as you stand your ground and learn how to overcome even larger challenges, you'll persevere whatever you put your mind to.

While it's not recommended to alter the structure of the spread (as it would defy the purpose of the Tree of Life layout), you can make a few modifications when reading it. For example, after reading cards 1-4, you can start interpreting cards 5-7, except in reverse order. Instead of your connection to the ancestors, you can learn first about your link to the other realms. This can come in handy if you want to establish a relationship with spiritual guides other than your ancestors.

Flower of Life Spread

Difficulty Rating: ★☆☆☆☆

The Flower of Life is another ancient symbol related to nature. It stands for growth and fertility, as the flower produces the seeds that give life. In Tarot, this symbol is linked to spiritual growth and self-empowerment through the renewal of one's life. The Flower of Life layout is a fantastic option for answering non-specific questions. While the ancient symbol has 19 overlapping circles, the Tarot spread is much simpler than that. It uses only six cards, each revealing specific influences in your life. They are as follows:

- The first card relates to the current energies ruling your mind, body, and spirit

- The second card indicates any external influences affecting future outcomes

- The third card denotes current challenges and things you need to let go of

- The fourth card reveals the strengths and personality traits you need to cultivate

- The fifth card symbolizes messages you've received from your spiritual guides

- The sixth card highlights expected future outcomes based on current actions

Casting the Cards

To cast the cards, place a round object in the middle of the space you're working on (altar, table, floor, etc.). This can be a plate, a piece of cloth, or anything that has a round shape. Arrange the six cards around it. Start by placing the first one on top of the round object. Moving clockwise, place the second and third cards on the right, the fourth one in the middle, and the fifth and sixth cards to the left of the object.

Interpretation

Let's say you've pulled the following cards:

1. Knight of Wands
2. The Judgment
3. Five of Cups
4. King of Swords
5. The Lovers
6. Nine of Pentacles

Revealing the Knight of Wands as your current energy card indicates you're ready for action. You're buzzing with positive energy and are prepared to take on any challenge. The Judgment card in the external influences position reveals that you feel judged by others for your actions, thoughts, and emotions. The Five of Cups indicates that you may even turn to self-pity due to the reactions you perceive from those around you. However, the next card, the King of Swords, highlights that you should focus on disciplining yourself to leave these thoughts behind instead of giving in to your grievances. Your spiritual guides are telling you to move on to work on establishing new and stronger relationships based on your values and mutual acceptance. And finally, the Nine of Pentacles reveals that by working hard towards your spiritual and personal goals, you'll be able to enjoy the fruits of your labor.

While the spread works best with general inquiries, you can also ask it open-ended questions. However, you should avoid asking specific questions. For example, instead of asking about the best way to move on from a relationship, you should ask what you can do to empower yourself. The answers will help you achieve your goal – even if they aren't specific – because through growth and empowerment, you can achieve everything.

Connect with Your Spirit Guides Spread

Difficulty Rating: ★★☆☆☆

A spiritual guide can be any spirit from this world or any other realm. The most common spirit guides are ancestral spirits, guardian angels, animal spirits, higher beings, and living spirit guides. Whoever your guides are, the following Tarot spread will help you form a meaningful connection with them, so you can work with them in the future.

Casting the Cards

Place the five cards face-down, forming a star. Begin by placing the first card at the top of the star, the second on the top left position, and the third on the top right. The fourth card goes into the bottom left position. The fifth one should make up the bottom right corner of the star. Here is what the cards represent:

- The first card symbolizes who the spirit is and what can they help you with

- The second card reveals the message your guide has for you at this moment

- The third card hints at certain parts of the message you might be afraid to hear

- The fourth card shows you how to be more open to your guides in the future

- The fifth card indicates how the information you've learned will contribute to your spiritual growth

Interpretation

Let's say you've pulled the following cards:

1. Queen of Cups.
2. Six of Swords.
3. The Magician.
4. The Justice.
5. Queen of Wands.

The Queen of Cups in the first position indicates that your spirit guide is a nurturing and compassionate person with whom you had a close relationship. It could be a family member you've always admired for their serene nature, and they're there to impart their wisdom regarding patience. Maybe you're too impatient to reach your goals and end up self-sabotaging your success. The Six of Swords shows that you're in a transitional period, which means you'll soon leave behind whatever is making you impatient. The Magician in this position suggests that you're afraid that leaving behind parts of yourself will hold you back from manifesting your desires. The Justice card indicates that if you're clear in communicating your intention to your guides, they can provide you with more straightforward messages in the future. The Queen of Wands signals that you can establish a meaningful relationship with your spirit guides by being determined to form a strong connection with them. Consequently, you will trust their messages even more in the future.

Connecting with your spirit guides is a very intuitive practice. Trusting your gut feelings during Tarot readings will go a long way in accurately interpreting messages. Take your time and consider what each card represents to you and your connection with your spiritual guide.

Spiritual Gift Spread

Difficulty Rating: ★★★☆☆

Each person has spiritual gifts, but not everyone is aware of theirs. You may be holding back from acknowledging your aptitudes because of fear, anxiety, or uncertainty. Or, you might not understand how to explore your spiritual skill or express them. This spread is designed to reveal your spiritual gifts and help you learn a little more about them. While this spread seems like a simple 5-card layout, it requires some introspective awareness, which takes some practice to develop.

Casting the Cards

Start by laying down the first card in the center, face down. Place the second one over it and the third one to its left. The fourth card goes below the first one, and the fifth one is on its right side. Here is what they represent:

- The first card symbolizes yourself and your relation to your spiritual gifts

- The second card reveals talents you are aware of

- The third card identifies any issues that are holding you back from using your gifts

- The fourth card denotes gifts you haven't acknowledged yet

- The fifth card hints at practices that can help you embrace your gifts

Interpretation

Let's say you've revealed the following cards:

1. The Hanged Man
2. Four of Wands
3. Eight of Wands
4. The Empress
5. Six of Wands

The Hanged Man in the central position indicates that you're feeling powerless in your situation. Perhaps you've sensed your spiritual gifts emerging but aren't sure how to deal with them. The Four of Wands signals that you're probably talented in creating a stable, loving environment for your loved ones. The Eight of Wands symbolizes impatience. In this instance, it means that even if you become aware of your gifts, you want them to develop instantly. Pulling the Empress into the fourth position means you aren't fully aware of how much you can do with your talents. The Six of Wands indicates that you can work toward expressing your gifts by seeing yourself as successful in the role that allows using them.

You can look at the theme you see emerging from the cards. For instance, you've seen three Wands cards in the example above, which means a lot of activity. It indicates that to successfully connect with your gifts, you might need to slow down and let things happen as they're naturally supposed to.

Shadow Work Spread

Difficulty Rating: ★★★☆☆

Many people put things they're afraid of, ashamed of, or embarrassed about to the back of their minds. Instead of confronting these issues, they're repressing them, creating a shadow self, which prevents them from reaching their full potential. However, facing your shadows can actually help dispel their harmful effects and enable you to create a more positive self-image. This layout is perfect for exploring the depths of shadow work, the practice of revealing one's shadows and working through them. Many shadow spreads exist, but this one is chosen for its simplicity. Yet, through five cards, it can provide a comprehensive insight into yourself.

Casting the Cards

Start by placing the first card face down in the middle of the space in front of you. Next, place the second card directly under it and the third one over it. Place the fourth card on the left side of the first and the fifth one on its right side. Here is what these cards represent:

- The first card will serve as a tool for identifying a shadow trait

- The second card will reveal why you held onto this shadow trait

- The third card symbolizes a hard truth you need to learn about the trait

- The fourth card hints at possible practical applications of the trait

- The fifth card reveals how to take care of yourself while exploring your shadow trait

Interpretation

Let's say you've revealed the following cards:

1. The Emperor
2. The Devil
3. Four of Cups
4. Eight of Wands
5. Queen of Swords

Having The Emperor in the shadow trait position indicates that your traits are structure and control. Perhaps you're trying to manage things you can't control, or maybe you have trouble establishing your authority. The Devil in the second position reveals that you've probably held onto this shadow trait because you're addicted to relying on it. The Four of Cups indicates that you've distanced yourself from your true desires due to your controlling ways. Because of this, you're now discontent with your life and are contemplating how to break the cycle. The Eight of Wands, in this context, reveals that you can still use your shadow trait in a challenging situation. When time is of the essence, your ability to control a situation and make quick decisions can go a long way toward success. Finally, the Queen of Swords tells you that the best way to take care of yourself during shadow work is to always be perceptive and open-minded.

For the best results, spend a little time with each card as you pull them and lay them out in the spread. While you're free to stay with the meanings mentioned here, make sure to take a few seconds to contemplate what each card means to you at that moment.

A Few Honorable Mentions

The Soul Activation Spread

Difficulty Rating: ★★☆☆☆

Casting and Interpretation

After choosing a card to depict you, lay it on the table. You'll place the following 3 cards below it, from left to right. Here is what all the card in this spread represents:

- The first card indicates the energy you want to manifest into the world

- The second card denotes past influences on your energy and future outcomes

- The third card represents who you are in the current time

- The fourth card will activate your spiritual growth

New Year's Tarot Spread

Difficulty Rating: ★★★★☆

Casting and Interpretation

You'll need eight cards. You'll lay the first three cards out face down, from left to right. Leaving a little space under them, place the fourth card in the middle and the fifth one on top of it in a horizontal position. The next card goes to the left of the fourth, while the seventh is placed on the right. Place the eighth card between the first and second rows in the middle. Here is what they mean:

- The first card depicts the biggest lessons you've learned during the year

- The second card highlights your most prominent achievement throughout the year

- The third card symbolizes the things you let go of last year

- The fourth card hints at experiences you can expect in the coming year

- The fifth card reveals major obstacles you'll encounter in the coming year

- The sixth card shows what you will focus on during the new year

- The seventh card transmits advice you should listen to for the coming year

- The eighth card reveals how your transition from the past year to the new one will be

Making Tough Choices Spread

Difficulty Rating: ★☆☆☆☆

Casting and Interpretation

In this simple spread, you'll lay the first three cards in a horizontal line, beginning from at the top and moving down. Then, you'll place the fourth card on the left and the fifth one on the right side of the second card. Here is how to interpret this layout:

- The first card is linked to your motivation and how whatever inspires you affects your decision

- The second card symbolizes the ideal outcome you expect to achieve under the current circumstances

- The third card reflects your core values and principles and how they affect your decision

- The fourth card shows one of the likely outcomes of following your current path

- The fifth card demonstrates another of the likely outcomes of following your current path

Chapter 9: Spreads for Work and Career

This chapter brings you spreads for work and career. While a few layouts in this chapter focus strictly on professional life, others have slightly different purposes. For example, you'll find spreads for establishing a work-life balance, getting along with your coworkers, and finding out what makes you happy career-wise.

Work-Life Balance Spread

Difficulty Rating: ★★☆☆☆

Finding the precarious balance between your professional and personal life is tricky. It comes down to your priorities, which must be set and adhered to. Otherwise, habits from one aspect of your life will seep into the other and vice versa. The following spread for a work-life balance acts as a bridge between situations, tasks, and relationships you prioritize in your life and what you're overlooking. It helps you understand what's out of balance, so you can resolve the issue.

Casting the Cards

Start by placing the first card on the upper part of the far left side of your table. On the lower part of the right side, you'll put the second card. Position the third card on the right side of the first one, just a little lower. Lastly, place the fourth one under the third one on the left side of the fourth card. Here is what these cards symbolize:

- The first card represents what you're currently prioritizing

- The second card shows what you need to pay more attention to

- The third card reveals why you prioritize certain things

- The fourth card tells you why you need to focus on things that require your attention

Interpretation

Let's say you've drawn the following cards:

1. Seven of Cups
2. Ace of Wands
3. Eight of Pentacles
4. The Tower

Seven of Cups in the first position indicates that you don't have priorities because you're trying to excel in all areas of life. However, because you have so many goals and tasks, you can't focus on a single one sufficiently to make it a priority. This card typically refers to one's personal life, showing that you have so many things going for you personally that it affects your professional development. This message is underlined by the Ace of Wands, telling you that what you need to prioritize is singling out one thing to focus on. This should be a smaller goal or task, so it wouldn't interfere with the rest of them. The Eight of Pentacles symbolizes that you're looking at the bigger picture. You're chasing big dreams, so you can't focus on smaller goals. The Tower tells you that the reason you can't focus on one thing is that you're afraid. You fear that by doing so, you'll neglect the other areas, and consequently, you'll fail to realize your biggest dreams.

While the first two cards are easy to decipher, the third and fourth need more attention. Make sure to look at their relationship to see if you can see any patterns. Sometimes there will be an evident conflict between the two reasons, which you can explore through additional readings.

Finding Opportunities Spread

Difficulty Rating: ★★★★☆

Whether you're unemployed or are looking to move on from your current position, job hunting can be challenging. Finding a suitable job prospect is hard enough, and getting through the interview and winning is even more problematic. This spread is designed to help you with the first part of that task, finding job opportunities suitable for your skills and preferences.

Casting the Cards

Lay down the first of the six cards you'll use face down in the middle of your table in a horizontal position. Place the second one on top of it in a vertical position. Visualizing a square around these two cards, place the third card in the top left corner of the square. Finish the spread by placing the fourth one in the top right corner, the fifth one in the bottom left corner, and the sixth card in the bottom right corner of your imaginary square. Here is what these cards represent:

- The first card points to your attitude regarding your job search, including preconceived expectations and their effects

- The second card shows the biggest obstacle you must overcome to find the best career opportunities

- The third card highlights your skills, including the ones you can offer to your employer, the ones you're using, and the ones you've overlooked

- The fourth card represents your secret weapon, something that helps distinguish you from all other applicants

- The fifth card tells you something you have to understand about your motivations before being successful in your job hunting

- The sixth card offers advice going forward in terms of what you should focus on and where you should spend your energy

Interpretation

Let's say you've revealed the following cards:

1. The Chariot
2. The Wheel of Fortune
3. King of Wands
4. Two of Cups
5. King of Swords
6. Knight of Pentacles

Drawing the Chariot in the first position indicates that you believe that finding the right job will give you more control over your life. While this may be partially true, you're too focused on this aspect and forget that you're supposed to be looking for something fulfilling. The Wheel of

Fortune tells you that your biggest obstacle will be fate. If you didn't get a job you were hoping to get, there is probably a reason for that. The King of Wands in your skills position is a good indicator of excellent leadership skills. You can persevere and work hard for your goals, not to mention to look at the big picture. You'll always do a thorough job, which is a desirable skill. Make sure to emphasize this skill to potential employers during your next job hunt. The Two of Cups is the partnership card, which means your secret weapon is being a good team worker. The King of Swords indicates that you need a little more discipline. When job hunting, you should listen to your head instead of following your heart. Your final advice comes from the Knight of Pentacles. This card symbolizes perseverance which means that by putting in the hard work, you'll be able to land your dream job.

This spread can reveal any obstacles that might obstruct your view of the best opportunities. When drawing on the cards, focus on identifying the internal barrier or issues that may arise later. For example, landing your dream job can mean relocating your entire family.

Finding Your Life Goals Spread

Difficulty Rating: ★★☆☆☆

If you want to learn more about your life's goals, this general-purpose spread is a valuable tool. Whether you're feeling stuck, undetermined about your position, or happy where you are currently in life, this layout will help you identify whether you're on the right track toward reaching your goals.

Casting the Cards

You'll need six cards. You'll place the first three in a row, face down, from left to right. Lay the fourth and fifth cards above the first row. The sixth one goes above the second row. Here is what these cards symbolize:

- The first card reveals why you choose certain job roles and what purpose they serve in your life
- The second card highlights the primary motivating forces that inspire you to do your best
- The third card indicates the responsibilities you're willing to take on, whether they're in the job description or not
- The fourth card tells you what projects you like to work on and what sort of work environment you prefer

- The fifth card shows the potential rewards you're interested in gaining from your new job, spiritually, financially, or otherwise
- The sixth card hints at where you are heading and what your future goals can bring to you

Interpretation

Let's say you've cast the following spread:

1. Three of Pentacles
2. Page of Swords
3. Four of Swords
4. Three of Cups
5. Ten of Wands
6. The World

If you've drawn the Three of Pentacles in your first position, you choose jobs where you will collaborate with others. You value teamwork and will always do your best to work well with your teammates. The Page of Swords in the second position means you're also driven by curiosity and have plenty of mental energy to work productively, even under stress. Four of Swords is a card that, in this instance, tells you that you're willing to take on tasks that require a lot of analysis and patience. You have the Three of Cups in your preferred environment position. It indicates that you prefer a close-knit community-type of work culture where you can form long-lasting friendships with your coworkers. The Ten of Wands suggest that your reward will be spiritual fulfillment. And while the rewards will come with even more responsibilities, the World card indicates that what waits for you at the end of the journey will be more than worth all your hard work.

No matter your results, it's always worth considering the bigger picture. Make sure to always look at all of the cards in your spread to see if there is a connection between them.

Career Shift Spread

Difficulty Rating: ★☆☆☆☆

Some say it's always a good idea to leave a job when you're still satisfied with your position. However, deciding when to change careers is never easy. The following spread will clarify where you are in terms of your professional goals, allowing you to decide whether you should look for a new opportunity.

Casting the Cards

You'll lay three of the seven cards in a horizontal line, starting from the left. Place the fourth and fifth cards under the first and second one in a second horizontal line. Lastly, put the sixth and the seventh card under the fourth and fourth ones, forming a third row. Here is what these seven cards symbolize:

- The first three cards represent options you should be contemplating for your next career
- The fourth card highlights your possible future career, letting you see how it looks
- The fifth card tells you what to do to have that career
- The sixth hints at things you need to let go of to move toward the desired career
- The seventh card indicates how your life will change when you start that career

Interpretation

Let's say you've revealed the following cards:

1. The Hermit
2. The Death
3. Knight of Wands
4. Five of Wands
5. Seven of Cups
6. Eight of Swords
7. King of Pentacles

The Hermit indicates that one of your future jobs could be related to work that requires using your intuition. The Death card denotes that another one of your prospects could be in a dynamic environment. The Knight of Wands supports this indicating that you're in for plenty of action in your new job. The Five of Wands tells you you're looking into plenty of competition in your future career. The Seven of Cups reveals that you'll need to look into your purposes and the choices you are willing to make to find your dream job. The Eight of Swords indicates that you're prone to self-victimization, and if you want to succeed, you'll need to stop this behavior. And lastly, the King of Pentacles shows you that landing your dream job means abundance and prosperity in your future.

One of the modifications you can make is to use only one card to reveal your future career. This way, the rest of your answers will be more specific. Or, you can do separate readings for all three suggested options after an initial one to clarify the answers you got on the last four positions.

Career Direction Spread

Difficulty Rating: ★☆☆☆☆

If you aren't sure whether your current career is heading in the right direction, this spread can clarify this matter. It will help you learn whether you'll still find this role fulfilling in the future or whether you should look into something more rewarding.

Casting the Cards

Place the first card face down in the middle of the space and arrange cards 2-5 around it. Start from the left corner and work in the clockwise direction filling each corner of an imaginary square. Here is what these cards mean for career direction:

- The first card represents your current career as a whole
- The second card hints at steps you'll need to take in your career
- The third card tells you how you'll know that you're taking the right steps
- The fourth card denotes the skills you'll need further in your career
- The fifth card shows what you can do to further your career

Interpretation

Let's say you've drawn the following cards:

1. The Fool
2. The Hanged Man
3. Six of Wands
4. Knight of Swords
5. Knight of Pentacles

As the first card of the Major Arcana, the Fool symbolizes the beginning of your journey. Your career is just beginning, and you still have a lot of learning to do. The Hanged Man indicates that your chosen profession will require some sacrifices. The Six of Wands is a card of success, which means you'll soon taste your first victory. When you do, you'll know you're on the right path. The Knight of Swords in the fourth position denotes that you'll make good use of your skills, like pursuing your goals, proving points, and letting others see things from your perspective. The Knight of Pentacles reassures you that the best way to further your career is to work hard for your goals.

You can modify your inquiry by being more specific with your question. For example, in the last question, you can ask whether taking a particular step will further your career.

You and Your Coworkers Spread

Difficulty Rating: ★☆☆☆☆

Sometimes it's difficult to get along with coworkers because you don't understand each other. This can affect your productivity and result in strained relationships at the workplace. This spread will help you uncover more about your coworkers and learn how to get along with them. The key is understanding your and your coworkers' needs and finding a bridge between them.

Casting the Cards

Draw three cards and lay them on the table, face down. Here is what they represent:

- The first card symbolizes your coworker's needs
- The second card denotes your own needs
- The third card illustrates an overlap between the two needs as a way of finding common ground

Interpretation

Let's say you've revealed the following cards:

1. Eight of Wands
2. Ten of Wands
3. Two of Pentacles

Drawing the Eight of Wands as your coworker's card means that they probably like to resolve everything through quick actions. And while they're only focusing on finishing the job as soon as possible, you see it as unnecessary rushing that can lead to mistakes. The Ten of Wands in the second position shows that you prefer to work hard, even if you have to do everything yourself. In fact, you may even take on a task from your coworker because you want to ensure it gets done accurately. The Two of Pentacles is a card linked to time management and adaptability. It could indicate that you should see your coworkers' traits as strengths instead of weaknesses. Perhaps it's good that they don't over-analyze things as you do. Otherwise, work would take much longer to get done.

Besides the images on the cards, you should also look at the bigger picture they represent. For example, here you have two Wands cards, which means you have two people with excellent work ethics and committed to their job. However, the two Wands are turning away from each other, which means they aren't on the same wavelength. The good news is you have a common ground, which isn't always the case. For example, the first two cards could stand in opposition, indicating that you and your coworker have nothing in common personality-wise. You can also alter this spread to include more than one coworker if needed. You'll just add a card for each coworker's needs.

A Few Honorable Mentions

Judgement Spread for Career Evaluation

Difficulty Rating: ★★☆☆☆

Casting and Interpretation

You'll lay the first card on the left side of your space and the second one under it, leaving a little space between them. The remaining cards (3-6) go next to the first two on the right side, starting around the middle of both cards. Here is what the cards in this layout mean:

- The first card represents past mistakes you've made in your professional life

- The second card denotes the successes you achieved in your professional life

- The third card indicates the lessons you've learned from the successes and the failures

- The fourth card shows new information you're learning or acknowledging

- The fifth card symbolizes your transformation after receiving the information

- The sixth card highlights the changes your transformation will bring to your professional life

The Emperor Spread for Standing up for Yourself

Difficulty Rating: ★★★★☆

Casting and Interpretation

Start by placing the first card on the right side of the table. Put the second one on the left side of the first one and the third on the right side of the first one. The fourth card goes under the first one, between the second and third cards. Cards five and six (using the same format as cards one and four) go on the left side, next to the second one. Here is what these six cards mean:

- The first card offers clarity on why you feel that you lack control in your workplace
- The second card shows what you have control over and how to use this control
- The third card symbolizes everything that's out of your control
- The fourth card represents everything you should stop tolerating and say no to moving forward
- The fifth card highlights everything you need to keep doing and pay more attention to
- The sixth card indicates everything that brings you joy and fulfillment in your career

Chapter 10: Create Your Own Tarot Spreads

This chapter is a step-by-step guide to help you create personalized Tarot spreads that align with your reading style. Here, you'll learn how to develop original positions, orders, and layouts based on a single question, problem, or goal. You'll also understand how to modify a ready-made Tarot spread if you don't want to create one from scratch.

Step 1: Know the Question and Pinpoint Your Goal

There are two factors you must consider when creating a tarot spread. You won't be able to create a spread without knowing the question needing to be asked and identifying the goal of the spread. Whether you're creating a spread for yourself for a client reading, it's a lot easier if you understand the question since it fulfills a current need. Determining the goal, however, could be more challenging. Goals hint at long-term, future needs. They shape our motives, actions, and even the questions that we have at the moment. The problem with identifying our goals is that they're not always acknowledged on a conscious level. People who have low levels of self-awareness might struggle to identify their goals. Many people find it hard to name their deepest desires. Fortunately, there are Tarot readings that can provide guidance on the subject.

Suppose you are doing the reading for someone else. In that case, you might not have a solid understanding of their goals and desires, especially if they feel uncomfortable sharing this type of information with you. In that case, you'll have to make do with the background knowledge you have. Try to use it to get a general idea of what they desire most in life. If they are dealing with a certain problem, be empathetic and try to relate to how they're feeling. Learning as much as possible about their desires and problems ensures that your reading is heading in the right direction and offers satisfactory information. Ultimately, the reading should provide a sense of clarity and even enlightenment.

If you're creating the Tarot spread for yourself, then this step will likely be easy. Take a moment to introspect and reflect on your past and current experience. You can also practice positive visualization to get a better grip on your goals and the future that you want for yourself. Now that you know the purpose of your Tarot spread, you can move on to the next step.

Step 2: Develop the Positions for Your Tarot Spread

This step requires a little effort and focus on your side. Creating Tarot spreads and developing positions requires you to take on the role of an investigator. Use all the information you have about the person you are reading to or the relevant information you have about yourself to come up with specific, narrowed-down questions. It helps to know what type of answers you need for clarity. Once you have the questions you need, break each one down into three distinct parts. The whole point of a Tarot reading is to tell a story or paint a picture in which you or your client act as the main characters.

Like any other story, your Tarot reading must illustrate the situation, the environment, the circumstances, the main problem, possible challenges, and the solution. This structure would make the reading more interesting and compelling and ensure that you deliver a comprehensive and detailed message. This is why you must have sufficient information about current affairs and any behaviors, personality traits, and past events that might influence the outcome.

Step 3: Expand Your Horizons

You might feel very confused about where to start, what type of information to gather, and how to ensure you receive all the answers you need. Your questions lay the foundation for the Tarot spread you'll be building. You need to pinpoint the pieces of context that will affect your reading. Too much knowledge can be confusing and might cause you to lose sight of the purpose of the spread. Too little information would result in an unsatisfactory reading.

The following questions will give you ideas regarding what to ask yourself or your client. When working with instruments of divination, you should always follow your intuition. Don't let these examples limit you; use them as sources of inspiration and tweak them and add to them as needed.

Ask yourself:

- What type of information am I seeking?

- What do I need to know at the moment?

- What do I think is hidden or concealed?

- Who is involved or plays a role in the situation I'm in?

- Where or who can I turn to for guidance and help?

- Where do I stand in my journey?

- What are the things that I can't control in life?

- How is my environment?

- How am I seen by others?

- What are the potential opportunities, and where can I find them?

- How am I approaching and dealing with the problem at hand?

Step 4: Target the Problem

When going through the questions mentioned in the previous step, you might be surprised by how easy it is to grasp the problem. However, you must remind yourself that what's easy to express and put into words is often very shallow and lacks depth or meaning. As you explore your personal journey and work with more clients, you'll find that the easily-articulated things often distract from the bigger picture – and the things that truly matter.

For instance, if you're going through a rough patch with your partner, you might think that your recurrent arguments, recent traumatic experiences, or other external factors are the main reasons behind the tension between you. You might not necessarily realize that something within either (or both) of you might be the root of the problem. Perhaps you have unresolved trauma, an unhealthy coping mechanism, or a detrimental behavioral pattern. For instance, an argument about whose turn it is to do the laundry might be really about your inability to communicate or clearly express your needs.

To be able to target the root problem, you should ask yourself (or your client) the following questions:

- Is there anything blocking you/me from moving forward?
- Are there any obstacles standing in our/my way?
- What are the things that you/I can change in your/my life?
- What is the biggest challenge you're/I'm facing at the moment?
- What is your/my deepest desire?
- What do you/I truly wish for?
- What is your/my greatest goal in life?
- What are things that you/I need to work on?
- Is there anything that you/I wish to develop in yourself/myself?
- What are some things that would bring you/me joy and happiness?
- What are your/my strengths and weaknesses?

Step 5: Come Up with a Solution

Tarot can be a very powerful tool if you set reasonable expectations for your readings. If you're expecting your cards to tell the future or uncover the unknown, then you'll be setting yourself up for disappointment. Tarot is a way to get clarity and guidance on your current position in life and the actions you can take to control your future and the circumstances at hand. It can give you insight into which road to take and the confidence you need to make things right. It is an empowering tool that allows you to focus on what you can do instead of lamenting your problems. If you're giving the reading to someone else, make sure to know their expectations and correct any misconceptions they might have about Tarot readings. Otherwise, they won't be satisfied with what you have to offer.

To find the solution to your problem, ask yourself the following questions:

- What can I do to alleviate the problem?

- Is there something that I need to redirect my attention to?

- How can I make the best use of potential opportunities?

- Is there something holding me back that I need to let go of?

- Is there a lesson that I need to learn?

- Where is this road leading me?

- Where or who can I turn to for helpful advice?

- What can help me overcome this roadblock?

Step 6: Create a Tarot Spread Layout

You don't need to ask yourself or your client all the questions mentioned above. Once you've decided on the most relevant and helpful ones and got the answers you need, you should start painting your picture. Think about the direction the story will take and the order in which all your answers will come up. Picture what your story will look like. Follow your intuition when creating your spread, laying them out in the shape of anything relevant to your spread's theme. A cross is a popular shape for anyone with many decisions to make. If you value balance or want to learn about both the positive and negative sides of the question or issue at hand, you can lay out your cards symmetrically. Many Tarot readings find that symmetrical and balanced layouts allow them to do better readings.

Remember, however, that while visual layouts can yield better-quality readings, they don't matter much. If you wish to give a quick reading, you can simply lay down the cards beside each other. If you want to know something in particular, you need to think about the order in which you lay down your cards; this is more important than their visual representation. The story you tell is the most important aspect of your Tarot spread, and the story is the reading itself. At its most basic level, a story is told by explaining the current circumstances, introducing the problem, and then coming up with a resolution.

Step 7: Give Your Tarot Spread a Try

To use your spread effectively, you must ensure that all the details tie in seamlessly. This is considered the most exciting part of the process, especially for those in design and user experience testing. In this step, you need to determine which parts are working, which ones are off, and how you can improve the overall quality of the spread. You'll find that the more readings you do with your Tarot spread, the more knowledge and ideas you'll learn regarding how to fix it up and refine it until you're satisfied.

Modify a Ready-Made Spread

There are many great Tarot spreads out there. You've probably encountered several you like but thought they were lacking in one area or another. Instead of creating your own spread from the start, you can modify it to suit you. Tweaking a spread doesn't have to be tedious; you can simply modify it by changing the numbering or the positional meaning. Some Tarot readers even argue that if you modify an existing spread, you create a brand-new one.

Modifying a Tarot spread requires you to make small changes that align with your reading style, your (or your client's) questions, and personal beliefs. You can modify a spread in several ways. Still, before you make any changes, you must think about its initial purpose. Analyze the cards' layout and positions and whether the spread successfully meets its initial purpose. If you're certain that it doesn't suit you, take a moment to ponder how it would better suit you.

The following are some points to consider:

- *The focus of the spread.* Do you need to change the intrinsic purpose of the spread so it suits your needs more effectively?

- *The positional meanings of the deck.* Do the positions of the cards align with your questions? Do you think they'll give you the answers you're looking for? Do you wish to add or remove some positions?

- *The layout of the spread.* Does the layout look right to you? Does it fit the changes you made in the positions? Would it be easier to read the cards if you changed the layout?

- *The number of cards.* According to your reading style, are the cards present too many or too few to give you an effective reading?

- *Techniques.* Which reading technique can you use to enrich your reading and make the best use of your spread?

Now that you know everything you need to know about creating Tarot spreads from scratch, you are ready to personalize the whole reading experience. Learning how to modify Tarot spreads so they fit your personal style makes you better at giving readings overall.

Conclusion

From a simple parlor game to one of the most effective divinatory tools, Tarot has come a long way since its introduction to society. That said, the most popular decks used today are still based on the ones created during the late 19th and early 20th centuries. The Rider-Waite deck, in particular, is heavily featured among the modern variants, and this book has introduced you to its structure and symbolism. You've learned about the meanings of the 22 Major Arcana cards and the 56 Minor Arcana cards and how you can apply them to the different aspects of your life.

You've also read about the importance of tuning in to your intuition when connecting with your deck. Tarot readings can teach you many things about yourself and how to persevere in life, but you'll need to form a connection with them. For beginners, steps like choosing the right deck, holding each card in your hands, and contemplating its meaning can go a long way in learning how to do Tarot readings. Because, more often than not, the messages you receive through the cards will be tied to what the cards mean to you rather than their general symbolism.

After providing plenty of advice on reading and interpreting the cards using your intuition, you were introduced to the most popular general spreads. The layouts with the lower number of cards are perfect for practicing basic Tarot reading skills. These will be the ideal stepping stone for more elaborate work. Mastering these will also give you the opportunity to seek answers to problems you encounter in different areas of life. Cards with higher numbers can offer you generalized advice on various matters.

If you want to explore specific matters in more depth, you can use the spreads provided. For example, you can do a reading for finding or strengthening love, self-care, and spiritual growth. These are all crucial elements of keeping your life balanced, but you can't forget about your professional life either. Feel free to use the spread supplied in the penultimate chapter to find answers for career development.

Another splendid option for finding answers to specific issues is to create your own spreads. Developing original positions based on your requirements, goals, or questions requires actively engaging your intuition from start to finish. This takes a lot of practice and time to master, but the final results will definitely be worth it. The best way to start is to modify existing spreads and see what your gut tells you about the new layouts and the results they deliver. Later on, you can decide whether you want to come up with entirely new spreads or stick to doing original ones. Either way, good luck on your Tarot journey and finding the answers you seek for your life.

If you enjoyed this book, I'd greatly appreciate a review on Amazon because it helps me to create more books that people want. It would mean a lot to hear from you.

To leave a review:

1. Open your camera app.
2. Point your mobile device at the QR code.
3. The review page will appear in your web browser.

Thanks for your support!

Here's another book by Mari Silva that you might like

Your Free Gift
(only available for a limited time)

Thanks for getting this book! If you want to learn more about various spirituality topics, then join Mari Silva's community and get a free guided meditation MP3 for awakening your third eye. This guided meditation mp3 is designed to open and strengthen ones third eye so you can experience a higher state of consciousness. Simply visit the link below the image to get started.

https://spiritualityspot.com/meditation

Or, Scan the QR code!

References

Part 1: Astrology and Relationships

Bennett, C. (1981). What is astrology? Sun Publishing.

Brown, M. (2021, August 11). What is astrology? A beginners' guide to the language of the sky. InStyle. https://www.instyle.com/lifestyle/astrology/what-is-astrology

How to know if you're truly compatible with someone, according to astrologers. (2022, April 18). Mindbodygreen. https://www.mindbodygreen.com/articles/synastry

Kelly, A. (2022, September 21). The trick to understanding astrological compatibility. The Cut. https://www.thecut.com/2022/09/zodiac-sign-compatibility-meaning.html

Patz, A. (2021, September 1). Zodiac compatibility: Signs that should and shouldn't date. Reader's Digest. https://www.rd.com/list/zodiac-signs-compatibility/

SueM. (2019, May 30). Jung on astrology. Jungian Center for the Spiritual Sciences. https://jungiancenter.org/jung-on-astrology/

Kahn, N. (2021, February 9). Your descendent sign can reveal A lot about your romantic life. Bustle. https://www.bustle.com/life/descendent-sign-meaning-astrology

Kelly, A. (2018, February 2). 12 zodiac signs: Dates and personality traits of each star sign. Allure. https://www.allure.com/story/zodiac-sign-personality-traits-dates

Kelly, A. (2022, May 30). Rising Sign: What is it, and what does it mean? The Cut. https://www.thecut.com/article/what-is-my-rising-ascendant-sign.html

Latreille, J. (2022, October 15). What your Sun sign in astrology says about you. Yoga Journal. https://www.yogajournal.com/lifestyle/astrology/sun-sign-meaning/

Robinson, K. (2022, May 26). Descendant in astrology: Meaning, signs, and more. Astrology.com. https://www.astrology.com/article/descendant-astrology/

The total beginner's guide to the zodiac's 12 moon signs, from astrologers. (2022, October 17). Mindbodygreen. https://www.mindbodygreen.com/articles/moon-sign-meaning

Your moon sign is the last piece of the astrology puzzle, so here's what it means. (2021, October 20). ELLE. https://www.elle.com.au/culture/moon-sign-meaning-26111

A beginner's guide to the 12 houses of the horoscope. (2020, August 31). Mindbodygreen. https://www.mindbodygreen.com/articles/the-12-houses-of-astrology

Lanyadoo, J. (2019, August 19). Here's everything you need to know about astrology houses. Cosmopolitan. https://www.cosmopolitan.com/lifestyle/a28700440/astrology-houses/

Outlook Web Desk. (2021, October 30). Role of different planets in horoscope. Outlook India. https://www.outlookindia.com/website/story/role-of-different-planets-in-horoscope/399275

Planet: All about planets in astrology. (n.d.). Astrosage.com. https://www.astrosage.com/planet/

Thomas, K. (2021, November 5). A guide to the planets in astrology and what they each represent. New York Post. https://nypost.com/article/astrology-planets-meaning/

Barros, A. (2021, August 28). Synastry 101: Where to Get + How to Read a Synastry Chart (but, like, not well, ok?) — hella namaste. Hella namaste. https://www.hellanamaste.com/blog/how-to-read-a-synastry-chart

How to read your synastry chart. (n.d.). Astro-charts.com. https://astro-charts.com/blog/2017/how-to-read-your-synastry-chart/

Quinn, S. (2017, November 17). Planets in synastry: A beginner's guide to relationship astrology. Everydayhealth.com; Everyday Health. https://www.everydayhealth.com/healthy-living/planets-synastry-beginners-guide-relationship-astrology/

Steve. (2021, January 27). How to read a synastry chart! The big questions answered. Vekke Sind. https://vekkesind.com/how-to-read-a-synastry-chart-the-big-questions-answered/

The AstroTwins. (2022, April 8). Synastry chart for couples: Compare two charts to make a "relationship chart." Astrostyle: Astrology and Daily, Weekly, Monthly Horoscopes by The AstroTwins; Astrostyle by the AstroTwins. https://astrostyle.com/astrology/synastry-relationship-chart/

Aries 101: Everything you need to know about the kickstarter of the zodiac. (2021, March 26). Mindbodygreen. https://www.mindbodygreen.com/articles/aries-sign-101

Aries and Taurus compatibility. (2021, October 2). GaneshaSpeaks. https://www.ganeshaspeaks.com/zodiac-signs/compatibility/aries-taurus/

Aries moon sign compatibility. (2015, April 19). Cafeastrology.com; Cafe Astrology .com. https://cafeastrology.com/moonsignariescompatibility.html

Astrology.Care - Aries Strengths and Weaknesses, Love, Family, Career, Money. (n.d.). Astrology.Care. http://astrology.care/aries.html

Astrology.Care - Taurus Strengths and Weaknesses, Love, Family, Career, Money. (n.d.). Astrology.Care. http://astrology.care/taurus.html

AstroMundus, & Happy, happy.com. pt. (2021, March 6). Descendant Sign - What it Means for Astrology? AstroMundus; SUEBI Digital Labs. https://astromundus.com/en/descendant-sign/

Brown, M. (2022, March 31). The most compatible — and most problematic — zodiac signs for a Taurus. InStyle. https://www.instyle.com/lifestyle/astrology/taurus-compatibility

Coughlin, S. (2018, November 6). What your astrological sign's "keyword" reveals about you. Refinery29. https://www.refinery29.com/en-us/2018/11/216100/astrology-zodiac-keywords-the-stars-within-you

Daruwala, C. B. (2021, December 1). Strengths and weakness of Taurus. Times Of India. https://timesofindia.indiatimes.com/astrology/zodiacs-astrology/taurus/strengths-and-weakness-of-taurus/articleshow/88026908.cms

Devon. (2021, June 18). Everything you need to know about your descendant sign. Rebel Circus. https://therebelcircus.com/astrology/descendantsign/

Douglas, M. (n.d.-a). Aries moon sign: What does it mean? Prepscholar.com. https://blog.prepscholar.com/aries-moon-sign

Douglas, M. (n.d.-b). Taurus moon sign: What it means for you. Prepscholar.com. https://blog.prepscholar.com/taurus-moon-sign

Everything to know about Taurus, the zodiac's stubborn-but-loving sign. (2021, May 4). Mindbodygreen. https://www.mindbodygreen.com/articles/taurus-101-personality-traits-compatability-and-more

Hutter, J. (2022a, December 6). 15 most common Aries weaknesses. So Synced - Personality Dating; So Synced. https://www.sosynced.com/15-most-common-aries-weaknesses/

Hutter, J. (2022b, December 17). 14 strengths & weaknesses of the Taurus zodiac sign. So Synced - Personality Dating; So Synced. https://www.sosynced.com/14-strengths-weaknesses-of-the-taurus-zodiac-sign/

Ibeh, C. (2020, October 2). Taurus symbol: Zodiac sign glyphs & meanings. YourTango. https://www.yourtango.com/2020337344/taurus-symbol-zodiac-sign-glyphs-meanings

Jessica. (2022, August 19). Aries descendant: Personality traits and compatibility. Symbolism & Metaphor. https://symbolismandmetaphor.com/aries-descendant/

Kahn, N. (2020, July 29). The ruling planet for your zodiac sign's meaning in astrology. Bustle. https://www.bustle.com/life/ruling-planet-zodiac-sign-meaning-astrology

Kahn, N. (2021a, August 10). Why Aries are the natural leaders of the zodiac. Bustle. https://www.bustle.com/life/aries-zodiac-biggest-strengths-astrologer

Kahn, N. (2021b, August 31). Why Taurus is one of the most loyal signs of the zodiac. Bustle. https://www.bustle.com/life/taurus-zodiac-biggest-strengths-astrologer

Kelly, A. (2018, February 2). 12 zodiac signs: Dates and personality traits of each star sign. Allure. https://www.allure.com/story/zodiac-sign-personality-traits-dates

Marz5SOS. (n.d.). The signs key phrases. Wattpad.com. https://www.wattpad.com/148780202-zodiac-signs-the-signs-key-phrases

Newhouse, E. (2019, November 12). A comprehensive guide to rising signs and what they actually mean. Allure. https://www.allure.com/story/rising-sign-personality-traits-astrology-ascendant-signs

Nunez, A. T. (2022, August 6). How your rising sign affects your relationships. YourTango. https://www.yourtango.com/zodiac/rising-sign-compatibility

Perkins, C. (2020, May 13). Here's your biggest pet peeve, according to your zodiac sign. Yahoo Life. https://www.yahoo.com/lifestyle/2020-05-13-heres-your-biggest-pet-peeve-according-to-your-zodiac-sign-241292858.html

Rose, K. (2020, August 22). What does the Aries symbol & glyph mean? YourTango. https://www.yourtango.com/2020336399/aries-symbol-zodiac-sign-glyphs-meanings

Ross, H., Clarke, J., Young, E., & Bishop, K. (2018, December 18). What is my ruling planet, according to the zodiac, and what does it mean for me? Repeller. https://repeller.com/ruling-planets-and-what-they-mean-for-you-according-to-the-zodiac/

Stardust, L. (2022a, February 18). Your Moon sign compatibility guide. Cosmopolitan. https://www.cosmopolitan.com/sex-love/a39139470/moon-sign-compatibility/

Stardust, L. (2022b, April 5). Aries sun sign: Personality traits, love compatibility and more. TODAY. https://www.today.com/life/astrology/aries-traits-personality-rcna22002

Stardust, L. (2022c, April 15). Taurus sun sign: Personality traits, love compatibility and more. TODAY. https://www.today.com/life/astrology/taurus-traits-personality-rcna24594

Steber, C. (2019, July 23). Your biggest pet peeve, based on your zodiac sign. Bustle. https://www.bustle.com/p/your-biggest-pet-peeve-based-on-your-zodiac-sign-18208104

Stewart, A. (2022, February 6). What planets rule each zodiac sign? POPSUGAR. https://www.popsugar.com/smart-living/what-planet-rules-each-zodiac-sign-48699351

Taurus Ascendant. (2023, January 4). Astroyogi. https://www.astroyogi.com/kundli/ascendant/taurus

Taurus moon sign compatibility. (2015, April 14). Cafeastrology.com; Cafe Astrology .com. https://cafeastrology.com/moonsigntauruscompatibility.html

Taurus sun sign compatability matches. (2015, April 13). Cafeastrology.com; Cafe Astrology .com. https://cafeastrology.com/taurussunsigncompatibility.html

The AstroTwins. (2016, August 18). Aries symbol and astrology sign glyph. Astrostyle: Astrology and Daily, Weekly, Monthly Horoscopes by The AstroTwins; Astrostyle by the AstroTwins. https://astrostyle.com/astrology/aries-symbol/

The AstroTwins. (2022, March 30). The Descendant in astrology: Your relationship "personality." Astrostyle: Astrology and Daily, Weekly, Monthly Horoscopes by The AstroTwins; Astrostyle by the AstroTwins. https://astrostyle.com/astrology/the-descendant/

The Pagan Grimoire. (2021, June 29). The Taurus symbol and its meaning in astrology. The Pagan Grimoire. https://www.pagangrimoire.com/taurus-symbol/

The zodiac sign Aries symbol - personality, strengths, weaknesses. (2018, February 5). Labyrinthos. https://labyrinthos.co/blogs/astrology-horoscope-zodiac-signs/the-zodiac-sign-aries-symbol-personality-strengths-weaknesses

The zodiac sign Taurus symbol - personality, strengths, weaknesses. (2018, February 5). Labyrinthos. https://labyrinthos.co/blogs/astrology-horoscope-zodiac-signs/the-zodiac-sign-taurus-symbol-personality-strengths-weaknesses

Wright, J. (2022, April 19). Aries compatibility: The best and worst zodiac matches. PureWow. https://www.purewow.com/wellness/aries-compatibility

(N.d.). Symbolspy.com. https://www.symbolspy.com/zodiac-symbols-text.html

AstroMundus, & Happy, happy.com. pt. (2021, March 6). Descendant Sign - What it Means for Astrology? AstroMundus; SUEBI Digital Labs. https://astromundus.com/en/descendant-sign/

Brown, M. (2020, April 17). Your Gemini zodiac sign guide: Everything to know about the curious air sign. InStyle. https://www.instyle.com/lifestyle/gemini-zodiac-sign

Brown, M. (2021, June 3). The most compatible — and most problematic — zodiac signs for a Cancer. InStyle. https://www.instyle.com/lifestyle/astrology/cancer-compatibility

Cancer moon sign compatibility. (2015, April 19). Cafeastrology.com; Cafe Astrology .com. https://cafeastrology.com/moonsigncancercompatibility.html

Coughlin, S. (2018, November 6). What your astrological sign's "keyword" reveals about you. Refinery29. https://www.refinery29.com/en-us/2018/11/216100/astrology-zodiac-keywords-the-stars-within-you

Daruwalla, C. B. (2022a, May 19). Gemini: Strengths and weaknesses. Times Of India. https://timesofindia.indiatimes.com/astrology/zodiacs-astrology/gemini/gemini-strengths-and-weaknesses/articleshow/91663530.cms

Daruwalla, C. B. (2022b, June 24). Gemini compatibility with Cancer. Times Of India. https://timesofindia.indiatimes.com/astrology/zodiacs-astrology/gemini/gemini-compatibility-with-cancer/articleshow/92429172.cms

Daruwalla, C. B. (2022c, August 29). Cancer: Strengths and weaknesses. Times Of India. https://timesofindia.indiatimes.com/astrology/zodiacs-astrology/cancer/cancer-strengths-and-weaknesses/articleshow/93857148.cms

Douglas, M. (n.d.). Gemini moon sign: What does it mean? Prepscholar.com. https://blog.prepscholar.com/gemini-moon-sign

Fellizar, K. (2021, April 5). Gemini & Cancer sign compatibility, according to astrologers. Bustle. https://www.bustle.com/life/gemini-cancer-zodiac-sign-compatibility-astrologers-love

Gemini zodiac sign: Symbols & facts. (2019, June 9). Cafeastrology.com; Cafe Astrology .com. https://cafeastrology.com/gemini-symbols.html

Hatch, M. (2021, March 10). The meaning of the Gemini symbol and zodiac sign glyph. YourTango. https://www.yourtango.com/2020337317/gemini-symbol-zodiac-sign-glyphs-meanings

Holmes, M. (2021a, April 7). Everything you need to know about Gemini risings. Cosmopolitan. https://www.cosmopolitan.com/lifestyle/a36041364/rising-gemini/

Holmes, M. (2021b, April 27). This is what a Cancer Rising is *really* like. Cosmopolitan. https://www.cosmopolitan.com/lifestyle/a36269056/cancer-rising/

Hutter, J. (2022a, December 17). 14 strengths & weaknesses of the Cancer zodiac sign. So Syncd - Personality Dating; So Syncd. https://www.sosyncd.com/14-strengths-weaknesses-of-the-cancer-zodiac-sign/

Hutter, J. (2022b, December 18). 14 strengths & weaknesses of the Gemini zodiac sign. So Syncd - Personality Dating; So Syncd. https://www.sosyncd.com/14-strengths-weaknesses-of-the-gemini-zodiac-sign/

Kahn, N. (2021a, September 8). Why Geminis are the great communicators of the zodiac. Bustle. https://www.bustle.com/life/gemini-zodiac-signs-biggest-strengths-astrologer

Kahn, N. (2021b, October 27). Cancer zodiac signs' biggest strengths, according to an astrologer. Bustle. https://www.bustle.com/life/cancer-zodiac-sign-biggest-strengths-astrologer

Marz5SOS. (n.d.). The signs key phrases. Wattpad.com. https://www.wattpad.com/148780202-zodiac-signs-the-signs-key-phrases

Meet Cancer: The nurturing & emotional water sign of the zodiac. (2021, June 22). Mindbodygreen. https://www.mindbodygreen.com/articles/cancer-sign-101

Miller, K., Levitan, H., & Inks, L. (2018, March 16). What your Moon sign says about your personality and how to find yours, according to astrologers. Women's Health. https://www.womenshealthmag.com/life/g19448039/what-is-my-moon-sign/

Montúfar, N. (2022a, May 16). If your Moon sign is Gemini, here's what astrology says about you. Cosmopolitan. https://www.cosmopolitan.com/lifestyle/a40010835/gemini-moon-meaning/

Montúfar, N. (2022b, May 20). If your moon sign is cancer, here's what astrology says about you. Cosmopolitan. https://www.cosmopolitan.com/lifestyle/a40061764/cancer-moon-meaning/

Muniz, H. (n.d.). The 7 fundamental Cancer traits and what they mean for you. Prepscholar.com. https://blog.prepscholar.com/cancer-traits-personality

Nunez, A. T. (2022, August 26). What your descendant sign reveals about you (and your soulmate). YourTango. https://www.yourtango.com/zodiac/descendant-sign

Ross, H., Clarke, J., Young, E., & Bishop, K. (2018, December 18). What is my ruling planet, according to the zodiac, and what does it mean for me? Repeller. https://repeller.com/ruling-planets-and-what-they-mean-for-you-according-to-the-zodiac/

Seigel, D. (n.d.). The 7 fundamental Gemini traits, explained. Prepscholar.com. https://blog.prepscholar.com/gemini-traits

Sharma, B. (n.d.). Cancer Ascendant: Know your Characteristics and Compatibility. Sunnyastrologer.com. https://sunnyastrologer.com/blog/cancer-ascendant

Stardust, L. (2022a, May 6). Gemini sun sign: Personality traits, love compatibility and more. TODAY. https://www.today.com/life/astrology/gemini-traits-personality-rcna27515

Stardust, L. (2022b, June 13). Cancer sun sign: Personality traits, love compatibility and more. TODAY. https://www.today.com/life/astrology/cancer-traits-personality-rcna33170

stargazer. (2021, March 11). Descendant in Gemini meaning: Your perfect relationship. Astrology. https://advanced-astrology.com/descendant-in-gemini/

Steber, C. (2019, July 23). Your biggest pet peeve, based on your zodiac sign. Bustle. https://www.bustle.com/p/your-biggest-pet-peeve-based-on-your-zodiac-sign-18208104

Tenorio, I. (2020, October 10). Cancer symbol: Zodiac sign glyphs & meanings. YourTango. https://www.yourtango.com/2020337440/cancer-symbol-zodiac-sign-glyphs-meanings

The AstroTwins. (2016a, September 13). Cancer symbol and astrology sign glyph. Astrostyle: Astrology and Daily, Weekly, Monthly Horoscopes by The AstroTwins; Astrostyle by the AstroTwins. https://astrostyle.com/astrology/cancer-symbol/

The AstroTwins. (2016b, September 13). Gemini symbol and astrology sign glyph. Astrostyle: Astrology and Daily, Weekly, Monthly Horoscopes by The AstroTwins; Astrostyle by the AstroTwins. https://astrostyle.com/astrology/gemini-symbol/

The zodiac sign Cancer symbol - personality, strengths, weaknesses. (2018, February 2). Labyrinthos. https://labyrinthos.co/blogs/astrology-horoscope-zodiac-signs/the-zodiac-sign-cancer-symbol-personality-strengths-weaknesses

The zodiac sign Gemini symbol - personality, strengths, weaknesses. (2018, February 5). Labyrinthos. https://labyrinthos.co/blogs/astrology-horoscope-zodiac-signs/the-zodiac-sign-gemini-symbol-personality-strengths-weaknesses

Trivedi, Y. (2021, July 30). A complete guide on Gemini ascendant, Gemini Rising: Find out how is a Gemini ascendant, Gemini Rising in love and marriage. EAstroHelp. https://www.eastrohelp.com/blog/gemini-ascendant-traits/

(N.d.). Symbolspy.com. https://www.symbolspy.com/zodiac-symbols-text.html

Astrologers, O. (n.d.). Leo Zodiac Sign: Horoscope, dates, Traits & personality. Zodiacsign.com. https://www.zodiacsign.com/zodiac-signs/leo/

Astrology, T. O. I. (2021, July 5). Leo Personality Traits: All the secrets you need to know. Times Of India. https://timesofindia.indiatimes.com/astrology/zodiacs-astrology/leo-personality-traits-all-the-secrets-you-need-to-know/articleshow/84131853.cms

Co – star: Hyper-personalized, real-time horoscopes. (n.d.). Costarastrology.com. https://www.costarastrology.com/zodiac-signs/leo-sign

Kaufman, A. (2022, October 20). "The perfectionists of the Zodiac." What to know about Virgo signs' personality traits. USA Today. https://www.usatoday.com/story/life/2022/10/20/virgo-zodiac-sign-key-personality-traits-dates/10485480002/

Kelly, A. (2018a, February 2). The personality of a Leo, explained. Allure. https://www.allure.com/story/leo-zodiac-sign-personality-traits

Kelly, A. (2018b, February 2). The personality of a Virgo, explained. Allure. https://www.allure.com/story/virgo-zodiac-sign-personality-traits

Ward, K. (2019, May 20). Virgo traits and personality explained. Cosmopolitan. https://www.cosmopolitan.com/uk/horoscopes/a28685194/virgo-traits/

Brown, M. (2020, June 30). Libra zodiac sign guide: Learn about the social air sign. InStyle. https://www.instyle.com/lifestyle/libra-zodiac-sign

Co – star: Hyper-personalized, real-time horoscopes. (n.d.). Costarastrology.com. https://www.costarastrology.com/zodiac-signs/libra-sign

Kelly, A. (2018a, February 2). Libra zodiac sign: Personality traits and sign dates. Allure. https://www.allure.com/story/libra-zodiac-sign-personality-traits

Kelly, A. (2018b, February 2). Scorpio zodiac sign: Personality traits and sign dates. Allure. https://www.allure.com/story/scorpio-zodiac-sign-personality-traits

Longacre, C. (n.d.). Scorpio Zodiac Sign. Almanac.com. https://www.almanac.com/content/scorpio-zodiac-sign

The Editors of Encyclopedia Britannica. (2022). Libra. In Encyclopedia Britannica.

Ward, K. (2019, May 20). Virgo traits and personality explained. Cosmopolitan. https://www.cosmopolitan.com/uk/horoscopes/a28685194/virgo-traits/

(N.d.). Lifestyleasia.com. https://www.lifestyleasia.com/ind/astrology/zodiacs/scorpio-zodiac-sign-personality-traits-and-more/

Quinn, S. (2017, November 15). The significance of the rising sign in your birth chart. Everydayhealth.com; Everyday Health. https://www.everydayhealth.com/healthy-living/significance-rising-sign-your-birth-chart/

Miller, K., Levitan, H., & Inks, L. (2018, March 16). What your Moon sign says about your personality and how to find yours, according to astrologers. Women's Health. https://www.womenshealthmag.com/life/g19448039/what-is-my-moon-sign/

Nunez, A. T. (2022, August 26). What your descendant sign reveals about you (and your soulmate). YourTango. https://www.yourtango.com/zodiac/descendant-sign

Ross, H., Clarke, J., Young, E., & Bishop, K. (2018, December 18). What is my ruling planet, according to the zodiac, and what does it mean for me? Repeller. https://repeller.com/ruling-planets-and-what-they-mean-for-you-according-to-the-zodiac/

AstroMundus, & Happy, happy.com. pt. (2021, March 6). Descendant Sign - What it Means for Astrology? AstroMundus; SUEBI Digital Labs. https://astromundus.com/en/descendant-sign/

Everything you need to know about the zodiac's most eclectic sign. (2022, January 17). Mindbodygreen. https://www.mindbodygreen.com/articles/aquarius

Kelly, A. (2018, February 2). Pisces zodiac sign: Personality traits and sign dates. Allure. https://www.allure.com/story/pisces-zodiac-sign-personality-traits

Meet Pisces: The go-with-the-flow psychic of the zodiac. (2021, March 12). Mindbodygreen. https://www.mindbodygreen.com/articles/pisces-sign-101

Quinn, S. (2017, November 15). The significance of the rising sign in your birth chart. Everydayhealth.com; Everyday Health. https://www.everydayhealth.com/healthy-living/significance-rising-sign-your-birth-chart/

Robinson, A. (n.d.). Aquarius compatibility: Which sign is the best match? Prepscholar.com. https://blog.prepscholar.com/aquarius-compatibility-signs

Stardust, L. (2022a, February 22). An in-depth guide to the Aquarius zodiac sign. Shape. https://www.shape.com/lifestyle/mind-and-body/astrology/aquarius-zodiac-sign

Stardust, L. (2022b, February 24). An in-depth guide to the Pisces zodiac sign. Shape. https://www.shape.com/lifestyle/mind-and-body/astrology/pisces-zodiac-sign

Part 2: Tarot Spreads

2019. "Get to Know Your New Deck with the Tarot Deck Interview Spread." Little Red Tarot. February 6, 2019. https://littleredtarot.com/tarot-deck-interview-spread/.

"Tarot 101 - How to Connect with Your New Tarot Deck." 2021. Labyrinthos. August 2, 2021. https://labyrinthos.co/blogs/learn-tarot-with-labyrinthos-academy/tarot-101-how-to-connect-with-your-new-tarot-deck.

8 of Cups meaning love, career, health, upright & reversed. (2021, March 15). MyPandit. https://www.mypandit.com/tarot/minor-arcana/suit-of-cups/eight-of-cups/

9 of Wands meaning, feelings, upright & reversed – guide. (2021, March 24). MyPandit. https://www.mypandit.com/tarot/minor-arcana/suit-of-wands/nine-of-wands/

A New Year's Tarot Spread - Lessons from the Past and Looking Ahead. (2018, December 30). Labyrinthos. https://labyrinthos.co/blogs/learn-tarot-with-labyrinthos-academy/a-new-years-tarot-spread-lessons-from-the-past-and-looking-ahead

Ace of Cups Tarot card meanings. (2011, December 22). Biddy Tarot. https://www.biddytarot.com/tarot-card-meanings/minor-arcana/suit-of-cups/ace-of-cups/

Ace of Cups. (n.d.). Astrotalk. https://astrotalk.com/tarot/ace-of-cups

Ace of Pentacles Tarot card meaning, love, feelings, upright & reversed. (2021, March 19). MyPandit. https://www.mypandit.com/tarot/minor-arcana/suit-of-pentacles/ace-of-pentacles/

Ace of Pentacles Tarot card meanings. (2011, December 22). Biddy Tarot. https://www.biddytarot.com/tarot-card-meanings/minor-arcana/suit-of-pentacles/ace-of-pentacles/

Ace of swords meaning, love, feelings, upright & reversed – guide. (2021, April 27). MyPandit. https://www.mypandit.com/tarot/minor-arcana/suit-of-swords/ace-of-swords/

Ace of Swords Tarot card meanings. (2011, December 22). Biddy Tarot. https://www.biddytarot.com/tarot-card-meanings/minor-arcana/suit-of-swords/ace-of-swords/

Ace of Wands Tarot card meanings. (2011, December 22). Biddy Tarot. https://www.biddytarot.com/tarot-card-meanings/minor-arcana/suit-of-wands/ace-of-wands/

Ace of Wands Tarot guide: Meaning, upright & reversed. (n.d.). Mypandit.com. https://www.mypandit.com/amp/tarot/minor-arcana/suit-of-wands/ace-of-wands/

Alecha Tarot Journals. (2019a). King of swords: Dotted tarot journal, dot grid journal, journaling diary, dotted writing log, tarot lovers dot grid notebook sheets to write inspirations, lists, goals. Independently Published.

Alecha Tarot Journals. (2019b). King of wands: Dotted tarot journal, dot grid journal, journaling diary, dotted writing log, tarot lovers dot grid notebook sheets to write inspirations, lists, goals. Independently Published.

Alecha Tarot Journals. (2019c). Page of pentacles: Dotted tarot journal, dot grid journal, journaling diary, dotted writing log, tarot lovers dot grid notebook sheets to write inspirations, lists, goals. Independently Published.

Amber, B., Lou, Linda, B., & Wille. (2022, November 6). 47 Best Tarot Card Decks Listed and Ranked. A Little Spark of Joy. https://www.alittlesparkofjoy.com/tarot-decks/

Astrotalk - online astrology horoscope prediction by astrologer. (n.d.). Astrotalk. https://astrotalk.com/tarot/knight-of-cups

Beth. (2014, June 18). Fool's journey: Create your own tarot spread. Autostraddle. https://www.autostraddle.com/fools-journey-create-your-own-tarot-spread-241932/

Beth. 2016. "Fool's Journey: Get to Know Your New Tarot Deck with the Interview Spread." Autostraddle. July 27, 2016. https://www.autostraddle.com/fools-journey-get-to-know-your-new-tarot-deck-with-the-interview-spread-346310/.

Breckon, I. (2010). Knight of swords. Old Street Publishing.

Bretton, J. D. (2017). Eight of cups: The tarot trilogy, book two. Splintered Sky Publishing.

Casey, N. (2022). King of cups: A dark college bully romance. Independently Published.

Chalex Tarot Journals. (2019a). Ace of swords: Tarot diary log book, record and interpret readings, daily draw journal. Independently Published.

Chalex Tarot Journals. (2019b). King of pentacles: Tarot journal diary log book, record and interpret readings, 3 tarot card spread journal. Independently Published.

Chalex Tarot Journals. (2019c). Knight of pentacles: Tarot diary log book, record and interpret readings, daily draw journal. Independently Published.

Chalex Tarot Journals. (2019d). Ten of pentacles: Tarot diary log book, record and interpret readings, daily draw journal. Independently Published.

Chalex Tarot Journals. (2019e). Ten of swords: Tarot diary log book, record and interpret readings, daily draw journal. Independently Published.

Chariot Tarot card meaning, upright, reversed & guide. (2021, April 5). MyPandit. https://www.mypandit.com/tarot/major-arcana/chariot/

Connect with Your Spirit Guides Tarot Spread. (2021, October 8). California Psychics. https://www.californiapsychics.com/blog/psychic-tools-abilities/tarot-oracle-and-angel-cards/connect-spirit-guides-tarot-spread.html

Crawford, C. (2019, December 21). How to Use a 3 Card Tarot Spread For Self Care —. The Self-Care Emporium. https://theselfcareemporium.com/blog/tarot-card-spread-self-care

Crawford, C. (2021, March 2). Finding work/life balance tarot spread —. The Self-Care Emporium. https://theselfcareemporium.com/blog/finding-worklife-balance-tarot-spread

DailyTarotGirl. (2012, July 22). Sharing Your Gifts ~ 5 Card Tarot Spread. Daily Tarot Girl. https://daily-tarot-girl.com/tarot-card-spreads/sharing-your-gifts-5-card-tarot-spread/

daysinspired. (2021, April 22). 5 Shadow Work Tarot Spreads to Uncover and Integrate Your Shadow Self. Days Inspired. https://daysinspired.com/shadow-work-tarot-spreads/

Death tarot card – meaning, upright-reverse, love, health & guide. (2021, March 19). MyPandit. https://www.mypandit.com/tarot/major-arcana/death/

Death Tarot card meanings. (2011, December 22). Biddy Tarot. https://www.biddytarot.com/tarot-card-meanings/major-arcana/death/

Death. (n.d.). Astrotalk. https://astrotalk.com/tarot/death

Devil Tarot card meaning, love, upright & reverse – complete guide. (2021, March 29). MyPandit. https://www.mypandit.com/tarot/major-arcana/devil/

Divination, E. L. (2019, November 18). Career Direction Tarot Spread. Emerald Lotus Divination. https://www.emeraldlotusdivination.com/blog/careerdirection

DLC Tarot Journals. (2019a). Five of swords: Tarot diary log book, record and interpret readings, daily draw journal. Independently Published.

DLC Tarot Journals. (2019b). Five of wands: Tarot journal diary log book, record and interpret readings, 3 tarot card spread journal. Independently Published.

DLC Tarot Journals. (2019c). Four of swords: Tarot diary log book, record and interpret readings, daily draw journal. Independently Published.

DLC Tarot Journals. (2019d). Nine of swords: Tarot journal diary log book, record and interpret readings, 3 tarot card spread journal. Independently Published.

DLC Tarot Journals. (2019e). Page of wands: Tarot diary log book, record and interpret readings, daily draw journal. Independently Published.

DLC Tarot Journals. (2019f). Queen of pentacles: Tarot diary log book, record and interpret readings, daily draw journal. Independently Published.

DLC Tarot Notebooks. (2019a). Ace of pentacles: Tarot diary log book, record and interpret readings, lined notebook journal for tarot lovers. Independently Published.

DLC Tarot Notebooks. (2019b). Ace of wands: Tarot diary log book, record and interpret readings, lined notebook journal for tarot lovers. Independently Published.

DLC Tarot Notebooks. (2019c). Eight of pentacles: Tarot diary log book, record and interpret readings, lined notebook journal for tarot lovers. Independently Published.

DLC Tarot Notebooks. (2019d). Eight of wands: Tarot diary log book, record and interpret readings, lined notebook journal for tarot lovers. Independently Published.

DLC Tarot Notebooks. (2019e). Four of pentacles: Tarot diary log book, record and interpret readings, lined notebook journal for tarot lovers. Independently Published.

DLC Tarot Notebooks. (2019f). Four of wands: Tarot diary log book, record and interpret readings, lined notebook journal for tarot lovers. Independently Published.

DLC Tarot Notebooks. (2019g). Knight of wands: Tarot diary log book, record and interpret readings, lined notebook journal for tarot lovers. Independently Published.

DLC Tarot Notebooks. (2019h). Nine of pentacles: Tarot diary log book, record and interpret readings, lined notebook journal for tarot lovers. Independently Published.

DLC Tarot Notebooks. (2019i). Nine of wands: Tarot diary log book, record and interpret readings, lined notebook journal for tarot lovers. Independently Published.

DLC Tarot Notebooks. (2019j). Page of cups: Tarot diary log book, record and interpret readings, lined notebook journal for tarot lovers. Independently Published.

DLC Tarot Notebooks. (2019k). Seven of pentacles: Tarot diary log book, record and interpret readings, lined notebook journal for tarot lovers. Independently Published.

DLC Tarot Notebooks. (2019l). Seven of wands: Tarot diary log book, record and interpret readings, lined notebook journal for tarot lovers. Independently Published.

DLC Tarot Notebooks. (2019m). Six of pentacles: Tarot diary log book, record and interpret readings, lined notebook journal for tarot lovers. Independently Published.

DLC Tarot Notebooks. (2019n). Six of wands: Tarot diary log book, record and interpret readings, lined notebook journal for tarot lovers. Independently Published.

DLC Tarot Notebooks. (2019o). Ten of wands: Tarot diary log book, record and interpret readings, lined notebook journal for tarot lovers. Independently Published.

DLC Tarot Notebooks. (2019p). Three of pentacles: Tarot diary log book, record and interpret readings, lined notebook journal for tarot lovers. Independently Published.

DLC Tarot Notebooks. (2019q). Three of swords: Tarot diary log book, record and interpret readings, lined notebook journal for tarot lovers. Independently Published.

DLC Tarot Notebooks. (2019r). Three of wands: Tarot diary log book, record and interpret readings, lined notebook journal for tarot lovers. Independently Published.

DLC Tarot Notebooks. (2019s). Two of pentacles: Tarot diary log book, record and interpret readings, lined notebook journal for tarot lovers. Independently Published.

DLC Tarot Notebooks. (2019t). Two of wands: Tarot diary log book, record and interpret readings, lined notebook journal for tarot lovers. Independently Published.

Donati, S. (2006). Queen of Swords. Bantam.

Douglas, C. N. (1986). Six of Swords. Del Rey Books.

Durose-Rayner, J. (2017). Queen of Cups: Part 1. New Generation Publishing.

Eight of Cups Tarot card meanings. (2011, December 22). Biddy Tarot. https://www.biddytarot.com/tarot-card-meanings/minor-arcana/suit-of-cups/eight-of-cups/

Eight of Pentacles meaning, upright & reversed - guide. (n.d.). Mypandit.com. https://www.mypandit.com/amp/tarot/minor-arcana/suit-of-pentacles/eight-of-pentacles/

Eight of Pentacles Tarot card meanings. (2011, December 22). Biddy Tarot. https://www.biddytarot.com/tarot-card-meanings/minor-arcana/suit-of-pentacles/eight-of-pentacles/

Eight of swords meaning, upright & reversed – complete guide. (2021, March 16). MyPandit. https://www.mypandit.com/hindi/tarot/minor-arcana/suit-of-swords/eight-of-swords/

Eight of Swords Tarot card meanings. (2011, December 22). Biddy Tarot. https://www.biddytarot.com/tarot-card-meanings/minor-arcana/suit-of-swords/eight-of-swords/

Eight of wands meaning, love, upright & reversed - MyPandit. (n.d.). Mypandit.com. https://www.mypandit.com/amp/tarot/minor-arcana/suit-of-wands/eight-of-wands/

Eight of Wands Tarot card meanings. (2011, December 22). Biddy Tarot. https://www.biddytarot.com/tarot-card-meanings/minor-arcana/suit-of-wands/eight-of-wands/

emeraldlotus. (2018, September 18). Tarot Spread - Career Shift. Emerald Lotus Divination. https://www.emeraldlotusdivination.com/blog/2018/09/18/tarot-spread-career-shift

Emperor Tarot meaning, upright & reversed. (2021, April 1). MyPandit. https://www.mypandit.com/tarot/major-arcana/empror/

Empress Tarot meaning, love, feelings, upright & reversed – guide. (2021, April 5). MyPandit. https://www.mypandit.com/tarot/major-arcana/empress/

Esra. (2022, May 9). What Tarot Deck Should I Start With? The Best Tarot Decks For Beginners. Lamucidesign.Com. https://lamucidesign.com/what-tarot-deck-should-i-start-with-the-best-tarot-decks-for-beginners/

Esselmont, B. (2018, August 30). Dealing with Difficult Colleagues Tarot Card Spread. Biddy Tarot. https://www.biddytarot.com/difficult-colleagues-spread/

Esselmont, B. (2018, October 4). 9 Sure-Fire Ways to Select a Tarot Deck That's Right for You. Biddy Tarot. https://www.biddytarot.com/selecting-a-tarot-deck/

Five of cups meaning, upright & reversed. (2021, March 22). MyPandit. https://www.mypandit.com/tarot/minor-arcana/suit-of-cups/five-of-cups/

Five of Cups Tarot card meanings. (2011, December 22). Biddy Tarot. https://www.biddytarot.com/tarot-card-meanings/minor-arcana/suit-of-cups/five-of-cups/

Five of Cups. (n.d.). Astrotalk. https://astrotalk.com/tarot/five-of-cups

Five of pentacles meaning, upright & reverse – complete guide. (2021, April 1). MyPandit. https://www.mypandit.com/tarot/minor-arcana/suit-of-pentacles/five-of-pentacles/

Five of Pentacles Tarot card meanings. (2011, December 22). Biddy Tarot. https://www.biddytarot.com/tarot-card-meanings/minor-arcana/suit-of-pentacles/five-of-pentacles/

Five of swords meaning, upright & reversed – complete guide. (2021, March 22). MyPandit. https://www.mypandit.com/tarot/minor-arcana/suit-of-swords/five-of-swords/

Five of Swords Tarot card meanings. (2011, December 22). Biddy Tarot. https://www.biddytarot.com/tarot-card-meanings/minor-arcana/suit-of-swords/five-of-swords/

Five of wands meaning, upright & reversed – guide. (2021, March 18). MyPandit. https://www.mypandit.com/tarot/minor-arcana/suit-of-wands/five-of-wands/

Five of Wands Tarot card meanings. (2011, December 22). Biddy Tarot. https://www.biddytarot.com/tarot-card-meanings/minor-arcana/suit-of-wands/five-of-wands/

Fool Tarot meaning, love, feelings, upright & reversed – guide. (2021, March 16). MyPandit. https://www.mypandit.com/tarot/major-arcana/the-fool/

Four of Cups meaning – upright & reverse guide. (2021, March 22). MyPandit. https://www.mypandit.com/tarot/minor-arcana/suit-of-cups/four-of-cups/

Four of Cups Tarot card meanings. (2011, December 22). Biddy Tarot. https://www.biddytarot.com/tarot-card-meanings/minor-arcana/suit-of-cups/four-of-cups/

Four of Cups. (n.d.). Astrotalk. https://astrotalk.com/tarot/four-of-cups

Four of Pentacles Tarot card meaning, upright & reversed. (2021, March 31). MyPandit. https://www.mypandit.com/tarot/minor-arcana/suit-of-pentacles/four-of-pentacles/

Four of Pentacles Tarot card meanings. (2011, December 22). Biddy Tarot. https://www.biddytarot.com/tarot-card-meanings/minor-arcana/suit-of-pentacles/four-of-pentacles/

Four of swords meaning, upright & reverse – complete guide. (2021, March 24). MyPandit. https://www.mypandit.com/tarot/minor-arcana/suit-of-swords/four-of-swords/

Four of Swords Tarot card meanings. (2011, December 22). Biddy Tarot. https://www.biddytarot.com/tarot-card-meanings/minor-arcana/suit-of-swords/four-of-swords/

Four of Wands meaning, love, upright & reversed - MyPandit. (n.d.). Mypandit.com. https://www.mypandit.com/amp/tarot/minor-arcana/suit-of-wands/four-of-wands/

Four of Wands Tarot card meanings. (2011, December 22). Biddy Tarot. https://www.biddytarot.com/tarot-card-meanings/minor-arcana/suit-of-wands/four-of-wands/

Getting Answers About Your Job Hunt - A Job Tarot Spread. (2018, January 29). Labyrinthos. https://labyrinthos.co/blogs/learn-tarot-with-labyrinthos-academy/getting-answers-about-your-job-hunt-a-job-tarot-spread

Getts, Alex. 2022. "How to Connect with Your Tarot Cards." Intuitive Souls. June 30, 2022. https://www.intsouls.com/blog/how-to-connect-with-your-tarot-cards.

Girl), Kate (daily Tarot. 2012. "How to Connect with Your Tarot Deck in 3 Easy Steps." Daily Tarot Girl. Kate (Daily Tarot Girl). November 22, 2012. https://daily-tarot-girl.com/learn-tarot/how-connect-with-your-tarot-deck-3-easy-steps/.

Hastings, L. (2020). Seven of swords. Hobeck Books. https://astrotalk.com/tarot/seven-of-swords

High Priestess Tarot meaning, love, money, health, upright & reversed. (2021, March 12). MyPandit. https://www.mypandit.com/tarot/major-arcana/priestess/

How to Choose the Right Tarot Deck for You. (2020, January 20). Labyrinthos. https://labyrinthos.co/blogs/learn-tarot-with-labyrinthos-academy/how-to-choose-the-right-tarot-deck-for-you

How to create your own tarot spreads: A step by step guide and infographic. (2017, November 29). Labyrinthos. https://labyrinthos.co/blogs/learn-tarot-with-labyrinthos-academy/how-to-create-your-own-tarot-spreads-a-step-by-step-guide-and-infographic

https://www.biddytarot.com/

https://www.throughthephases.com/easy-three-card-Tarot-spreads/

Husband, T. (2016, April 8). Before Fortune-Telling: The History and Structure of Tarot Cards. The Metropolitan Museum of Art. https://www.metmuseum.org/blogs/in-season/2016/tarot

Jaiswal, R. (2022, October 9). How Many Tarot Cards In A Deck? The Island Now. https://theislandnow.com/how-many-tarot-cards-in-a-deck/

Judgement Tarot card meanings. (2011, December 22). Biddy Tarot. https://www.biddytarot.com/tarot-card-meanings/major-arcana/judgement/

Judgement Tarot Card Spread - A Tarot Spread for Reflection and Evaluation. (2021, March 2). Labyrinthos. https://labyrinthos.co/blogs/learn-tarot-with-labyrinthos-academy/judgement-tarot-card-spread

Judgement Tarot meaning, love, feelings, upright & reversed – guide. (2021, March 30). MyPandit. https://www.mypandit.com/tarot/major-arcana/judgement/

Judgement. (n.d.). Astrotalk. https://astrotalk.com/tarot/judgement

Jung And The Tarot. (n.d.). Meta-religion.com. https://www.meta-religion.com/Esoterism/Tarot/jung_and_the_tarot.htm

Justice Tarot card meanings. (2011, December 22). Biddy Tarot. https://www.biddytarot.com/tarot-card-meanings/major-arcana/justice/

Justice Tarot meaning, love, money, career, health, emotions, upright and reverse. (2021, July 21). MyPandit. https://www.mypandit.com/tarot/major-arcana/justice/

Justice. (n.d.). Astrotalk. https://astrotalk.com/tarot/justice

Kali, A. (2022, October 2). 10 things to know about tarot reading for marriage and relationships. Www.top10.com; Top10.com. https://www.top10.com/psychic-reading/tarot-readings-for-love

Kernick, S. (2018). The Hanged Man. Arrow Books.

Kim. 2018. "9 Ways to Connect and Bond with Your Tarot Cards." TarotLuv. September 19, 2018. https://tarotluv.com/blog/9-ways-to-connect-and-bond-with-your-tarot-cards/.

King of cups meaning, upright-reversed, feelings & guide! (2021, March 31). MyPandit. https://www.mypandit.com/tarot/royal-arcana/suit-of-cups/king-of-cups/

King of Cups Tarot card meanings. (2011, December 22). Biddy Tarot. https://www.biddytarot.com/tarot-card-meanings/minor-arcana/suit-of-cups/king-of-cups/

King of pentacles meaning, love, feelings, upright & reversed. (2022, November 3). MyPandit. https://www.mypandit.com/tarot/royal-arcana/suit-of-pentacles/king-of-pentacle

King of Pentacles Tarot card meanings. (2011, December 22). Biddy Tarot. https://www.biddytarot.com/tarot-card-meanings/minor-arcana/suit-of-pentacles/king-of-pentacles/

King of swords meaning, feelings, upright & reversed – complete guide. (2021, March 29). MyPandit. https://www.mypandit.com/tarot/royal-arcana/suit-of-swords/king-of-swords/

King of Swords Tarot card meanings. (2011, December 22). Biddy Tarot. https://www.biddytarot.com/tarot-card-meanings/minor-arcana/suit-of-swords/king-of-swords/

King of Wands Tarot card meanings. (2011, December 22). Biddy Tarot. https://www.biddytarot.com/tarot-card-meanings/minor-arcana/suit-of-wands/king-of-wands/

King of Wands Tarot meaning, love, upright & reversed – complete guide. (2021, March 30). MyPandit. https://www.mypandit.com/tarot/royal-arcana/suit-of-wands/king-of-wands/

Knight of cups meaning, love, feelings, upright & reversed – guide. (2021, March 29). MyPandit. https://www.mypandit.com/tarot/royal-arcana/suit-of-cups/knight-of-cups/

Knight of Cups Tarot card meanings. (2011, December 22). Biddy Tarot. https://www.biddytarot.com/tarot-card-meanings/minor-arcana/suit-of-cups/knight-of-cups/

Knight of pentacles meaning, love, upright & reversed – complete guide. (2021, March 25). MyPandit. https://www.mypandit.com/tarot/royal-arcana/suit-of-pentacles/knight-of-pentacles/

Knight of Pentacles Tarot card meanings. (2011, December 22). Biddy Tarot. https://www.biddytarot.com/tarot-card-meanings/minor-arcana/suit-of-pentacles/knight-of-pentacles/

Knight of swords meaning, love, upright & reversed – complete guide. (2021, March 30). MyPandit. https://www.mypandit.com/tarot/royal-arcana/suit-of-swords/knight-of-swords/

Knight of Swords Tarot card meanings. (2011, December 22). Biddy Tarot. https://www.biddytarot.com/tarot-card-meanings/minor-arcana/suit-of-swords/knight-of-swords/

Knight of wands meaning, love, feelings, upright & reversed. (2021, March 26). MyPandit. https://www.mypandit.com/tarot/royal-arcana/suit-of-wands/knight-of-wands/

Knight of Wands Tarot card meanings. (2011, December 22). Biddy Tarot. https://www.biddytarot.com/tarot-card-meanings/minor-arcana/suit-of-wands/knight-of-wands/

Leah. 2021. "8 Ways to Connect with Your Tarot Cards (or Reconnect with Your Deck)." Leah Vanderveldt. June 2, 2021. https://thenourishexchange.com/2021/06/8-ways-to-connect-with-your-tarot-cards-or-reconnect-with-your-deck/.

Love tarot card meaning, upright & reverse – complete guide. (2021, March 13). MyPandit. https://www.mypandit.com/tarot/major-arcana/lovers/

Luna Luna Staff. (2019, November 11). All The Ways You Can Use Tarot for Self-Care. Luna Luna Magazine. http://www.lunalunamagazine.com/dark/how-to-use-tarot-for-self-care

Macdonell, F. K. (2009). The fool's journey. iUniverse.com. http://www.learntarot.com/journey.htm

Magician Tarot meaning, love, feelings, upright & reversed – guide. (2021, April 5). MyPandit. https://www.mypandit.com/tarot/major-arcana/magician/

Making Tough Choices - A 5 Card Tarot Spread for Decision Making. (2018, September 11). Labyrinthos. https://labyrinthos.co/blogs/learn-tarot-with-labyrinthos-academy/making-tough-choices-a-5-card-tarot-spread-for-decision-making

Makino, E. B. (1994). Six of cups: A circle of stories. Earth Books.

Manifestor, M. (2020, October 28). How tarot cards work: The fool's journey & story of the major Arcana. Liz Roberta. https://lizroberta.com/2020/10/28/how-tarot-cards-work-the-fools-journey-story-of-the-major-arcana/

Milliner-Waddell, J. (2021, October 22). The Best Tarot and Oracle Decks, According to Tarot Readers and Astrologers. The Strategist. https://nymag.com/strategist/article/best-tarot-card-decks.html

Minor Arcana Tarot card meanings. (2011, December 18). Biddy Tarot. https://www.biddytarot.com/tarot-card-meanings/minor-arcana/

Moon tarot meaning, upright, reversed & guide. (2021, March 16). MyPandit. https://www.mypandit.com/tarot/major-arcana/moon/

Moore, J. K. (2007). Seven of cups. Wild Rose Press.

Munson, A. M. (2020). Five of pentacles: A bad granna mystery. Independently Published.

Nine of Cups meaning, love, upright & reversed. (2021, March 26). MyPandit. https://www.mypandit.com/tarot/minor-arcana/suit-of-cups/nine-of-cups/

Nine of Cups Tarot card meanings. (2011, December 22). Biddy Tarot. https://www.biddytarot.com/tarot-card-meanings/minor-arcana/suit-of-cups/nine-of-cups/

Nine of Cups. (n.d.). Astrotalk. https://astrotalk.com/tarot/nine-of-cups

Nine of pentacles meaning, love, feelings, upright & reversed. (2021, April 1). MyPandit. https://www.mypandit.com/tarot/minor-arcana/suit-of-pentacles/nine-of-pentacles/

Nine of Pentacles Tarot card meanings. (2011, December 22). Biddy Tarot. https://www.biddytarot.com/tarot-card-meanings/minor-arcana/suit-of-pentacles/nine-of-pentacles/

Nine of Swords meaning, feelings, upright & reversed. (2021, March 23). MyPandit. https://www.mypandit.com/tarot/minor-arcana/suit-of-swords/nine-of-swords/

Nine of Swords Tarot card meanings. (2011, December 22). Biddy Tarot. https://www.biddytarot.com/tarot-card-meanings/minor-arcana/suit-of-swords/nine-of-swords/

Page of cups meaning, love, feelings, upright & reversed – guide. (2021, March 26). MyPandit. https://www.mypandit.com/tarot/royal-arcana/suit-of-cups/page-of-cups/

Page of Cups Tarot card meanings. (2011, December 22). Biddy Tarot. https://www.biddytarot.com/tarot-card-meanings/minor-arcana/suit-of-cups/page-of-cups/

Page of pentacles meaning, love, feelings, upright & reversed – guide. (2021, April 5). MyPandit. https://www.mypandit.com/tarot/royal-arcana/suit-of-pentacles/page-of-pentacles/

Page of Pentacles Tarot card meanings. (2011, December 22). Biddy Tarot. https://www.biddytarot.com/tarot-card-meanings/minor-arcana/suit-of-pentacles/page-of-pentacles/

Page of swords meaning, feelings, upright & reversed – guide. (2021, March 30). MyPandit. https://www.mypandit.com/tarot/royal-arcana/suit-of-swords/page-of-swords/

Page of Swords Tarot card meanings. (2011, December 22). Biddy Tarot. https://www.biddytarot.com/tarot-card-meanings/minor-arcana/suit-of-swords/page-of-swords/

Page of wands meaning, love, feelings, upright & reversed – complete guide. (2021, March 26). MyPandit. https://www.mypandit.com/tarot/royal-arcana/suit-of-wands/page-of-wands/

Page of Wands Tarot card meanings. (2011, December 22). Biddy Tarot. https://www.biddytarot.com/tarot-card-meanings/minor-arcana/suit-of-wands/page-of-wands/

Queen of cups meaning, upright & reversed – complete guide. (2022, November 3). MyPandit. https://www.mypandit.com/tarot/royal-arcana/suit-of-cups/queen-of-cups-meaning-upright-reversed-complete-guide/

Queen of Cups Tarot card meanings. (2011, December 22). Biddy Tarot. https://www.biddytarot.com/tarot-card-meanings/minor-arcana/suit-of-cups/queen-of-cups/

Queen of pentacles meaning, love, upright & reversed – complete guide. (2021, March 31). MyPandit. https://www.mypandit.com/tarot/royal-arcana/suit-of-pentacles/queen-of-pentacles/

Queen of Pentacles Tarot card meanings. (2011, December 22). Biddy Tarot. https://www.biddytarot.com/tarot-card-meanings/minor-arcana/suit-of-pentacles/queen-of-pentacles/

Queen of swords meaning, love, upright & reversed – complete guide. (2021, March 19). MyPandit. https://www.mypandit.com/tarot/royal-arcana/suit-of-swords/queen-of-swords/

Queen of Swords Tarot card meanings. (2011, December 22). Biddy Tarot. https://www.biddytarot.com/tarot-card-meanings/minor-arcana/suit-of-swords/queen-of-swords/

Queen of wands meaning, upright & reversed - guide. (n.d.). Mypandit.com. https://www.mypandit.com/amp/tarot/royal-arcana/suit-of-wands/queen-of-wands/

Queen of Wands Tarot card meanings. (2011, December 22). Biddy Tarot. https://www.biddytarot.com/tarot-card-meanings/minor-arcana/suit-of-wands/queen-of-wands/

Rajatnayartopastrologer. (2017, July 7). Some amazing benefits of tarot card reading. Medium. https://medium.com/@rajatnayartopastrologer/some-amazing-benefits-of-tarot-card-reading-2131225a9b51

Reeder, B. S. (2015). Page of Swords. Createspace Independent Publishing Platform.

Roethle, S. C. (2017). Queen of Wands. Vulture's Eye Publications.

Rose, M. (2019). Tarot card meanings: The absolute beginner's guide to tarot card reading. Kontakt Digital.

Rosslee, J. (2022, July 31). Soulmate Tarot Spread explained: How to read this tarot spread? Tarot Technique. https://tarottechnique.com/tarot-spreads/soulmate-tarot-spread/

Sawyer, Eva. n.d. "Interviewing Your Tarot Deck." Tucumcari Tarot. https://www.tucumcaritarot.com/blog/nice-to-meet-you-insert-deck-name-here.

Seven of Cups meaning – upright & reversed. (2021, March 18). MyPandit. https://www.mypandit.com/tarot/minor-arcana/suit-of-cups/seven-of-cups/

Seven of Cups Tarot card meanings. (2011, December 22). Biddy Tarot. https://www.biddytarot.com/tarot-card-meanings/minor-arcana/suit-of-cups/seven-of-cups/

Seven of Pentacles meaning, love, feelings, upright & reversed – guide. (2021, March 26). MyPandit. https://www.mypandit.com/tarot/minor-arcana/suit-of-pentacles/seven-of-pentacles/

Seven of Pentacles Tarot card meanings. (2011, December 22). Biddy Tarot. https://www.biddytarot.com/tarot-card-meanings/minor-arcana/suit-of-pentacles/seven-of-pentacles/

Seven of Swords meaning, feelings, upright & reversed. (2021, March 23). MyPandit. https://www.mypandit.com/tarot/minor-arcana/suit-of-swords/seven-of-swords/

Seven of Swords Tarot card meanings. (2011, December 22). Biddy Tarot. https://www.biddytarot.com/tarot-card-meanings/minor-arcana/suit-of-swords/seven-of-swords/

Seven of Wands Tarot card meanings. (2011, December 22). Biddy Tarot. https://www.biddytarot.com/tarot-card-meanings/minor-arcana/suit-of-wands/seven-of-wands/

Seven of Wands tarot guide – upright & reversed. (2021, March 26). MyPandit. https://www.mypandit.com/tarot/minor-arcana/suit-of-wands/seven-of-wands/

Siday, L. (2022, September 5). Tree of Life Tarot Spread Guide. Tarot Technique. https://tarottechnique.com/tarot-spreads/tree-of-life-tarot-spread-guide/

Six of Cups Tarot card meanings. (2011, December 22). Biddy Tarot. https://www.biddytarot.com/tarot-card-meanings/minor-arcana/suit-of-cups/six-of-cups/

Six of Cups Tarot guide – upright & reversed. (2021, April 3). MyPandit. https://www.mypandit.com/tarot/minor-arcana/suit-of-cups/six-of-cups/

Six of pentacles meaning, love, feelings, upright & reversed – guide. (2021, March 31). MyPandit. https://www.mypandit.com/tarot/minor-arcana/suit-of-pentacles/six-of-pentacles/

Six of Pentacles Tarot card meanings. (2011, December 22). Biddy Tarot. https://www.biddytarot.com/tarot-card-meanings/minor-arcana/suit-of-pentacles/six-of-pentacles/

Six of swords meaning, love, upright & reversed – complete guide. (2021, March 26). MyPandit. https://www.mypandit.com/tarot/minor-arcana/suit-of-swords/six-of-swords/

Six of Swords Tarot card meanings. (2011, December 22). Biddy Tarot. https://www.biddytarot.com/tarot-card-meanings/minor-arcana/suit-of-swords/six-of-swords/

Six of wands meaning, love, upright & reverse - guide. (n.d.). Mypandit.com. https://www.mypandit.com/amp/tarot/minor-arcana/suit-of-wands/six-of-wands/

Six of Wands Tarot card meanings. (2011, December 22). Biddy Tarot. https://www.biddytarot.com/tarot-card-meanings/minor-arcana/suit-of-wands/six-of-wands/

Skibbins, D. (1957). Eight of swords. Griffin.

Stewart, G. C. (2017). The Hierophant. Andesite Press.

Strength Tarot card meanings. (2011, December 22). Biddy Tarot. https://www.biddytarot.com/tarot-card-meanings/major-arcana/strength/

Strength. (n.d.). Astrotalk. https://astrotalk.com/tarot/strength

Suit of Pentacles Tarot card meanings. (2013, March 10). Biddy Tarot. https://www.biddytarot.com/tarot-card-meanings/minor-arcana/suit-of-pentacles/

Suit of Swords Tarot card meanings. (2011, December 15). Biddy Tarot. https://www.biddytarot.com/tarot-card-meanings/minor-arcana/suit-of-swords/

Suit of Wands Tarot card meanings. (2011, December 15). Biddy Tarot. https://www.biddytarot.com/tarot-card-meanings/minor-arcana/suit-of-wands/

Tarot Card Reading. (n.d.). Astrotalk. https://astrotalk.com/tarot

Tarot de Marseille by Vieux Monde Express. (n.d.). Buyolympia. https://buyolympia.com/Item/tarot-de-marseille-deck

Tarot, M. (2013, March 26). The Soul Activation Spread for Spiritual Growth. Mister Tarot. https://www.mistertarot.com/tarot-spirituality/

Tempera, J. (2022, September 22). How To Do Beginner Tarot Card Spreads, According To Experts. Women's Health. https://www.womenshealthmag.com/life/a41319340/beginner-tarot-spreads/

Temperance Tarot card meanings. (2011, December 22). Biddy Tarot. https://www.biddytarot.com/tarot-card-meanings/major-arcana/temperance/

Temperance Tarot guide – meaning, upright, reversed & love. (2021, March 25). MyPandit. https://www.mypandit.com/tarot/major-arcana/temperance/

Temperance. (n.d.). Astrotalk. https://astrotalk.com/tarot/temperance

Ten of Cups Tarot card meanings. (2011, December 22). Biddy Tarot. https://www.biddytarot.com/tarot-card-meanings/minor-arcana/suit-of-cups/ten-of-cups/

Ten of Cups. (n.d.). Astrotalk. https://astrotalk.com/tarot/ten-of-cups

Ten of Pentacles meaning, upright & reversed - guide. (n.d.). Mypandit.com. https://www.mypandit.com/amp/tarot/minor-arcana/suit-of-pentacles/ten-of-pentacles/

Ten of Pentacles Tarot card meanings. (2011, December 22). Biddy Tarot. https://www.biddytarot.com/tarot-card-meanings/minor-arcana/suit-of-pentacles/ten-of-pentacles/

Ten of Swords Tarot card meaning, love, feelings, upright & reversed. (2021, March 30). MyPandit. https://www.mypandit.com/tarot/minor-arcana/suit-of-swords/ten-of-swords/

Ten of Swords Tarot card meanings. (2011, December 22). Biddy Tarot. https://www.biddytarot.com/tarot-card-meanings/minor-arcana/suit-of-swords/ten-of-swords/

Ten of wands meaning, upright & reversed - guide. (2021, March 19). MyPandit. https://www.mypandit.com/tarot/minor-arcana/suit-of-wands/ten-of-wands/

Ten of Wands Tarot card meanings. (2011, December 22). Biddy Tarot. https://www.biddytarot.com/tarot-card-meanings/minor-arcana/suit-of-wands/ten-of-wands/

The Chariot Tarot card meanings. (2011, December 22). Biddy Tarot. https://www.biddytarot.com/tarot-card-meanings/major-arcana/chariot/

The Chariot. (n.d.). Astrotalk. https://astrotalk.com/tarot/the-chariot

The Devil Tarot card meanings. (2011, December 22). Biddy Tarot. https://www.biddytarot.com/tarot-card-meanings/major-arcana/devil/

The Devil. (n.d.). Astrotalk. https://astrotalk.com/tarot/the-devil

The Emperor Tarot card meanings. (2011, December 22). Biddy Tarot. https://www.biddytarot.com/tarot-card-meanings/major-arcana/emperor/

The Emperor Tarot Card Spread - A Tarot Spread for Claiming Personal Power. (2021, February 5). Labyrinthos. https://labyrinthos.co/blogs/learn-tarot-with-labyrinthos-academy/the-emperor-tarot-card-spread

The emperor. (n.d.). Astrotalk. https://astrotalk.com/tarot/the-emperor

The Empress Tarot card meanings. (2011, December 22). Biddy Tarot. https://www.biddytarot.com/tarot-card-meanings/major-arcana/empress/

The Empress. (n.d.). Astrotalk. https://astrotalk.com/tarot/the-empress

The Fool –. (2011, October 21). Tarot Elements. https://tarotelements.com/tarot-card-meanings/major-arcana/fool/

The Fool Tarot card meanings. (2011, December 23). Biddy Tarot. https://www.biddytarot.com/tarot-card-meanings/major-arcana/fool/

The Hanged Man Tarot card meaning, feelings, upright & reversed. (2021, April 1). MyPandit. https://www.mypandit.com/tarot/major-arcana/hanged-man/

The Hanged Man Tarot card meanings. (2011, December 22). Biddy Tarot. https://www.biddytarot.com/tarot-card-meanings/major-arcana/hanged-man/

The Hermit Tarot card meanings. (2011, December 22). Biddy Tarot. https://www.biddytarot.com/tarot-card-meanings/major-arcana/hermit/

The Hermit tarot guide – upright & reverse guide. (2021, March 22). MyPandit. https://www.mypandit.com/tarot/major-arcana/hermit/

The Hermit. (n.d.). Astrotalk. https://astrotalk.com/tarot/the-hermit

The Hierophant Tarot card meanings. (2011, December 22). Biddy Tarot. https://www.biddytarot.com/tarot-card-meanings/major-arcana/hierophant/

The High Priestess meaning - major Arcana tarot card meanings. (2017, March 6). Labyrinthos. https://labyrinthos.co/blogs/tarot-card-meanings-list/the-high-priestess-meaning-major-arcana-tarot-card-meanings

The High Priestess Tarot card meanings. (2011, December 22). Biddy Tarot. https://www.biddytarot.com/tarot-card-meanings/major-arcana/high-priestess/

The High Priestess. (n.d.). Astrotalk. https://astrotalk.com/tarot/the-high-priestess

The Lovers. (n.d.). Astrotalk. https://astrotalk.com/tarot/the-lovers

The magician –. (2011, October 21). Tarot Elements. https://tarotelements.com/tarot-card-meanings/major-arcana/magician/

The Magician meaning - major Arcana tarot card meanings. (2017, March 6). Labyrinthos. https://labyrinthos.co/blogs/tarot-card-meanings-list/the-magician-meaning-major-arcana-tarot-card-meanings

The Magician Tarot card meanings. (2011, December 22). Biddy Tarot. https://www.biddytarot.com/tarot-card-meanings/major-arcana/magician/

the magus. (n.d.). Tumblr.
https://sylvaetria.tumblr.com/post/164609909472/flower-of-life-tarot-spread-current-energies

The Major Arcana Tarot card meanings. (2017, February 2). Tarot.com.
https://www.tarot.com/tarot/cards/major-arcana

The Minor Arcana tarot cards. (2016, February 19). Tarot.com.
https://www.tarot.com/tarot/cards/minor-arcana

The Moon Tarot card meanings. (2011, December 22). Biddy Tarot.
https://www.biddytarot.com/tarot-card-meanings/major-arcana/moon/

The moon. (n.d.). Astrotalk. https://astrotalk.com/tarot/the-moon

The Star Tarot card meanings. (2011, December 22). Biddy Tarot.
https://www.biddytarot.com/tarot-card-meanings/major-arcana/star/

The Strength tarot guide – upright & reversed. (2021, April 6). MyPandit.
https://www.mypandit.com/tarot/major-arcana/strength/

The suit of cups tarot card meanings. (2020, January 28). Labyrinthos.
https://labyrinthos.co/blogs/tarot-card-meanings-list/the-suit-of-cups-tarot-card-meanings

The suit of pentacles tarot card meanings. (2020, January 28). Labyrinthos.
https://labyrinthos.co/blogs/tarot-card-meanings-list/the-suit-of-pentacles-tarot-card-meanings

The suit of swords tarot card meanings. (2020, January 28). Labyrinthos.
https://labyrinthos.co/blogs/tarot-card-meanings-list/the-suit-of-swords-tarot-card-meanings

The Sun Tarot card meaning – upright & reverse guide. (2021, March 18).
MyPandit. https://www.mypandit.com/tarot/major-arcana/sun/

The Sun Tarot card meanings. (2011, December 22). Biddy Tarot.
https://www.biddytarot.com/tarot-card-meanings/major-arcana/sun/

The Sun. (n.d.). Astrotalk. https://astrotalk.com/tarot/the-sun

The three of Pentacles Tarot guide – upright & reversed. (2021, April 5).
MyPandit. https://www.mypandit.com/tarot/minor-arcana/suit-of-pentacles/three-of-pentacles/

The Three of Swords Tarot guide – upright & reversed. (2021, March 16).
MyPandit. https://www.mypandit.com/tarot/minor-arcana/suit-of-swords/three-of-swords/

The Tower Tarot card meanings. (2011, December 22). Biddy Tarot.
https://www.biddytarot.com/tarot-card-meanings/major-arcana/tower/

The tower. (n.d.). Astrotalk. https://astrotalk.com/tarot/the-tower

The World Tarot card meanings. (2011, December 22). Biddy Tarot.
https://www.biddytarot.com/tarot-card-meanings/major-arcana/world/

The World Tarot meaning – upright & reversed. (2021, March 25). MyPandit. https://www.mypandit.com/tarot/major-arcana/world/

The World. (n.d.). Astrotalk. https://astrotalk.com/tarot/the-world

Thoth Tarot 101: Let This Amazing Deck Guide Your Life. (2021, September 16). A Little Spark of Joy. https://www.alittlesparkofjoy.com/thoth-tarot/

Three Career Tarot Spreads for Finding Your Path and Calling. (2016, December 1). Labyrinthos. https://labyrinthos.co/blogs/learn-tarot-with-labyrinthos-academy/three-career-tarot-spreads-for-finding-your-path-and-calling

Three of Cups meaning, love, upright and reversed – complete guide. (2021, March 16). MyPandit. https://www.mypandit.com/tarot/minor-arcana/suit-of-cups/three-of-cups/

Three of Cups Tarot card meanings. (2011, December 22). Biddy Tarot. https://www.biddytarot.com/tarot-card-meanings/minor-arcana/suit-of-cups/three-of-cups/

Three of Cups. (n.d.). Astrotalk. https://astrotalk.com/tarot/three-of-cups

Three of Pentacles Tarot card meanings. (2011, December 22). Biddy Tarot. https://www.biddytarot.com/tarot-card-meanings/minor-arcana/suit-of-pentacles/three-of-pentacles/

Three of wands meaning, love, feelings, upright & reversed – guide. (2021, May 5). MyPandit. https://www.mypandit.com/tarot/minor-arcana/suit-of-wands/three-of-wands/

Three of Wands Tarot card meanings. (2011, December 22). Biddy Tarot. https://www.biddytarot.com/tarot-card-meanings/minor-arcana/suit-of-wands/three-of-wands/

Tramble, Rashunda. 2021. "10 Ways to Connect with Your New Tarot Deck —." Stay Woke Tarot. July 13, 2021. https://www.staywoketarot.com/blog/10-ways-to-connect-with-your-new-tarot-deck.

TrulyLiving. 2018. "How to Attune a Deck of Cards for Divination." Truly Living with Lisa Rose | Soul Coach & Reiki. February 12, 2018. https://www.trulyliving.net/how-to-attune-a-deck-of-cards-for-divination/.

Two of cups meaning, upright & reversed – complete guide. (2021, March 23). MyPandit. https://www.mypandit.com/tarot/minor-arcana/suit-of-cups/two-of-cups/

Two of Cups Tarot card meanings. (2011, December 22). Biddy Tarot. https://www.biddytarot.com/tarot-card-meanings/minor-arcana/suit-of-cups/two-of-cups/

Two of Cups. (n.d.). Astrotalk. https://astrotalk.com/tarot/two-of-cups

Two of Pentacles Tarot card meanings. (2011, December 22). Biddy Tarot. https://www.biddytarot.com/tarot-card-meanings/minor-arcana/suit-of-pentacles/two-of-pentacles/

Two of Pentacles. (2021, March 16). MyPandit. https://www.mypandit.com/hindi/tarot/minor-arcana/suit-of-pentacles/two-of-pentacles/

Two of swords meaning, upright & reverse – complete guide. (2021, March 23). MyPandit. https://www.mypandit.com/tarot/minor-arcana/suit-of-swords/two-of-swords/

Two of Swords Tarot card meanings. (2011, December 22). Biddy Tarot. https://www.biddytarot.com/tarot-card-meanings/minor-arcana/suit-of-swords/two-of-swords/

Two of Swords. (n.d.). Astrotalk. https://astrotalk.com/tarot/two-of-swords

Two of Wands Tarot card meanings. (2011, December 22). Biddy Tarot. https://www.biddytarot.com/tarot-card-meanings/minor-arcana/suit-of-wands/two-of-wands/

Two of Wands tarot guide – upright & reversed. (2021, March 23). MyPandit. https://www.mypandit.com/tarot/minor-arcana/suit-of-wands/two-of-wands/

What does The High Priestess Tarot card mean? (2019, August 29).

What does The Magician Tarot card mean? (2019, August 29).

Wheel of Fortune Tarot card meanings. (2011, December 22). Biddy Tarot. https://www.biddytarot.com/tarot-card-meanings/major-arcana/wheel-of-fortune/

Wheel of Fortune tarot meaning, love, upright & reversed – complete guide. (2021, March 26). MyPandit. https://www.mypandit.com/tarot/major-arcana/wheel-of-fortune/

Wheels of fortune. (2006). New Scientist (1971), 191(2566), 85. https://doi.org/10.1016/s0262-4079(06)60311-4

Wigington, P. (n.d.). A Brief History of Tarot. Learn Religions. https://www.learnreligions.com/a-brief-history-of-tarot-2562770

Wille. (2020, July 31). Ten of Cups tarot card meaning. A Little Spark of Joy. https://www.alittlesparkofjoy.com/ten-of-cups-tarot-card-meanings/

Wille. (2021, February 5). 9 easy tarot Love spreads to spread the Love. A Little Spark of Joy. https://www.alittlesparkofjoy.com/tarot-love-spreads/

Wille. (2021, November 16). Four of Swords tarot card meaning: Love, health, money & more. A Little Spark of Joy. https://www.alittlesparkofjoy.com/four-of-swords-tarot-card-meaning/

Yotka, S. (2016, August 4). Tarot 101: A Beginner's Guide. Vogue. https://www.vogue.com/article/tarot-101-beginner-guide-how-to-small-spells

Image Sources

1   https://unsplash.com/photos/EdULZpOKsUE

2   RootOfAllLight, CC BY-SA 4.0 <https://creativecommons.org/licenses/by-sa/4.0>, via Wikimedia Commons https://commons.wikimedia.org/wiki/File: Chinese_Zodiac.png

3   https://unsplash.com/photos/m4-7DngV2Yo

4   ESO/M. Kornmesser, CC BY 4.0 <https://creativecommons.org/licenses/by/4.0>, via Wikimedia Commons https://commons.wikimedia.org/wiki/File: Planets_everywhere_(artist%E2%80%99s_impression).jpg

5   BoH, CC BY-SA 4.0 <https://creativecommons.org/licenses/by-sa/4.0>, via Wikimedia Commons https://commons.wikimedia.org/wiki/File:Freedman_Leary_1951.png

6   Christian Hoffmann, CC BY-SA 4.0 <https://creativecommons.org/licenses/by-sa/4.0>, via Wikimedia Commons https://commons.wikimedia.org/wiki/File:Partnerhoroskop_Synastrie_Radix_Grafik.jpg

7   https://pixabay.com/illustrations/star-sign-aries-horoscope-design-4374404/

8   https://openclipart.org/detail/233294/taurus-2

9   https://openclipart.org/detail/233277/gemini-2

10 https://pixabay.com/illustrations/star-sign-cancer-horoscope-design-4374406/

11 https://pixabay.com/illustrations/star-sign-lion-horoscope-design-4374408/

12 https://pixabay.com/illustrations/star-sign-virgin-horoscope-design-4374409/

13 https://openclipart.org/detail/233296/libra-2

14 https://pixabay.com/illustrations/star-sign-scorpio-horoscope-design-4374412/

15 https://pixabay.com/illustrations/star-sign-contactors-horoscope-4374413/

16 https://pixabay.com/illustrations/star-sign-capricorn-horoscope-4374414/

17 https://pixabay.com/illustrations/aquarius-star-sign-horoscope-759383/

18 https://pixabay.com/illustrations/star-sign-fishes-horoscope-design-4374416/

19 Image by Mira Cosic, Astrologer from Pixabay https://pixabay.com/photos/tarot-cards-magic-fortune-telling-991041/

20 Roberto Viesi, CC BY-SA 4.0 <https://creativecommons.org/licenses/by-sa/4.0>, via Wikimedia Commons https://commons.wikimedia.org/wiki/File:The_Major_Arcana_by_Roberto_Viesi.jpg

21 Image by Virgo Gem from Pixabay https://pixabay.com/illustrations/el-tonto-tarot-tarjeta-magia-6016940/

22 Image by Virgo Gem from Pixabay https://pixabay.com/illustrations/el-mago-cartas-de-tarot-tarot-mago-6103696/

23 Image by Virgo Gem from Pixabay https://pixabay.com/illustrations/tarot-tarot-cards-magic-fortune-6246912/

24 Image by Virgo Gem from Pixabay https://pixabay.com/illustrations/emperatriz-carta-de-tarot-s%c3%admbolo-6016923/

25 Image by Virgo Gem from Pixabay https://pixabay.com/illustrations/tarot-cartas-de-tarot-el-emperador-6129696/

26 Image by Virgo Gem from Pixabay https://pixabay.com/illustrations/el-hierofante-tarot-tarjeta-magia-6016942/

27 Image by Virgo Gem from Pixabay https://pixabay.com/illustrations/cartas-de-tarot-tarot-amantes-magia-6103697/

28 Image by Virgo Gem from Pixabay https://pixabay.com/illustrations/carruaje-tarot-tarjeta-magia-6016921/

29 Image by Virgo Gem from Pixabay https://pixabay.com/illustrations/tarot-cartas-de-tarot-fuerza-6129685/

30 Image by Virgo Gem from Pixabay https://pixabay.com/illustrations/ermita%c3%b1o-tarot-tarjeta-magia-6016941/

31 Image by Virgo Gem from Pixabay https://pixabay.com/illustrations/tarot-cartas-de-tarot-6129686/

32 Image by Virgo Gem from Pixabay https://pixabay.com/illustrations/tarot-cartas-de-tarot-justicia-6129675/

33 Image by Virgo Gem from Pixabay https://pixabay.com/illustrations/tarot-cartas-de-tarot-justicia-6129675/

34 Image by Virgo Gem from Pixabay https://pixabay.com/illustrations/cartas-de-tarot-tarot-muerte-magia-6103718/

35 Image by Virgo Gem from Pixabay https://pixabay.com/illustrations/templanza-tarot-tarjeta-magia-6016917/

36 https://freesvg.org/devil-tarot-card

37 Image by Virgo Gem from Pixabay https://pixabay.com/illustrations/tarot-cards-tarot-tower-magic-6103701/

38 Image by Virgo Gem from Pixabay https://pixabay.com/illustrations/tarot-cards-tarot-star-magic-cards-6103699/

39 Image by Virgo Gem from Pixabay https://pixabay.com/illustrations/tarot-cards-tarot-moon-magic-cards-6103698/

40 Image by Virgo Gem from Pixabay https://pixabay.com/illustrations/tarot-cards-tarot-sun-magic-cards-6103700/

41 Image by Virgo Gem from Pixabay https://pixabay.com/illustrations/tarot-tarot-cards-judgement-cards-6129676/

42 Image by Virgo Gem from Pixabay https://pixabay.com/illustrations/tarot-cards-tarot-world-magic-6103702/

43 Photo by Viva Luna Studios on Unsplash https://unsplash.com/photos/king-of-diamonds-playing-card-0-7oZdFHf-I

44 Photo by petr sidorov on Unsplash https://unsplash.com/photos/D3SzBCAeMhQ

45 Photo by Kayla Maurais on Unsplash https://unsplash.com/photos/1t2Kjo4Smpc

46 carbonnyc, Attribution 2.0 Generic, CC BY 2.0, <https://creativecommons.org/licenses/by/2.0/deed.en> https://www.flickr.com/photos/carbonnyc/5101424798

www.ingramcontent.com/pod-product-compliance
Lightning Source LLC
Chambersburg PA
CBHW060822050726
47601CB00014B/213